Institut International de Philosophie
International Institute of Philosophy

Philosophy of Education
Philosophie de l'éducation
Pädagogische Philosophie

edited by/édité par/herausgegeben von

Prof. Dr. Peter Kemp
(Institut International de Philosophie &
Department of Education, Aarhus University)

Volume/Band 2

LIT

POLITICS IN EDUCATION

edited by

Peter Kemp and Asger Sørensen

LIT

Cover Illustration © Nyoman Nuarta: *Horizon* 2000
(Polester resin 83 × 30 × 40).

The illustration is taken from the book: Nyoman Nuarta, edited by Jim Supangkat, published by The Garuda Wisnu Kencana Foundation, Jakarta, 2001

Gedruckt auf alterungsbeständigem Werkdruckpapier entsprechend
ANSI Z3948 DIN ISO 9706

Bibliographic information published by the Deutsche Nationalbibliothek
The Deutsche Nationalbibliothek lists this publication in the Deutsche Nationalbibliografie; detailed bibliographic data are available in the Internet at http://dnb.d-nb.de.

ISBN 978-3-643-90253-5

A catalogue record for this book is available from the British Library

Klosbachstr. 107
CH-8032 Zürich
Tel. +41 (0) 44-251 75 05
Fax +41 (0) 44-251 75 06
e-Mail: zuerich@lit-verlag.ch
http://www.lit-verlag.ch

LIT VERLAG Dr. W. Hopf
Berlin 2012
Fresnostr. 2
D-48159 Münster
Tel. +49 (0) 2 51-620 320
Fax +49 (0) 2 51-23 19 72
e-Mail: lit@lit-verlag.de
http://www.lit-verlag.de

Distribution:
In Germany: LIT Verlag Fresnostr. 2, D-48159 Münster
Tel. +49 (0) 2 51-620 32 22, Fax +49 (0) 2 51-922 60 99, e-mail: vertrieb@lit-verlag.de

In Austria: Medienlogistik Pichler-ÖBZ, e-mail: mlo@medien-logistik.at

In Switzerland: B + M Buch- und Medienvertrieb, e-mail: order@buch-medien.ch

In the UK: Global Book Marketing, e-mail: mo@centralbooks.com

THE I.I.P. COLLECTION ON PHILOSOPHY OF EDUCATION

EDITORIAL

"Philosophy of Education" is a philosophy focusing on education. Specifically, how is education possible in a multicultural world, where new problems raised by new technologies in communication and production challenge traditional thinking across all national and regional borders? They challenge the role of the teacher, the educational relationship, the social and institutional conditions of education and the importance of education for the future of society: for ethical and social justice, for cosmopolitan upbringing and for the climate and the environment in general.

These are the main problems considered in the Collection on "Philosophy of Education" sponsored by the International Institute of Philosophy.

Peter KEMP.

TABLE OF CONTENTS

INTRODUCTION

Peter KEMP and Asger SØRENSEN

Education is the conscious formation (or *Bildung*) of human beings to enable them to live together with other human beings. Thus, no education can avoid being political. Still, the question is in what sense education is political and whether all education must be politics, or, if not, to what extent politics must be made the explicit *telos* of formation and upbringing, and what the relationship might be between the principles needed for education and those of the political sphere. Today, after the successive collapse of the modern models of the good society – first, eastern bloc socialism and, then, neo-liberal market society, the question is what the standards should be for education and especially what the relation should be between these standards and politics. Are we, for instance, to raise human beings to become citizens of a civic republic, a world society, or a league of nations? Can education limit itself to local concerns, or must it transcend limits to become international, transnational, or even global? Should we educate to a global social democracy?

*

This collection of articles tries to grapple with these questions, although in very different ways. The articles in the first section are mainly historical perspectives on the politics of education from Antiquity to the Enlightenment. The second section consists of critical investigations into the ideology of education from the perspectives of the marginalized in various senses. In the third section, focus is on the universities, which today have become a battlefield in the international fight over education. The fourth section aims at providing some reasons and suggestions for hoping for a brighter future for education from a political perspective.

HISTORY

Evanghelos Moutsopoulos considers the views of education contained in Proclus' interpretation in his *Commentary on Plato's Republic* of the musico-political theory of Damon, a Pythagorean thinker who in 443 B.C. in Athens was prosecuted for his teachings, which, allegedly, had been too conservative and, hence, dangerous to democracy. Damon was banished from the city but not without defending himself before the Areopagus in a speech, which became known as the *Areopagiticus*. This speech became notorious, because Plato provides long citations from it, inspiring both Aristotle and Philodemus. Damon insisted upon the need to avoid musical innovations. The idea was that traditional standards had a beneficial effect on the soul of the young man and future citizen by communicating the principle of equality to his consciousness; whereas, removing such standards would necessarily entail the elimination of fundamental city laws. Proclus saw this effect at three levels: an aesthetic level, a psychological level, and a political level. However, despite the changes in musical education that occurred during the half-millennium from Damon's era up to the middle of the 5th century A.D., when Proclus wrote his *Commentary*, Damon's doctrine on musical education remained unchanged, since it had been transmitted exclusively through literary sources. This tells us that the idea of political equality, considered as an inalienable right of the citizen, has been implied from the very beginning in the Greek conception of education through music.

Blaise Bachofen discusses the educational importance of work for Locke and Rousseau. Apparently, Rousseau was inspired by Locke, but, so Bachofen argues, Rousseau actually subverts the legitimacy of Locke's position. For Locke, it is important to argue that education should aim at keeping the child active. The body as well as mental faculties should be trained to become a tool for all kinds of useful ends; and, for Locke, this is beneficial to the child, whom he considers a spontaneous pragmatist. Rousseau is also preoccupied with educating the child to become active but not in the same instrumental sense. Whereas Rousseau emphasizes being, Locke emphasizes 'being for.' The contrast becomes even more marked, since Locke denounces laziness as a vice; whereas, for Rousseau, idleness is a virtue. Bachofen calls attention to the difference in educational aim – namely, between Locke's gentleman, who is supposed to fulfill his social role, and Rousseau's man, who has value independent of the contemporary social organization. This analysis makes it possible for Bachofen to argue that Locke considers manual occupation as simply leisure for the gentleman, who should primarily be raised to administer his fortune by keeping his account books. Rousseau, on the other hand, wants Emile to learn a trade, which will enable him to earn his living. This makes it possible for Emile to experience and, thus, discover the true logic of property and economy, namely, alienation. Whereas Locke argues normatively for work as legitimizing property, Rousseau demonstrates how, in reality, property rights overrule the ideological legitimacy put forward by Locke. So, for Emile, Bachofen argues, it becomes possible to know that people may work without actually gaining any profit from their labor, just as other people may profit without working. And, when it comes to education, Locke actually let children learn about property rights through gifts, not by work. By focusing on work, Bachofen is able to demonstrate a crucial difference between Locke's approach to education and Rousseau's, even though they might appear similar at first.

Jørgen Huggler analyses Immanuel Kant's essay *Towards Perpetual Peace*, which is famous for its promotion of cosmopolitanism as citizenship of world. In Kant's *On Education*, cosmopolitanism is claimed to be the overall educational goal, but *Towards Perpetual Peace* actually rejects the prerequisite of world citizenship, namely, the idea of a world government earlier advocated by Kant himself. The point is that it is perpetual peace that is the overall goal, and Huggler emphasizes that Kant does not think of this as a utopian project but as a task to be completed, the goal of which we are steadily approaching. To promote the process, Kant formulates six preliminary articles in the form of prohibitions such as a ban on military intervention, uncivilized warfare, national debt, etc. These articles outline a path of progression from the natural state to the civilized state of law, and the three definitive articles define the institutions necessary to maintain peace: not only cosmopolitanism but also republicanism and federalism. It is the combination of these three spheres of law that, according to Kant, secures peace. However, they also mutually restrict and thus balance each other. To justify his optimism, Kant points first to the nature of human desire, which spurs human beings to enter into stable commercial and legal relations. More importantly, however, Kant thinks that the just ordering of states in accordance with national and international law will make peace sustainable. Kant has often been accused of being dangerously naïve and confusing morality with politics. For Huggler, therefore, it is important to emphasize that Kant clearly distinguishes between law and morality in his argument and that the restrictions put on cosmopolitan rights do not mean giving up cosmopolitan ideas. In fact, he argues that the cosmopolitanism is given a sharper and more reflected expression than in Kant's earlier works.

Athanasia Glycofrydi-Leontsini focuses on the ideas of citizenship education connected to the revival of Greek thought in the epoch of the Neohellenic Enlightenment and early Romanticism of the 18th and early 19th centuries. It was a time of modernization and innovative education in both secondary and higher education that was opened up for free thought and cultural, social, and political change in institutions and ways of life. Many new ideas were introduced through translations of English, French, and German philosophy and literature. In particular, Greek scholars and teachers were interested in moral thinking for guiding moral education according to Enlightenment and early Romantic ideas. One of these ideas was that of the "beautiful soul" described in writings by Rousseau, Schiller, and Wieland. Wieland created the *Bildungsroman* in which he combined Platonic and Christian allegories and myths with Greek ideals and British moral theory. In this epoch, Greek intellectuals were interested in virtue ethics and ethics about care for oneself as well as for others and the importance of character education for politics. At that time, the Greek philosopher Eugenios Voulgaris, who had studied seven years in Germany (Halle and Leipzig), translated Voltaire and advocated toleration, freedom of thought, and "freedom to read," had a great influence. However, the most important writer for the regeneration and re-education of Greeks was the physician and political theorist Adamantios Korais, who came to Paris in 1788 when he was 50 years old, became closely tied to the new regime's intellectual supporters, and stayed there for the rest of his life (he died in 1833). He was an editor of classical texts and believed in the importance of classical studies for a liberal education in general, stressed the Aristotelian archetype of "kalos-k'agatos" (the connection of beautiful and good) and contributed thereby to the establishment of an independent and modern Greek state. It follows that the Neohellenic Enlightenment can provide us a good foundation for liberal and social reform of the individual and society.

CRITIQUE

Enrique Dussel presents the idea of "conscientisation" in the educational thought of Paulo Freire. Education is a relation between an educator and an educand and, for Freire, the primary goal of education is the liberation of the oppressed. Education must, therefore, be part of a real transformation of the structures that so far have maintained education as reproducer of existing injustices. What is important for both Freire and Dussel is that the process of conscientisation is a dialogical process that includes both the educator and the educand. All education begins from a perceived reality of the educand, but this reality must be criticized in order to achieve a critical consciousness. One of the obstacles to this process, which must be overcome, is the fear of freedom of many oppressed. In order to show the paths to freedom to the oppressed, the educator must engage with the educand, avoiding discourses *about* the objects of education. The educator must learn the world of the educand in order to be able to interpret the reality critically. According to Freire, the oppressed are thus not the objects of education but the subjects. Still, in relation to their own society, the oppressed are excluded victims who, as such, constitute a social exteriority. In relation to discourse ethics, therefore, Dussel emphasizes that educational dialogue must always have content – namely, that the world has to be transformed. For Freire, the denunciation of the oppressors is at the same time a proclamation of their narratives as myths; this denunciation is, therefore, also a proclamation of the imagination and creation of a possibly more humane future.

Bhuvan Chandel and *Tuktuk Ghosh* bring out the prime importance of education explicitly stated by Marx in his third thesis on Feuerbach in which he states the materialist doctrine about which "it is essential to educate the educator himself." The article aims to explicate the intimate bond between politics and philosophy, and attention is called to the role of action in changing the world and the precondition of conceiving action only in the context of a truthful consciousness of social reality. It is emphasized how the ideas of truth and freedom are central to the Marxist perspective as social goals to be achieved for human fulfillment. It is argued that a radical reconstruction of society is necessary for a truly human society based on a conception of ethical humanism declaring that humanity is in each one of us and centers around the basic reverence for man and life. Chandel and Ghosh remind us of the importance of the concern for suffering humanity and that the endless urge for a unity of mankind can be conceived as the cognitive requirement to examine the historical and socio-economic dimensions of social reality. As they emphasize, happiness and freedom cannot be class-bound; they must be for a universal humanity. As such, 'freedom' from the realm of 'historical necessity' can be attained only by the transcendence of alienation and servitude, which in fact defines the spirit of Marxist ideology. Such teachings, it is argued, found a sizeable space in the educational curricula of many countries of the world, and this forged a strong link between the political primacy of Marxism and education.

Per Jepsen raises with Theodor W. Adorno the question of why the theory of *Bildung*, or formation of the human being, as it was developed by educators during the Enlightenment could not prevent the barbarism of Nazism and Fascism in the 20th century. He considers education, whether it is children's education or adult education, as the "facilitation of possibilities of human self-expression and action through the widening of knowledge and reflection," which means that the philosophy of education is a part of practical philosophy about the values and goals of human action. It follows that education as a human practice in general presupposes the idea of individual autonomy, which only makes sense if there are options for human action and forms of life. The question of why the education project of the Enlightenment failed then becomes a question about the conditions for the failure of the project of its practical philosophy. Jepsen claims that, according to Adorno, these conditions are essentially political. This was not taken into account by philosophers who, like Kant, understood education as pure cultivation of freedom, since freedom was understood as an unrestricted human capacity and not as an activity that only society makes possible. It was not recognized that freedom presupposes political forms. Therefore, the project of cultivation or *Bildung* that was a part of the emancipatory project of the Enlightenment was doomed to fail. Adorno characterised this form of *Bildung* or cultivation as half-cultivation or half-education *(Halbbildung)* in his essay *Theorie der Halbbildung*. It is part of a culture that understood freedom as domination over inner and outer nature. However, by this mastery of nature, Enlightenment culture reproduced the barbarity from which it tried to escape and, finally, became the victim of fascism and anti-semitism. This culture could not be an antidote to totalitarianism, because its education was only a half-education without subjective identification with society and without individual capacity for critique and resistance. There were no political forms that could favour this capacity and strengthen human autonomy.

UNIVERSITY

Gordon Finlayson explains how the university was born in European culture in the Middle Ages and how it has survived many crises by being able to renew and adapt itself to different political conditions. Now, however, it is threatened by a storm that might undermine its very existence as an institution of free research and teaching. Since the beginning of the 19th century, universities have flourished more and more and were not seen as barriers but as pillars for the Industrial Revolution and the emergence of strong nations. They survived two World Wars and supported the rebuilding of the European economy during the Cold War. However, today, the question is whether they can survive the Management Revolution, which means that only economic values count and that all management must follow the leadership model in business. The consequence is that researchers and teachers themselves are not considered capable of determining their own work. It all started in 1979 in the UK, when Margaret Thatcher's government was elected and wanted to reduce the cost of bureaucracy in social institutions. This government did not attack the universities directly, but some university leaders thought that they could avoid major government surgery by making cuts themselves, and they hired professional managers to assist them in making the best efficiency reviews. They also introduced audits on research to check that the practice in universities was proceeding properly. And this became a very powerful tool in the corporate governance of university activities. Add to this the creation of peer review panels, whose rankings were used to allocate quality-related research funding of each institution, so that the government was assured that it was getting "value for money." As a result, the universities prioritised research over teaching and abandoned small group teaching as "inefficient." The general marketization that was initiated by Thatcher was intensified by the new Labour government in the 1990s. The Conservative policy was to reduce economic input into universities, since they wanted to save money. New Labour did not only want to increase the economic output of universities but also to change the nature of that output by a radical regulation of universities that challenged the very idea of the university. They were not only to become business-like but to become businesses. Therefore, university senates were downsized and mostly replaced by small councils with a "majority of lay members" and small senior management executive committees. But, as Gordon Finlayson points out, universities cannot survive if, for instance, peer-reviews are made by people who are not peers. He also reminds us that it is extremely difficult to predict the impact of research. For example, nobody could know that academic research in mathematics and logic would give birth to informatics and computing. He concludes that there is little evidence that the transformation of universities over the last four decades has improved their excellence in teaching and research.

María José Guerra Palmero also calls attention to the consequences of globalization on education and research, taking Spanish universities as an example of this colonization of the life-world by the market and bureaucracy. She argues that neoliberal slogans function as an ideological cover-up for a reality of authoritarian routines of monitoring and control. In focus is the Bologna process, as it has been implemented administratively in Spain, i.e. in haste, without due reflection, multiplying bureaucratic procedures, without economic support, and thus usurping resources earmarked for education and science. With the current unemployment in Spain, this means more students, fewer teachers, and thus heavier workloads and stress. In order to make Spain's education system comparable to the rest of Europe, a competence model for university teaching has been introduced, but it only aims at training professionals; the passion for learning is not considered relevant. Palmero quotes Boaventura Sousa Santos questioning whether European standardization will mean the end of university diversity and innovation. One of the devices introduced is a teaching guide, which is conceived of by university administrators as a contract, which sometimes must even be signed by the teacher. The guides present themselves as tools, but in reality they discipline the teaching in details unheard-of until now. Following Deleuze, Palmero argues that what we see is actually control societies replacing disciplinary societies. Ironically, in Spain, the universities never got to the point of abandoning the disciplinary model, but now control is added. The only hope is the rebellion of the youth.

Tong Shijun demonstrates that the idea of the university has universal appeal. Currently in China universities are being established in a pace never experienced in the western hemisphere, and China has already years ago overtaken the US in rate of enrolment in higher education. This development has of course been accompanied by reflections on the idea of the university, and Tong quotes some of the presidents of the best Chinese universities for their views as well as some of the mottos of these universities. Tong in particular refers to Meng Xiancheng, who as university president in the 1930'ies argued for the importance of knowledge creation in contrast to the Chinese tradition of knowledge conservation, just as he emphasized the role of the university as an educator and its importance for the development of society following the demands of democracy. Tong discusses what it means for modern Chinese universities to be under the Leadership of the Party Committee, and he admits that the tensions between the classical western ideas of the university and modern China may not be easily resolved. Still he argues that party leadership secures the dual purpose of a university as an elite research institution committed only to truth and as a school, which also pay attention to disadvantaged groups under norms of justice and fairness. Tong argues that the current development of the universities reflects the increasing need for cultural self-awareness in modern China. Following these considerations he reminds us that the idea of the university was introduced in China during the time of Western imperialism, and this aspect he thinks must deserve some attention.

HOPE

D. P. Chattopadhyaya calls attention to how nations that emerged during the recent past often considered education as the only instrument of progress and social change. A reminder is given as to how democratic-socialistic educational policies, national objectives, and national development were discussed in the light of this. It is argued that the individual and social fulfillment of the nation can be achieved by dedication to national development and through a deepening of national consciousness. The idea is that the latter can be facilitated through an understanding and re-evaluation of the cultural heritage of a nation and that faith in achievements in the future can strengthen the bond between individuals and society. This is followed up by a matrix for a socialist morality, which is worked out on the basis of an idea of universal human nature expounded by Marx. Chattopadhyaya emphasizes how Marx thinks of the uniqueness of man as a conscious, free, social, creative, purposive, and aesthetic being for whom freedom was a necessary precondition for fulfillment. It is argued that Marx's conceptual framework implies that such freedom could only be possible in a socialistic society. The article concludes with the hope that the illumination of what is meaningful for human life and society above will provide an adequate ground for further philosophical reflection in the domain of the philosophy of education.

Sergio Cremaschi departs from the Aristotelian conception of practical philosophy in which perspective ethics is politics. This concept of politics, however, conflicts with modern instrumental conceptions of politics and the idea of *Realpolitik*. Still, the importance of the classical notion of politics has been recognized institutionally by the recent establishment of citizen education in post-fascist democracies such as Italy and Spain. Cremaschi calls attention to a tradition of civic education often forgotten – namely, the teaching of secular ethics in early modern Europe, especially from the 15th century until the end of the 18th, i.e. in the time of the Renaissance and the Enlightenment. Apart from Aristotle, the basic literature was Cicero's teaching of social and political duties, but Samuel von Pufendorf also contributed with a normative perspective based on the natural law tradition. His book was a basic textbook for 150 years but largely forgotten after 1800, rejected by both the Kantian and the utilitarian perspectives. Kant himself also proposed a purely moral catechism for teaching all the virtues and vices. The idea was that morality should be taught separately from the Lutheran catechism, but Kant never realized the project himself and, after the Enlightenment in Europe, the church took over the teaching of morality again in most countries. By calling attention to this European tradition for secular civic education, Cremaschi wants to argue against not just the right of one religion to define ethics and morality but also against the political bias of the modern idea of civic education. Instead, one should focus on ethics, demonstrating it by examples from all of the high cultures of the globe.

Asger Sørensen presents Émile Durkheim's idea of education in order to clarify the ideal role of the State for a democracy in which individuals can develop their autonomy and freedom. According to Durkheim, modern societies in his time, i.e. the beginning of the 20th century, are in crisis, and this crisis is both economic and moral. It is economic because trade, industry, entrepreneurship, etc., are conducted more and more beyond morality in such a way that the whole society becomes 'demoralized.' Therefore, he believes that the economy must become 'moralized,' i.e. regulated, and the only actor capable of doing that is the State. People do not live as isolated individuals, they live in groups in particular societies. And the most organized group in a society is the State, which as the organ for social deliberations and organization is the group that controls other groups. It is because of this structure that the State is supposed to 'moralize' the economy and cure social disease that consists in the lack of morality. If this is true, as Durkheim believes, then the State is not a threat to human freedom, as it has been claimed by liberal and post-modern writers. On the contrary, it is a supporter of freedom. If the State has been considered a danger to individual autonomy, it is because of the conception of the individual as a monad and not, as in Durkheim's view, a social creation that has rights and value as a person given by the society. And that means that the State creates individuals through its educational measures and secures their freedom in its core. It is true that, in 1893, Durkheim thought that the State was not necessary for human freedom, but after 1902, he was convinced that the State should be a counterbalance to suppressive groups such as families, clans, and religious communities that enslave individuals if they are not protected by the State. According to Durkheim and Sørensen, the State also protects the individual against capitalism, against private decisions that do not serve social life, because it is the rational part of society protecting it against itself by rational education. Discipline is the basic condition of this education, but it should be without corporal punishment, since it must be a preparation for democracy, which prescribes inhibitions but also offers much freedom. To Durkheim, in principle, the ideal state would be the global state, but that might not be possible. Nevertheless, every State must aim to realize the ideals of humanity as an expression of true patriotism. This is the task of moral education, which takes reason and science as its basis for making individuals autonomous and giving them the power to counter the tyranny of capitalism.

Peter Kemp wants to counter the current dehumanization of education with an emphasis on the good life, as it is conceived in ethics, and the idea of global justice as a world order of national and transnational laws. Such a project is, of course, challenged by all kinds of obstacles and barriers, and in this connection Kemp calls attention to Mireille Delmas-Marty, who through the four volumes of her *The Imaginative Forces of Law*, published in French, scrutinizes the possibilities of realizing a global legal community. The biggest challenge, however, is another law: namely, the law of the market. Kemp reminds us that Kant thought of commercial relations as contributing to peace, but this is not possible to believe anymore – neither for Delmas-Marty nor for Kemp. Kemp presents two major challenges in the current state of affairs: first, the emerging world order as a system of competitive states; second, the fear of the Other. The idea of the competitive state has been conceived by the Danish political scientist, Ove Kaj Pedersen. The point is that, on one hand, states increasingly think of themselves as commercial agents on a global market but, on the other hand, all kinds of organizations within each society tend to be organized in accordance with the ideal of being commercially competitive. Kemp and Pedersen, thus, want to call attention to the pervasiveness of the idea of competition in many different kinds of social relations. The generalized fear of the Other is a result of the increased focus on terrorism, and the problem is that fear is now thought of as legitimizing the individual and collective right to self-defence, which has actually led to an acceptance of torture. With Delmas-Marty, Kemp notes that, even though fear may make people stick together, fear is always insufficient to give meaning to human action. As a basic opposition, they propose solidarity to counter the values of the market. This, however, is not sufficient. Against the prevalent political discourse of achieving a balance between security and freedom, they remind us that human rights must never be taken for granted. A new humanism must be developed that is open and plural; it must overcome the law of the market as well the fear of the Other. Only then can politics and education triumph over the logic of the market, and for this project, we need imaginative forces.

*

In the midst of a global financial, social, and ecological crisis, it might be comforting to remind ourselves of what we as human beings have actually achieved during the last millennium. In the continued *praxis* of education, we have been able to display the finest traits of humanity, and it is remarkable that generation after generation – in spite of war, hunger, and terror – have been able to pass on to the their children ideals, values, and norms that help us maintain our hopes for the future of humanity. Education is the activity in which human beings become human, and this mode of being has so far shown itself to be remarkably successful. Actually, the general marketization of our educational institutions threatens us today, and this threat is more serious than ever. But whatever the solution may be, education is essential to democracy, and responsibility has to be part of it.

HISTORY

EDUCATION IN VIEW OF A VALID GOVERNANCE ACCORDING TO PROCLUS

Evanghelos MOUTSOPOULOS

I have often disserted on philosophy in ancient Greece,[1] notably on the transmission of the musico-political theory of the Pythagorean Damon of Oa, known through his fragments, mainly contained in Plato's *Republic*, although they are echoed in Aristotle and even in Philodemus[2] and Proclus who tries to comment Damon's *Areopagiticus*, some 930 years after it had been held (in 443 B.C.) and had caused his exile, or, at least, what Plato boosts to be able to report on it.[3]

What Plato, as a philosopher, is interested in and what he particularly retains from Damon's teaching is the teaching of philosophy as an initiation to a sane political life which has to be prepared through a correct musical education in order to predispose the young individual to virtue by habit, thanks to the exclusive practice of musical forms proven for their beneficial action on the soul of the future citizen. It is precisely this theoretical duality, which qualifies Plato's appreciation of Damonianism, that Proclus validates in his *Commentary on the Republic*,[4] by underlining the effects produced by such or such musical aspect or element on the soul. One should however beware: almost one thousand years after Damon, Proclus must have been the witness of real disruptions in the realm of music. The theoreticians of the Hellenistic period had highly contributed to cause a confusion, each one of them interpreting in his own way an already fluid theory as old as the age of Pericles, as far as

---

[1] Cf. Moutsopoulos, E. (1959) *La musique dans l'œuvre de Platon*. Paris : P.U.F.; 2nd ed. 1989; Idem (1975) *La philosophie de la musique dans la dramturgie antique. Formation et structure*. Athènes; 2nd ed., Paris: Vrin, 1999.

[2] Cf. Lasserre, F. (1954) *Plutarque, De la musique*. Olten/Lausanne: UrsGraf: 74-79; Plato, *Rep*., III, 398 d; 399 c. Cf. Moutsopoulos, E. (1998) "L'éducation musicale, culture morale et politique chez Aristote," *in* idem, *Philosophie de la culture grecque*. Athènes: Académie d'Athènes: 182-194; Idem (2009) "La philosophie de la musique dans l'ancien stoïcisme," *Festschrift für Klaus Oehler*. Wiesbaden: Pragmata: 707-711.

[3] Cf. *Rep*., III, 424 c.

[4] Cf. ed. W. Kroll, vol. I, Leipzig: Teubner, 1899; vol. II, 1901.

the so-called "harmonies" are concerned. The confusion lasts through the Middle Ages, even up to our days.[5] In fact, supposing that our knowledge about Greek rhythmic is almost complete thanks to the poetic metrics, on the contrary, the modes of Greek music are still and will remain for us almost a *terra incognita*.

Thus, Proclus moves in this domain on a "livresque" plane, so to speak, and approaches an issue whose technical data he is unable to fully understand and, hence, to correctly appreciate, though he extracts the philosophical significance that Plato had wanted to give them.[6] The same will occur, several centuries later, in a series of anonymous epigrams referring to the modes of Byzantine music and qualifying their ethical character. "Harmonies" (modes), as Damon considered them, were rather condensed formulas, similar to Hindu *ragas* or to Arabic *maqams*, which were thought to foster dispositions entailing moral attitudes.[7]

Under these conditions, three different, though connected, levels may be distinguished. At each one of them Proclus expresses himself as a commentator of Plato who, in his turn, is supposed to report a dialogue reflecting Damon's teaching: (i) an *aesthetic* level with its adherent technical aspects; (ii) a *psychological* level comprising, among others, a pedagogical aspect; and (iii) a *political* level which is believed to result from the satisfactory behavior of individuals at the former levels.[8] The respective values to safeguard would be *beauty*, *virtue*, mainly as *courage*, and *justice*.[9]

(i) At the *aesthetic* level, the particularities of each of the elements composing a musical form as a whole become obvious, notably melody and rhythm. To their *excellence* Plato's *Protagoras* already acknowledged a vital necessity.[10] Melody and rhythm are irrational components to which, unlike what occurred in Plato's time, when musicians tended to promote instrumental music, the rational element of the *logos* (=both *word* and *reason*) should be added, Proclus confirms,[11] since for him too, ancient musical forms should not be abandoned to the profit of virtuosity. For, according to Damon, changes in

---

[5] Cf. Chailley, J. "Le mythe des modes grecs," *in Acta Musicologica*, 28 / IV: 137-163.
[6] Cf. *Philebus*, 17 c-d.
[7] Cf. Moutsopoulos, E. *La musique*...: 69 sq.; Idem, "Modal 'Ethos' in Byzantine Music," *in Akten des Internat. Byzant. Kongr.*, vol. 2,7 (32). Wien, 1981: 3-6.
[8] Cf. idem (1994) *Poïésis et Technè*, vol. 3, *Évocations et résurgences*. Montréal: Montmorency: 86-92.
[9] Cf. idem, *Variations sur le thème du kairos*: 156-165; Idem (1978) *Philosophical Questionings*, vol. 2, *Retrospectives and Restructurings*. Athens: Univ. Press: 122-125.
[10] Cf. *Protag.*, 326 b.
[11] Cf. Proclus, *in Rempubl.*, I, 56, 1, 8-9; 11-12 (K.). Cf. Plato, *Laws VII*, 700 a sq.

music entail changes in fundamental political structures.[12] Such a hierarchy of musical elements and forms is, then, politically justified.[13]

(ii) At the *psychological* level, it is understood that music influences the soul by penetrating into it through the body. In the *Timaeus* Plato formulates a very original, though complicated, theory about hearing which takes into consideration his theory on the tripartition of the soul, as it is exposed in the *Republic*. Sensible music reflects intelligible harmony which only educated people are able to capture, while non educated, experience only a mere pleasure from it.[14] In his *Commentary* Proclus adds that it is imperative not to be satisfied with appearances, but that one should try to elevate himself up to their homologous *intelligibilia*, which convene to one's own intellect.[15] Such an attitude is equivalent to elevating oneself towards the universal reasons that dominate the ascension until the very truth.[16] Proclus also insists upon the pedagogical character of musical practicing which helps shaping the soul of the future citizen who must become courageous in order to be ready to efficiently defend his city. Hence the significant role of musical education which consists in accustoming the youth to prefer and practice the musical forms that the experts and the governors of the city consider as the best ones in order to inculcate into them the virtues requested.[17] The role of the governors in establishing the educational programs in music together with educators themselves is enhanced even to the detriment of the latter.[18] Nevertheless, it is a matter of justice that both parts equally participate in this process. Equity requires that neither governors fail to display enough culture nor musicians choose to stay out of the city affairs; for, in both cases, they would not be able to adequately cooperate.[19] Matters which should be taught would be chosen by excluding those which should not. Those selected should favor the acquisition of qualities becoming to virility. To the other rhythmic patterns attributed by Plato to Damon, Proclus cites the *pariambis* as the viril rhythm *par excellence*.[20] At the opposite, one should situate forms that would

---

[12] Cf. Ryffel, H. (1949) *Metabole politeion*. Der Wandel der Statsverfassungen, *Noctes Romanae* (Bern), 2: 52 sq. Damon, fr. 14 (Lasserre: 77); Plato, *Rep.*, IV, 424 c; Proclus, *in Rempubl.*, I, 61; (K.) 219, 1-8; cf. Moutsopoulos, E. (2004) *La philosophie de la musique dans le système de Proclus*. Athens: Academy of Athens: 32, n. 116 and 43, n. 57.

[13] Cf. Proclus, *in Rempubl.*, I, 56, 7-14 (K.).

[14] Cf. *Rep. IV*, 443 d; *Tim.*, 61 a-b; 80 a-b; *Theaetetus*, 155 e.

[15] Cf. *in Rempubl.* I, 63, 10-15 (K.).

[16] Cf. *ibid.*; 60, 3-6 (K.); Moutsopoulos, E. (1985) *Les structures de l'imaginaire dans la philosophie de Proclus*. Paris: Les Belles Lettres; 2nd ed. Paris: L'Harmattan, 2006: 56 sq.

[17] Cf. *in Rempubl.*, I, 59, 27 sq. (K.).

[18] Cf. *ibid.*, I, 54, 7-9.

[19] Cf. *ibid.*, I, 54, 16-22.

[20] Cf. *ibid.*, I, 61, 2-11. According to Epicharmus, 75 (Ahrens), the *pariambus* (note the difference in the vocabulary, which shows how distant Proclus is from classical antiquity) would consist out of a long syllable followed by four short ones.

become to female attitudes, e.g. lamentations, or to convivial relaxations.[21] The major concern of the governors being how to assure a correct civic instruction to the youth, it is necessary that monitors in music be able to designate which forms are adequate to the required values and which, as nocive, are not, so that the youth be aware of the difference and seek for the former while rejecting the others; for, any mixture would be unacceptable and condemnable, since it would imitate incompatible ways of life, whose coexistence would turn out to be pernicious.[22]

(iii) At the *political* level, the principal quality inherent to musical forms selected by the authorities of the city resides, according to Proclus, in their regularity, manifested through the equality of their rhythmical elements which are, in turn, concordant with the metric elements of the poetic texts. The principle of equality is, thus, communicated to the consciousness of the young citizen who is called to apply this principle during his whole life. The *enhoplian* rhythm would be proper to reinforce the warrior's impetus rather than to educate him in depth, but it however might contribute to the welfare of the city in case of danger. It suggests an armed warrior's dance figuring courage during combat. Nevertheless its teaching should be provisionally isolated from the curriculum and postponed until the youth reaches the adequate age. The dactylic rhythm would be the most convenient, adequate to the heroic hexameter which is proper to the epic poetry and which expresses an equilibrate measure "adorned with equality."[23]

The analytical explanation of this justification immediately follows: one and only one "*harmony*," *i.e.* "mode," is convenient, the *dorian* (but which one, indeed?),[24] and only one rhythm, the *dactylic* (in this case Proclus is very precise). Together, they form a shape of equality and balance, since they are elements communicating thanks to their structural adequacy in musical practice. "Harmony" and rhythm display common features, equivalence between them and equality in their respective divisions: in the first case, two equal tetrachords; in the second case, the rise and its complement being of strictly equal duration, independently from the number their particular elements are composed of. This excludes any excess or deficiency and imposes a rigorous measure by eliminating at the same time any risk of falling into irrationality. One remarks here the Damonian germ of what will be developed by Aristotle in an accomplished theory of the citizen's musical education.[25] Proclus, however, does not seem to care about this fact. He clearly establishes that the theory in question directly derives from Damon whose Plato was the first, though late, heir, since several details, if not a major part of its es-

---

[21] Cf. *in Rempubl.*, I, 61, 22-23 (K.).

[22] Cf. *ibid.*, I, 54, 9-16; I, 63, 21-28; 64, 6 (K.).

[23] Cf. *ibid.*, I, 62, 9-12 (K.).

[24] Cf. *ibid.*, I, 62, 17-27 (cf. *supra*, n. 5); I, 62, 3-17 (K.).

[25] Cf. *supra*, n. 2.

sential core have skipped his attention. The long series of philosophers, musicians, erudites and even poets of all kinds, who have held back some parts of the theory, have transmitted them to Proclus along the centuries that separate him from his main source. This temporal distance is the principal reason of Proclus' partial misunderstandings of the theory, all of which grew more serious due to the fast evolution of musical language because of post-Hellenistic contributions. Even so, Proclus steadily maintains the ethico-political and educational principles of Damonism, which had already been treasured by Plato, and applies them to his own conception of equality considered as an inalienable right of the citizen who must be conscious of it at the earliest.

The Man of Business, the Craftsman and the Citizen
The Social Destination of Humanity in the Pedagogical Theories of Locke and Rousseau

Blaise Bachofen

Locke and Rousseau both have had great influence on the thinking about education in the modern period. In this article I will argue that their pedagogical theories may best be understood by examining the place given to work in the process of education. What value do they assign to the ideas of activity, occupation, trade and 'business'[1] – to use a term that we often find used by Locke in his *Thoughts Concerning Education*? More concretely, what skills or professions do Locke and Rousseau recommend for the education of children and young adults? We will see that this area of questions will show up very different choices, and negate the impression of a strong convergence between the theses of Locke and Rousseau.

Even if Rousseau has read Locke very closely, and takes up for himself a number of his analyses and chains of reasoning, he also distinguishes himself from Locke on some decisive points. As is often the case with the authors to whom he seems the closest, he subverts the very theses which he seems to be continuing in his own thought. On the one hand, Rousseau gives less weight than Locke to activity for its own sake – the "busy humour"[2] – and makes *idleness* an essential part of the definition of Man's state of completion. But on the other hand, he gives much greater importance than Locke to learning a skill, and to the capacity to produce economic riches by oneself, through labour. This learning is also inseparable from the child's discovery of the social and political relations within which all economic activity takes place.

---

[1] We must give this term, as used by Locke, a larger sense than that in which it used in current English (a narrow use, for which Locke uses the term "affairs"): "business," in Locke's vocabulary, is very generally the fact of being busy, active, occupied or employed with something; it is the fact of not remaining idle and unproductive.

[2] See Locke, J. *Some Thoughts Concerning Education* (abbr. *Education*), § 152. Oxford: Clarendon Press, 1989: 211.

***

EDUCATION AS ŒUVRE

Nature, understood as what is there before any modification produced by human will and as something that produces its effects spontaneously, cannot on its own suffice to give direction to the existence of Man. Both Locke and Rousseau, however, recognize the value in the notion of 'nature' as a theoretical and practical model, and that is not incompatible with the need to educate people, nor the desire to educate them even better than is ordinarily done.

"Men's happiness or misery is most part of their own making," writes Locke from the first lines of *Thoughts Concerning Education.* "I may say, that of all the men we meet with, nine parts of ten are what they are, good or evil, useful or not, by their education."[3] Now, as it is directed by reason and by experience, this work of transformation of man by man that is education may be considered philosophically, and thus torn away from custom, relativism and the arbitrary. Rousseau is not very far from Locke on this point. For him no less than for Locke, education is an art, an art which is attentive to nature but which principally employs the work of reason applied to experience to defeat the arbitrary quality of custom. This is why Rousseau writes in Book IV that "Much art is required to prevent man in society from being altogether artificial."[4] The domestic education proposed by Locke and Rousseau is an education according to "nature,"[5] but this means understanding the word "nature" in a sense not to be confused either with pure spontaneity or with the absence of culture: "We must not confuse what is natural[6] in a state of savagery with what is natural in civilized life."[7] This, we must remark, is a first and essential element in forming a concept of the role of work in the definition of humanity's state of completion.

Education itself is said to be a kind of work, and this is true not only for the pedagogue, but for the pupil too. The connecting thread for most of the precepts developed by Locke, which provide constant inspiration for Rousseau, is that the pedagogue must make the pupil work at becoming his own teacher. Education, before transmitting any instruction or precept whatsoever, must seek to exercise in the child those faculties

---

[3] *Education*, § 1: 83.

[4] Rousseau, J.-J. *Emile*, transl. Barbara Foxley. London: Everyman, 1993, Book IV: 336.

[5] See *ibid.*, Book I: 6.

[6] B. Foxley translates the French term "*naturel*" by "suitable." I have replaced this with a more faithful translation here.

[7] *Emile*, Book V: 441.

which will allow it to discover for itself the precepts and knowledge which will make it into an accomplished and autonomous individual.

Most of the concrete pedagogical recommendations given by Locke, which in turn inspired Rousseau, flow from the idea that education is work twice over: the difficult work of the pedagogue, and the work of the pupil, who becomes his own work-piece. Remembering only the key items, we find in Locke, before Rousseau, a subordination of scientific instruction to practical training: "You will wonder, perhaps, that I put learning last, especially if I tell you I think it the least part."[8] The first and most important part of education is practical or moral, but it consists less of training the child and inculcating principles of action than in getting it to master itself and to enter into full possession of itself; to become its own master by working constantly on itself from earliest life.[9] This acquisition of a controlled relationship of the child with itself rests on the exercise and appropriation by the child of its own faculties, whether physical or intellectual.

Most of the prescriptions of Locke and Rousseau concerning physical education, and the precepts of health here clearly rest on the need to train the child in a skilful use of its own body.[10] This means that the child must exercise its physical faculties in order to make its body a familiar and appropriate tool, available for all kind of useful ends. The same logic applies when it comes to the child's intellectual training.[11]

Mastering the methods of acquisition of knowledge may be described as a continual exercise by the child of its faculties of knowledge, and thus here too as a work the child carries out on itself. And this work, prior to its intellectual application, is in a way applied to the body and to the sense-experience, as the body and the sense-experience are what is closest and known the most immediately to the child, and are the tools for the construction of the self, which the child can make use of in the most autonomous manner. Access to abstraction must pass through the mediation of doing and perceiving, in order for it to become something produced by the child itself rather than a finished product merely to be consumed. Rousseau thus advises cultivating and using the "reason of sense-experience" ["raison sensitive"] which is "man's first reason" and which "serves as a foundation for the reason of the intelligence," as "our first

---

[8] *Education*, § 147: 207.

[9] See *ibid.*, §§ 112 and 200: 172 and 255.

[10] See notably *ibid.*, §§ 3: 5-10, 15, 21 and 22: 84-90, 88-89, 93-94, 97-98 and 98-99; *Emile*, Book. I and II: 24-26, 49, 107-110, 115 and 125-127.

[11] *Education*, § 195: 249 and 251.

teachers in natural philosophy are our feet, hands, and eyes."[12] In this he takes his inspiration from Locke, who writes that "the reasons that move [children] [...] may (if I may say so) be felt, and touched."[13] The "reason of sense-experience" places the acquisition of knowledge in a dynamic of appropriation of things for the use of the child itself.[14]

WHAT IS THE USE OF THAT?

But these evident convergences are not the whole story: while Rousseau knows "the philosopher Locke" ["le sage Locke"][15] very well, and is often inspired by him, to the point where he sometimes seems to offer a mere copy of his thought, he also distances himself from Locke on some essential questions, to the point where they sometimes take entirely opposite positions.

To understand this, we must consider the question of the *ends* of education. We have seen that Rousseau shares with Locke the desire to make the child into its own teacher, by training it to make its own dispositions in order to make its faculties both effective and available for all useful ends. This being established, the whole question is one of knowing to what ends and to what uses the child, and when the child becomes an adult, should order its faculties and its activities. On this point, we may consider that Rousseau adopts a point of view that is more complex than Locke's. This is a recurrent aspect of his thought, notably in *Emile*: seeking to make a fresh start in defining what is useful, by aiming at what is *truly* useful.

One example is very illuminating on this point. Locke writes that "When any new thing comes in their way, children usually ask the common question of a stranger: *What is it?* [...] The next question usually is: *What is it for?*"[16] Children should thus be understood as spontaneously pragmatic and this spontaneous pragmatism would be an immediately effective instrument which is available to the educator. But Rousseau would seem to be a better observer of children, as we see in the following passage from Book III of *Emile*:

> As soon as we have contrived to give our pupil an idea of the word "Useful," we have got an additional means of controlling him [...]. "What is the use of that?" In future this is the sacred formula, the formula by which he and I test every action of our lives. This is the question with which I invariably answer

[12] *Emile*, Book II: 106-107.
[13] *Education*, § 81: 142.
[14] See especially *ibid.*, § 166: 219; *Emile*, Book II and III: 95, 107, 147-148, 169-172, 176.
[15] *Emile*, Book II: 108.
[16] *Education*, § 120: 184-185.

> all his questions; it serves to check the stream of foolish and tiresome questions with which children weary those about them.[17]

Unlike Locke, Rousseau does not think that the child would spontaneously form either a desire for what is useful, or even less – and this is the essential point – a precise idea of what actually deserves to be qualified as useful. He considers that the notion of 'utility' can only be *acquired* through the intermediary of the work of education, which opposes the spontaneous movement of the child's mind. And he gives the reason for this: what is useful only makes sense with reference to a certain idea of the destination of man himself, an idea of 'manhood' ["l'état d'homme"][18] to which the child can only move from far away, in a mode of becoming. Now, this idea, by definition, will apply for as long as the person is in the process of becoming (which is to say that he has never finished addressing himself), and assumes a reflexive relationship of the individual with itself. The idea of a human destination is constructed in a problematic manner, and is subject to the changing interplay of conformism and imagination, or on the other hand to reason or authentic sentiment. In other words, the desire for the 'useful,' which is determinative in the value accorded to all the forms the work can take (from this long term work of self-transformation which is education, to the more short-term and concrete activities to which the child devotes itself), is presented not as a *response* or solution: on the contrary it is necessary to bring out an awareness of a contingency in the determination of what a man must be and what he must do, and thus in his need to *decide* on what use he will make of himself.

To set out in broad strokes the gaps that this difference of points of view produces between the two authors, we may show that Rousseau is opposed to Locke on two main points. 1. While Locke declares that his aim is to make the child into a "man of business," Rousseau introduces among the aims of education and the ends of humanity an essential place for idle pastimes and the enjoyment of *being*, with nothing added, that is to say, without it *'being for'* a goal outside oneself. 2. Whereas Locke writes clearly that his pupil, born a gentleman, must be educated to fill his native function in an appropriate manner – that is, the function of a gentleman – Rousseau, who also describes the education of a child who "came of a good family"[19] seeks, quite to the contrary, to free him from the destination society had defined for him in advance, and more general-

---

[17] *Emile*, Book III: 169-170.

[18] *Ibid.*, Book I: 10.

[19] *Ibid.*: 23.

ly to liberate him from any predetermined status and function at all, to make of him a 'man' in general, and (because the contingent condition of man as linked to other men by social and political ties has become over the course of history a universal necessity for men) also a 'citizen'. These two aspects of education determine two fundamentally different conceptions of the relationship of the individual to work, understood here in a restricted manner as the activity of transforming nature.

BUSINESS OR IDLENESS?

It is interesting to note a very revealing hesitation in Locke's text, a sort of constant equivocation between these two theses. Locke definitely affirms that children naturally possess a "busy humour," and he gives a certain number of examples of this. The child is naturally animated by a "busy inquisitiveness"[20] and is in a general manner provided with a disposition to apply himself without lassitude to multiple activities, however demanding or difficult they may be, but simply on condition that these vary regularly.[21] But from another perspective, he several times considers the hypothesis that children are naturally indolent and lazy, so that it is necessary to use coercive means with them; and even insists on many occasions on the need for the educator to use all possible means against the danger – one of the most serious – of the tendency to laziness.[22]

We find a good illustration of the ambiguous anthropological status of the "busy humour," meaning the active or pro-work humour, in the judgement that Locke makes on certain peoples, who precisely lack this inclination to industry. In Chapter V of the *Second Treatise of Government*, Locke writes that:

> God, when he gave the world in common to all mankind, commanded man also to labour, and the penury of his condition required it of him. God and his reason commanded him to subdue the earth, i.e. improve it for the benefit of life, and therein lay out something upon it was his own, his labour.[23]

Locke notes that this commandment – both divine and supremely rational – is not universally observed:

> Several nations of the Americans [this refers to native Americans] are rich in land, and poor in all comforts of life [...]. Nature [has] furnished [them] as liberally as any other people, with the materials of plenty, i.e. a fruitful soil, apt to produce in abundance, what might serve for food, raiment, and delight;

[20] *Education*, § 118: 183.

[21] *Ibid.*, § 152: 210-211.

[22] See especially *ibid.*, §§ 124 and 126-127: 186-187 and 188-189.

[23] Locke, J. *Second Treatise on Government* (abbr. *Second Treatise*), Chap. V, § 32. London: Everyman, 1993: 130.

> yet for want of improving it by labour, have not one hundredth part of the conveniences we enjoy: and a king of a large and fruitful territory there feeds, lodges, and is clad worse than a day labourer in England.[24]

We can understand here why, in the text from *Thoughts Concerning Education* relating to the "busy humour," the normative and descriptive registers become confused. This shows the problems created by the attempt at the naturalisation of what we can see in reality to be a philosophical choice relating to the proper destination of humanity. If the work of exploiting nature is 'useful,' it is not so in an absolute sense (and anyway, how should we think of an absolute 'utility'?), but in a relative sense, that is, relative to a certain destination that is attributed to humanity. The question which must then be posed, though it is one that Locke does not look at as a problem in its own right, is that of the value of that destination. Rousseau, however, sets himself precisely the task of taking a fresh look at this question.

So, while he also insists on the child's natural taste for activity and spontaneous curiosity, while he advises strengthening the child's spirit of ingenuity and enterprise, he in fact limits himself to setting as the final purpose for the child that he should learn to become a man who is principally occupied, active and socially 'useful': a "man of business." Social utility must be a constant preoccupation in the mind of the tutor, as we will see, but the child must not be educated in view of a hypothetical social function without which he would see his existence struck with uselessness and insignificance. This is not a matter of abandoning the child to indolence. It is rather a question of never subordinating the activities of childhood to a future and hypothetical final purpose, where nothing guarantees that this will correspond to the actual destination of the child when he becomes a man, and where there is not even a guarantee that the child will live long enough to profit from it.[25]

To be present in the present, to take the time to live each of life's ages according to its own needs, and not with the preoccupation of what it is leading to: this ideal, which is opposed to the disturbed and agitated tyranny of the spirit of foresight, is not for Rousseau reserved to early childhood. It must be stressed in the educational choices related to the period of childhood, but this is because it is what man lacks the most *in all his ages* to be happy and not to miss out on his own life. True happiness assumes a wisdom that is almost completely opposite to what Locke describes under this term:

---

[24] *Ibid.*, § 41: 135.

[25] *Emile*, Book II: 50-51 and 84. *Cf.* Locke, *Education*, § 126: 188.

> What is human wisdom? Where is the path of true happiness? The mere limitation of our desires is not enough, for if they were less than our powers, part of our faculties would be idle, and we should not enjoy our whole being; neither is the mere extension of our powers enough, for if our desires were also increased we should only be the more miserable. True happiness consists in decreasing the difference between our desires and our powers, in establishing a perfect equilibrium between the power and the will. Then only, when all forces are employed, will the soul be at rest and will man find himself in his true position.[26]

This adjustment of the desires to the faculties excludes seeking the conditions for happiness in seeking some indefinite perfection of the faculties, a perfection slaved to the futile chase after desires that falsely pretend to be needs. "If a man were content to live," writes Rousseau further, "he would live happily."[27] We know that he tried this himself: according to the *Confessions*, he thought he could attain such a perfect happiness on the island of Saint-Pierre: "Such was my resolution, and it was there I hoped to execute the great project of the indolent life to which I had until then consecrated the little activity with which Heaven had endowed me."[28] He gave the attempt a famous *aperçu* in the *Reveries*[29].

Working the faculties, exercising them to put oneself into a state of more perfect freedom in disposing oneself, must not be confounded with the fact of applying oneself to torture to make oneself available to usages subjugated to the self. One must not be surprised that Rousseau, in diametrical opposition to Locke's judgment on the American Indians, affirms that the age of 'savage nations,' who did not yet know of the economy of production and who were satisfied with the consumption of goods offered spontaneously by nature, was "the happiest and the most lasting epoch" of the history of humanity.[30]

THE GENTLEMAN AND THE CRAFTSMAN

In view of the preceding analyses, how should we understand the importance that Rousseau accords to Emile learning a trade? How should we understand the role that he so often assigns to work as the only means

---

[26] *Emile*, Book II: 52.

[27] *Ibid.*: 53.

[28] Rousseau, J.-J. *The Confessions*, Book XII, transl. W. Conyngham Mallory. New York: Tudor Publishing Company, 1928: 1008.

[29] Rousseau, J.-J. *The Reveries of the Solitary Walker*, Fifth Walk, transl. Charles E. Butterworth, *The Collected Writings of Rousseau*, Vol. 8. Hanover/London: University Press of New England, 2000: 46.

[30] Rousseau, J.-J. *Discourse on Inequality* (abbr. DI), 2nd part, transl. V. Gourevitch, *The Discourses and Other Early Political Writings*. Cambridge: Cambridge University Press, 1997: 167.

of legitimising ownership of goods, meaning not only superfluous riches, but even the goods which are the most necessary for subsistence? If the "great project" of his own existence was always, as he said, to lead an "indolent life," why does he write in *Emile* that "Man in society is bound to work; rich or poor, weak or strong, every idler is a thief"?[31]

Locke, as I have said, gives as the end of the education he describes the purpose of forming a "gentleman."[32] One should not understand by this, at least not principally, a refined man. A "gentleman," or, as Rousseau says about Emile, a man who "came of a good family," is first of all an owner, someone who will inherit and who is placed in a dominant economic position. Now, if Locke and Rousseau alike undertake to educate an heir to riches, that is, for Locke, with the aim of teaching him to learn to keep his position and to occupy it as well as possible (he says himself that he has written a treatise of education "suited to our English Gentry").[33] For Rousseau, the aim is on the contrary to make of him a 'man', that is, to tear him away from that privileged condition.[34] And the need to work takes on an entirely different meaning according to which of these two frameworks it occupies: paradoxically, only Emile, who is not trained to become a man of business, will really experience the obligation to work with his body and to transform nature, thus giving work its full meaning as the force that legitimates wealth. But to understand this, we must make a detour into the complex analysis that Rousseau offers of the political status of work.

At first sight, one might be tempted to compare Rousseau's advice to parents to have their children learn a trade[35] with what Locke says on this point in *Thoughts Concerning Education.* In fact, Locke, against the prejudices of his aristocratic readers, not only recommends mastering some kind of manual work, but like Rousseau he gives pride of place to agriculture and carpentry.[36] However, the significance of this requirement is not the same in the two cases. Locke sees a manual occupation as a kind of leisure or relaxation for the pupil; but for Emile, it is really a trade, learnt from those who practise it to earn their living in workshops,[37]

---

[31] *Emile*, Book III: 189.

[32] See especially *Education*, The Epistle Dedicatory to Clarke: 80.

[33] *Ibid.*

[34] "I should not be sorry if Emile came from a good family. He will be another victim snatched from prejudice" (*Emile*, Book I: 23).

[35] See *ibid.*, Book III: 190.

[36] See *Education*, § 204: 257; *Emile*, Book III: 181, 190 and 195-196.

[37] See *Emile*, Book III: 178.

and its aim is to provide him with an honourable means of subsistence in the social order.[38]

So even if Locke, in the *Second Treatise*, considers that "the labour of his body, and the work of his hands"[39] is the foundation of the right that an individual has over his goods, for the gentleman of the *Thoughts Concerning Education*, and therefore for the property-holder, the work of his body is in reality simply a luxury. For the gentleman, the relationship between the concrete use of the body allowing the creation of wealth and the possession of wealth is so far mediated by the social relationships of production that the concrete work of transforming nature is relegated to a spare time activity. The proof of this is that the true trade the child must learn, for Locke (understanding 'trade' not in the sense of a skill whose purpose is to relax him while at the same time preventing him from allowing his time pass without employment of some kind, but rather as an *economic activity*) is that of an accountant or manager. Locke advises fathers to initiate their sons progressively into their "affairs;"[40] and at the end of the work, he recommends teaching the child the art of keeping account books.[41] An accomplished gentleman is one who knows how to maintain and produce further fruit from an economic patrimony that has already been acquired.[42]

The economic education of Emile is conceived in quite another spirit. We know from reading the sequel to *Emile*, that Emile ends up losing the wealth he has inherited[43]. But this choice is not just one of spite, connected to contingent circumstances (the treason of his wife Sophie). It has a much deeper meaning. Since his childhood, Emile has been put in a situation where he must ask himself about the true foundation of property (and therefore of his own inheritance), and on the true connection between work and property. What Emile has been initiated into is not, like Locke's pupil, a simple economic technical skill or ability, aimed at maintaining and confirming his social status, and more generally the existing social order. Emile has discovered, through some key mo-

---

[38] See *ibid.*, Book III: 187-192.

[39] *Second Treatise*, Chap. V, § 27: 128.

[40] See *Education*, §§ 96-97: 159-160.

[41] See *ibid.*, §§ 210-211: 260-262.

[42] We may remember something particularly significant on this point : something that Locke considers as something very serious, namely the unhappiness of a father whose son has the ambition – or, still worse, the talent – to become a poet (see *Education*, § 174: 230-231).

[43] See *Emile and Sophie; or The Solitaries*, 1st Letter, transl. C. Kelly and A. Bloom, *The Collected Writings of Rousseau*, Vol. 13 (Hanover and London: Dertmouth College Press, 2010): 710.

ments in his education, both the true logic of the economic order as an order of alienation, and the ethical problems raised by participation in that order of things. His relationship with work is thus to be understood in the light of this double growth of awareness. Two developments in *Emile* should be considered and related to each other here, as Rousseau himself invites us to do. In Book III, when the pupil is about fifteen, learning the carpenter's trade is the opportunity to make Emile understand the great principles of economics: mainly those concerning the division of labour, exchange, exchange value and use value, and currency.[44] But Rousseau specifies that "all these ideas hang together, and their foundation has already been laid in early childhood with the help of Robert the gardener. All we have now to do is to substitute general ideas for particular, and to enlarge these ideas."[45]

Indeed, in Book II Robert the gardener plays a role in a little scene of initiation bearing on the most fundamental of all economic principles, that of property. On that occasion, Emile is put in a situation that makes him understand something essential, of which the discoveries he will make later on concerning the division of labour and exchange will only be an extension and a confirmation. Helped by Robert the gardener, the governor initiated Emile in a conception of ownership at once very Lockean in its inspiration and at the same time, in its final consequences, something that subverts the Lockean project of rooting established ownership patterns in natural law. So that Emile can understand what the right of ownership means, he is taken by the governor to cultivate a bean plant by himself, for him to see the concrete prolongation of his work, and so that he can judge that he possesses the bean plant with a right comparable to his right over his own body.[46] This is a literal application of the thesis of Chapter V of the *Second Treatise*, according to which ownership is a natural right of the individual as long as it is based on "the labour of his body, and the work of his hands." But the lesson received by Emile is in reality more complex ("he is greatly mistaken," writes Rousseau).[47] Robert the gardener, the owner of the land cultivated by Emile, destroys the plantation and thus makes Emile understand the gap, and even the contradiction, between this theoretical foundation of ownership (real work carried out by an individual) and its real basis. Robert owns the earth that Emile has worked; so any relationship between work and

---

[44] See *Emile*, Book III: 177-190.

[45] *Ibid.*, Book III: 182.

[46] See *ibid.*, Book II: 73-74.

[47] *Ibid.*, Book II: 74.

property is in reality subordinated to the relationship among those who are property-owners and those who are only owners of their own strength as workers.[48]

On the small scale, Emile discovers what Rousseau describes in detail in the *Discourse On Inequality*: the expropriation of the greatest number by a small number which has taken possession of the land and the other means of production. From this original expropriation an illegitimate and limitless inequality results, based on the exploitation of men who possess nothing but their own bodies. This also leads to "war" and "misery."[49] We see how the ideas we find in Book III of *Emile* serve as a prolongation of this first experience in Book II. The reality of the division of labour is comparable to the reality of ownership, and is moreover the direct consequence of that reality: in what presents itself as a social collaboration where everybody wins, some people in fact work without gaining any profit from their work, while others profit from it without working.

On this point, a very revealing difference appears between the texts on education of Locke and Rousseau. While Rousseau has borrowed the principles of his theory of the natural law of property from Locke (where property would be a natural right if it was really and directly derived from the work carried out by an individual), it is remarkable that Locke has no plan to employ this practical mediation to make the child understand and respect the principle of an individual right to property. When, in *Thoughts Concerning Education*, he addresses this issue, he gives the two following pieces of advice:

> The safest way to secure honesty, is to lay the foundations of it early in liberality, and an easiness to part with to others whatever they have or like themselves. [...] And since children seldom have any thing but by gift, and that for the most part from their parents, they may be at first taught not to take or keep any thing but what is given them by those, whom they take to have power over it.[50]

What gives the child the idea of ownership is not here the process of creation of the good possessed – this should be work, if we believe what is said in the *Second Treatise* – but the means of acquisition of this idea is the *transmission* of property from individual to individual. Property is

---

48 See *ibid.* : 74-75. For a more complete analysis of this educational sequence and its political implications, see Bachofen, B. (2002) *La Condition de la liberté. Rousseau, critique des raisons politiques*, Chap. II. Paris: Payot: 131-148.

49 *DI*, 2nd part: 161.

50 *Education*, § 110: 170-171.

thus not essentially conceived as the fruit of labour, but as a status attaching a determined good to a determined person. The child becomes aware that things do not belong to everybody equally *by giving and receiving* and by discovering that by these two acts, the status of the good is modified. By giving, I cease to be the owner of a good with free disposition of it; and by receiving, I become the owner and the giver ceases to own it. That is why, when he receives a good, the child should only take it if he is aware that the person giving it has the right to give it, meaning that this person is its owner. Ownership is thus at root essentially conceived as the subtraction of a good from the common property, and the absorption of this good into the private sphere of individual disposition, without consideration for what might effectively and originally have legitimized this appropriation.

Rousseau knows this passage from *Thoughts Concerning Education* very well. He criticizes it thoroughly in *Emile*,[51] and replaces it, as we have seen, with the experience of concrete bodily labour transforming nature. I have said that Rousseau was more Lockean than Locke, and that by doing this he subverted the Lockean theory of property. He is more Lockean than Locke when he takes his theory of the natural right of ownership at its face value: he actually makes Emile work, not just when he is five years old, with the bean plant, but also later on, by teaching him the trade of carpentry. This study is the occasion for an initiation relating to questions of economic justice and injustice, which stands *against* the conclusions of Locke relating to the foundation of established property. Emile in fact understands on this occasion that "no father can transmit to his son any right to be of no use to mankind" and that "the man who eats in idleness what he has not himself earned, is a thief."[52] Far from serving to cover all right to established property with the appearance of a right that is natural, and thus sacred, the *real* link between work and property serves to introduce into reflections on rights a principle of radical criticism of the established order. Emile becoming an artisan symbolizes, at the individual level, the ideal of a social order where "no citizen is so very rich that he can buy another, and none so poor that he is compelled

[51] For a child to deal carefully with his own affairs, says Rousseau, "the first idea he needs is [...] property [...]. It is useless to enumerate his clothes, furniture, and playthings; although he uses these he knows not how or why he has come by them. To tell him they were given him is little better, for giving implies having; so here is property before his own, and it is the principle of property that you want to teach him; moreover, giving is a convention, and the child as yet has no idea of conventions. [...] We must therefore go back to the origin of property [...]" (*Emile*, Book II: 73).

[52] *Ibid.*, Book III: 189.

to sell himself."[53] In other words, a social order organized so that "work is always necessary and never useless."[54]

***

In all rigour, says Rousseau against Locke, the 'nature' of man does not require him to work, and certainly does not require him to torture himself into working. But in the social order in which Emile is constrained to live, in a world irreversibly modified by the techniques of production, by economic exchanges and above all universally conquered by the principles of land ownership and the social division of labour,[55] there is both a need and a duty to work. This necessity and this duty are ordered by complex political and social contingencies, and by reflexive, critical work on these contingencies. The problem of the status of work makes the meaning of this distinction explicit, by revealing the horizon towards which the whole of Rousseau's thought relating to the education of man as a citizen is orientated. The difficult learning of liberty integrates two dimensions that cannot be dissociated in the civil state, namely the independence of the individual, and the awareness of his social and political responsibilities.

[53] *The Social Contract*, Book II, Chap. XI, transl. V. Gourevitch, *The Social Contract and Other Later Political Writings* (Cambridge: Cambridge University Press, 1997): 78.
[54] Rousseau, J.-J. *Political Economy*, transl. V. Gourevitch, *The Social Contract and Other Later Political Writings*: 23.
[55] See *Emile*, Book III: 187.

Cosmopolitanism and Peace in Kant's Essay on 'Perpetual Peace'

Jørgen Huggler

Introduction

Immanuel Kant's book *Zum ewigen Frieden. Ein Philosophischer Entwurf* (*Toward Perpetual Peace. A Philosophical Sketch* [or Project]) first appeared in 1795.[1] What Kant sketches is the necessary and sufficient conditions for a lasting termination of the state of war among states, and, a path which can lead from a discorded state of nature among political bodies to a state of law, where war between these powers is prohibited. Along with other texts by Kant, the book is famous for its contribution to cosmopolitanism. However, Kant's essay on *Perpetual Peace* rejects the idea of a world government (earlier advocated by Kant himself), and the essay contains together with a substantial argument for cosmopolitan rights the most rigorous philosophical formulation of the limitations of the cosmopolitan law ever. Which reasons does he give for these restrictions? This is the question dealt with below. After some remarks on the setting of his book (sect. I) Kant's 'preliminary' and 'definitive' articles for a treaty of peace are examined (sect. II-III). Kant's arguments for cosmopolitan rights and his limitations of these to a right of visiting are discussed and related to Jacques Derrida's objections against Kant's lack of ethical concern about hospitality (sect. IV). After that, the very sophisticated discussion of the relation between politics and morality which Kant himself presents in *Toward Perpetual Peace* is analysed (sect. V). Against Derrida's ethicism as well as against so-called political realism it is concluded that neither did Kant suspend ethical concerns in order to be politically efficient nor did he confuse politics with morality. His restrictions on cosmopolitan rights do not give up his cosmopolitan ideas. In fact, cosmopolitanism is given a sharper and more reflected expression than in his earlier works (sect. VI).

---

[1] With kind permission from Springer Science+Business Media: *Studies in Philosophy and Education*, Cosmopolitanism and Peace in Kant's Essay on 'Perpetual Peace', Vol. 29 (2010): 129-140. © Springer Science+Business Media B. V. 2009. – References to *Zum ewigen Frieden/Toward Perpetual Peace* refer to the pages of the Akademie-Ausgabe VIII, and the second edition (1796). References to other of Kant's works are to the first edition (A) or to the second edition (B). Texts: Kant (1796, 2006).

I

Kant's focus on the demands of reason and on the presuppositions of peace has been read by the posterity as a mixture of sinister realism and bright utopian thinking.[2] Kant himself opens with a *captatio benevolentiae*, anticipating the sardonic claim that his book is just another scholarly utopia, because peace is only possible for the dead, whereas the living, and in particular the rulers of states, continue strife, as realised by every practical politician. This introduction recognises a division of labour between the politician and the philosopher, clearing the philosopher from being charged with dangerous interference in the affairs of government. To a reader of Kant's article on "Theory and Practise," this admission, however, is no confession at all: If a theory is of no use in practice, it is because the theory was not good enough as *theory*, not because theory as such has no *validity for practice*.[3]

Kant's essay is structured as a peace treaty, a rhetorical form well suited to the subject. At first he sets forward six 'preliminary articles,' negative or prohibiting articles in which he lists conditions that initially must be satisfied in international politics in order to make a radical armistice possible, not just any truce, but a perpetual peace. Kant goes on by formulating three so-called 'definitive articles,' positive prescriptions for the legal state that is required for peace to be durable. He formulates orders within three fields: constitutional law, law of nations, law of world citizenship. Then follows a first supplement concerning the *guarantee for the realisation* of perpetual peace, *viz.* that just as nature forces humans to organise themselves in states, nature will also force these states into a state of peace. In the second edition from 1796, a second supplement explains that this treaty must contain a subtle 'secret article,' which states that the philosophers, a group that rarely come under suspicion for their ability to conspire (possibly due to their inability to come to terms on any other issue whatsoever), should be allowed to contribute to the enlightenment of the rulers through public debate, which cannot do any harm, in order to inform the states that are prepared to go to war about the possibility of peace. The text ends with an appendix in two parts, the first of which concerns the conflict between morality and politics with respect to perpetual peace, while the second deals with the possibility of harmony between morality and politics based on a transcendental concept of public

---

[2] Cf. the historical studies: Lettevall (2001), Cavallar (1992).

[3] Kant, I. "Ueber den Gemeinspruch: Das mag in der Theorie richtig sein, taugt aber nicht für die Praxis," A 202.

law, *viz.* a theory considering how the relation between people and among states shall be, i.e. that it endures the light in perfect publicity.

Kant's efforts in this book (and later)[4] very clearly anticipate the charge of utopism laid at his door. He articulates a path to a political realisation of his notion of public law, which is not an empty idea *("keine leere Idee, sondern eine Aufgabe, die nach und nach aufgelöst, ihrem Ziele [...] beständig näher kommt"* (386, B 112)). Politics is conceived as "executive jurisprudence" *("ausübender Rechtslehre")*, as the applied doctrine of right or as a "practical doctrine of law" ('practical' meaning a practical use or realisation of the doctrine) (370, B 71). Kant's book on *Perpetual Peace* was written shortly after Prussia's separate peace treaty in Basel 1795 and subsequent withdrawal from the alliance against revolutionary France. Presumably Kant was at least superficially aware of the anti-utopian criticism against the revolution expressed by Edmund Burke (in his *Reflections on the Revolution in France* (1790)), translated into German in 1793. Although Kant does not mention Burke or his translator Friedrich Gentz, he refers in a very deprecatory manner to Jacques Mallet du Pan (353 note, B 28) whose *Considérations sur la nature de la Révolution de France* (1793) was translated by Gentz in 1794.

The achievements of the revolution in France (and perhaps also the results of the revolution in North-America)[5] seem pivotal for Kant's optimism in the book. Around that nucleus, a progress leading to an international league of republics – a pacific federation *("Friedensbund (foedus pacificum)")* – can begin, aiming at the end of *all* wars, not the end of merely *one* war (356, B 35). In some parts of his works Kant attempted to interpret the rebellion in France more as a legitimate development rather than as a revolution.[6] However, it would be subreptious to consider Kant's discourse as a defence of democracy or of the sovereignty of the people. Kant does not mention any 'democracy' or so-called 'republic' of

---

[4] Cf. Kant, Immanuel *Der Streit der Fakultäten* (1798), A 156 ff.

[5] An interesting recent study is Ossipow (2008). Ossipow argues that Kant has used a lot of silent quotations from a German translation of Emerich de Vattel's *Le droit de gens* (1758) in questions concerning international law, and in addition, Kant in his remarks concerning the internal organisation of republics was astonishing close to expressions in David Hume's *Essays* and unexpectedly also to phrases in a particular article (n° 51) published in the American *Federalist Papers* by Publius, i.e. James Madison [or Alexander Hamilton?] (1788). However, the influence of the political writings of Aristotle, Locke and Montesquieu present in the *Federalist Papers* weakens Ossipow's observation.

[6] Kant, Immanuel *Metaphysik der Sitten*, Rechtslehre, A 176 ff. In *Toward Perpetual Peace*, Kant thinks it just to punish the rebels, but without legitimacy to restore the pre-revolutionary political conditions (372 f., B 77 f.).

antiquity worthy of the term 'rule of law': they all eventually degenerated into despotism (353, B 29). What could promote the endurance of peace is not such a democracy. As a form of government, democracy is in principle, according to Kant, a despotism, because "it establishes an executive power in which 'all' decide for or even against one who does not agree; that is, 'all', who are not quite all, decide" – a contradiction of the general will with itself and with freedom, he points out.[7] Kant actually speaks in favour of the importance of having a representative form of government, i.e. *republics*, and by that term he refers to states ruled by law, i.e. which separates the executive and the legislative power (352, B 25). According to Kant, in the essay on "Theory and Practise" from 1793,[8] the laws of such republics must be "*as if*" they could have been made by the subjects themselves.[9] The same criterion is used in *Toward Perpetual Peace* (350 note, B 21). Only thus can they meet the strict standards of legitimacy. In the book on *Perpetual Peace* Kant adds another fundamental criterion, human right, implying freedom, not to be reduced to a tool, and the right to mutual communication (345, B 8 f.; 350, B 21; 366, B 60; cf. 353 note, B 27).[10]

---

[7] "Unter den drei Staatsformen [i.e. Autokratie, Aristokratie & Demokratie] ist die der *Demokratie* im eigentlichen Verstande des Worts notwendig ein *Despotism*, weil sie eine exekutive Gewalt gründet, da alle über und allenfalls auch wider Einen (der also nicht miteinstimmt), mithin alle, die doch nicht alle sind, beschließen; welches ein Widerspruch des allgemeinen Willens mit sich selbst und mit der Freiheit ist" (352, B 26).

[8] Kant, I. "Ueber den Gemeinspruch: Das mag in der Theorie richtig sein, taugt aber nicht für die Praxis," A 250.

[9] Kant admired the achievements of the revolution because it allowed for a more righteous and fair development than the old regime did. A positive view on the development in France is predominant in Kant, and it distinguishes him from many other voices in Germany at that time. Nevertheless, the idea of the sovereignty of the people made an escalation of war possible. The recruitment of soldiers was facilitated immensely by the invention of 'conscription.' In *Vom Kriege* Carl von Clausewitz called that phenomenon "The People in Arms" (Volksbewaffnung): "In the civilized parts of Europe, war by means of popular uprisings [*Volkskrieg*, war by means of the people] is a phenomenon of the nineteenth century. It has its advocates and its opponents. The latter object to it either on political grounds, considering it as a means of revolution, a state of legalized anarchy that is as much of a threat to the social order at home as it is to the enemy; or else on military grounds, because they feel that the results are not commensurate with the energies that have been expended" [...] "[A] popular uprising should, in general, be considered as an outgrowth of the way in which the conventional barriers *[seine alte künstliche Umwallung]* have been swept away in our lifetime by the elemental violence of war *[das kriegerische Element]*. It is, in fact, a broadening and intensification of the fermentation process known as war." Carl von Clausewitz, *On War*. M. Howard & P. Paret transl. Princeton: Princeton University Press, 1976/1984: 479 [From the 26th chapter of the sixth book].

[10] Cf. Kant, I. "Ueber den Gemeinspruch: Das mag in der Theorie richtig sein, taugt aber nicht für die Praxis", A 233 ff. & A 267 f.

II

The Preliminary Articles, the six negative clauses early in the essay, are:

> 1. Peace shall be more than just another pause in the war. Peace presupposes that the reasons for future hostility are totally removed.
> 2.The ties that bind a state to a particular community of people or 'society of men' shall be respected, and hiring-out of troops shall be prohibited. Princes shall have no opportunity to acquire other states by inheritance, exchange, purchase or donation.
> 3. In time standing armies shall be abolished, and there shall not be accumulated considerable fortunes, i.e. economic means that can be liberated to be used for warfare and thus must be considered as a threat to other states.
> 4. Unproportioned national debts to foreign states shall not be contracted (misusing credit to build up dominant economical power and to indulge poverty on other states in case of bankruptcy).
> 5. Violent interference with the constitution of another state is prohibited as far as it is not in a state of anarchy.
> 6. Prohibited are acts of war which make trust in future peace impossible such as use of assassins, poisoners, breach of capitulation and incitement to treason.

It would seem that common sense would approve of these preliminary articles, but some historical comments are revealing. Article 3 can be interpreted as an objection against the militarised absolutistic Prussian state, as it had been since Kant's youth and the wars 1740-48. Article 5 can be read as a warning against interference in revolutionary France (Saner 1995) or alternatively as an objection against the interference of Prussia, Austria and Russia in the division of Poland in 1772, 1793 and 1795 (Cf. Klemme's editorial notes in his edition of Kant 1796). However, Kant's argumentation is not historical or time-bound, but a principled discourse. For instance, he considers the danger of war connected to the expensive rearmament and the costs of maintaining standing armies, and the threats and dangers connected with big war chests and excessive governmental spending on the military, i.e. not for development of infrastructure and improvement of the situation of the citizens. The protests against the actual lack of reason are mobilised by Kant to point out the paths to peace in the hope that reason can change political practise. Articles 1, 5 and 6 imply strict prohibition, and differ from articles 2, 3 and 4 whose point is to prevent future misconduct, not to demand immediate changes of the things not fulfilling the articles. To Kant, perpetual peace does not mean a perpetual standstill; it means an epoch-making, definitive farewell to war as an instrument of politics among states. The point of the preliminary articles is to allow the will to peace to make a difference that matters. Therefore they outline the condition for a lasting termination of the state of war. They outline *a path of progression* from a natural state among political bodies where war is the insuspensible condition to an (anti-Hobbesian) state of law, where war between political bodies is prohibited.

III

The Definitive Articles, Kant's positive orders, define the institutions necessary for a definitive peace. These are:

> 1. The constitutional law of every state should be *republican.*
> 2. The law of nations should be founded on a *federation of free states.*
> 3. The law of world citizenship shall be *limited* to conditions of universal hospitality.

The *Republican* article is related to Kant's contractual understanding of society. The legitimacy of government relies on the fact that it gives everyone the freedom to seek his own happiness, insofar as it does not encroach on the right of others to do the same (350 note, B 20). The republican form of government implies that a decision concerning war cannot be made without the consent of the citizens. From the citizens' position, such a decision is not an easy one, because they have to bear the consequences themselves. Therefore republicanism is an obstacle against warfare. However, as mentioned above, Kant does not talk about democracy, but about government by law. Perhaps he feared that the explosive enthusiasm of a mob would make war more ferocious and cruel than war among kings.

The *Federal* article points out that having a republican rule of law in common leads to an insight in shared interests and therefore to the joint concern for a federal connection – a particular league of nations, restricted to the limited task of being a league of peace (356, B 34 f.) – among states which are free in the republican way. Kant does not demand a vertical subjection under a mega-state.[11] Nature itself is against such an institution: diversity of languages and religions are among the obstacles (367, B 64). Although a universal monarchy seems to be an effective guard of peace, Kant is sceptical because monarchy tends to develop into a despotic regime, powerful enough to ignore the rule of laws. Even if the idea of international law presupposes many independent states potentially in a state of war, this is rationally preferable to the dangerous lack of freedom in the universal monarchy. Kant suggests a horizontal develop-

[11] Matthias Lutz-Bachmann considers this rejection of a world republic as "inconsistent with Kant's own assumptions." However, Lutz-Bachmann neglects the difference between the arguments in *Zum ewigen Frieden* and those in Kant's earlier works (Lutz-Bachmann1997).

ment of a fellowship among states that share the same form of government and enjoying similar civil rights. According to Kant, a world republic would be governed in a despotic manner and its rule would be anarchical, that is without law (352, B 26; cf. 373 note, B 79). It would destroy the division between legislative and executive power, make representation impossible and reduce citizens to subjects.

The *Cosmopolitan* article seems to introduce a seminal legal construction, *the law of world citizenship*. It is seminal because the individuals are given rights that are not bound to a particular state. In fact, Kant has made important contributions to develop different aspects of the idea of cosmopolitanism. This idea pervades many aspects of his thinking in texts such as "Idee zu einer allgemeinen Geschichte in weltbürgerlicher Absicht," Achter Satz (1784), *Metaphysik der Sitten* (1797), Rechtslehre § 62,[12] *Der Streit der Fakultäten* (1798), the "Lectures on Pedagogic," etc.[13] In his "Idee zu einer allgemeinen Geschichte in weltbürgerlicher Absicht," 7. Satz, Kant remarked that the attempt to create a perfect internal organisation of the state can only remain incomplete, unless it deals with the problem of the legal relations between states. In that essay, his means to a lasting end to all war between states was a world government (A 398 f.). However, in comparison to Kant's earlier writings (1784-93), the conception in *Toward Perpetual Peace* seems to be founded on deeper considerations, *viz.* the problem of combining a mega-state with freedom. In consequence, Kant had to adopt and to substantiate the thought of a slow growth of international peace dependent on the development of republican states. Such considerations sharpened his views on cosmopolitanism. On the other hand, they implied a limitation on cosmopolitanism that diverged from the optimistic views about the possibility for a future development and perfection of the humankind in Kant's earlier philosophy of history and in his pedagogical lectures. We may ask for the reasons for that limitation.

IV

In the essay on *Perpetual Peace*, the idea of cosmopolitanism is subordinated to the political aim of achieving peace. Kant does not speak about propagating an international law superior to national law. On the contra-

---

[12] "[die] Vernunftidee einer *friedlichen*, wenn gleich noch nicht freundschaftlichen, durchgängigen Gemeinschaft aller Völker auf Erden, die untereinander in wirksame Verhältniss kommen können, ist nicht etwa philanthropisch (ethisch), sondern ein *rechtliches* Prinzip" (Kant 1798, A 229/B 259).

[13] Cf. Kemp (2005).

ry, his point is to confine the claims of cosmopolitanism to hospitality, which is the right of a stranger not to be treated as an enemy when he arrives in the land of another (state). Nevertheless, Kant contributes with a substantial new argument for cosmopolitan rights based on the space needed for a human being on the limited surface of the Earth. In *Toward Perpetual Peace* Kant writes:

> As in the previous articles, we are concerned here with *right* [*Recht*, law], not with philanthropy, and in this context *hospitality* (a host's conduct to his guest) means the right of a stranger not to be treated in a hostile manner by another upon his arrival on the other's territory. If it can be done without causing his death, the stranger can be turned away, yet as long as the stranger behaves peacefully where he happens to be, his host may not treat him with hostility. It is not the *right of a guest* [to be a permanent visitor, *Gastrecht*] that the stranger has a claim to (which would require a special, charitable contract stipulating that he be made a member of the household for a certain period of time), but rather a right to visit *[Besuchsrecht]*, to which all human beings have a claim, to present oneself to society by virtue of the right of common possession of the surface of the earth. Since it is the surface of a sphere, they cannot scatter themselves on it without limit, but they must rather ultimately tolerate one another as neighbours, and originally no one has more of a right to be at [be present on] a given place on earth than anyone else. (Colclasure transl.: 82) (357 f., B 40.)

Reinhard Brandt has pointed out the importance laid in *Metaphysik der Sitten* §§ 4-9 (AB 59 ff.) on the human *body* and its being in need of a place to occupy. The human body is in need of a place, although it cannot claim to have that place as its possession.[14] In the book on *Perpetual Peace*, this idea is not developed in detail. However, it is used here in combination with the idea of the communal possession of the Earth's surface. Based on that, Kant argues that you have the right to visit (and to ask for asylum) in another country. However, it does not give occasion to claim a right of being welcomed as a child (i.e. a native) of the state. This signifies a *de facto* recognition in Kant of the states as the proprietors of a territory. In his general remarks to 'the preliminary articles' where Kant prohibits a "manner of acquisition," his prohibition does not concern the status of possession, e.g. of the territory on which the state exists (347, B 14 f.; cf. 344, B 7). However, such *de facto* possession is distinguished from a strict *de jure* claim. Acquisitions made in a state of nature (where there is no legal authority) can be transformed into lawful possession in a civil society, although the manner of acquisition did not meet the stand-

[14] Brandt (1995). He writes: "wer also gegen seinen eigenen Willen an das Ufer eines Landes getrieben wird, hat das Recht des Besuchs, weil er einen Boden unter seinen Füßen braucht" (144 f.).

ards of law that qualify a civil society.[15] In the essay on *Perpetual Peace* this clause is not made explicit in the specific context of cosmopolitan law, although it could easily be expressed in here as well. This means that Kant chooses to be silent in regard to some fundamental question of cosmopolitan justice. He is not unaware of the problematic and unjust situation.

One may be astonished by this restriction, because Kant's ethics underlines the unlimited dignity of man as a rational being, and in his pedagogical lectures and in the essay on philosophy of history, he aims for the unrestricted development of the humankind, a realisation of the human possibilities as not limited by a national or local scope, but rather cosmopolitan in orientation and outlook. The utopian ideas in Kant's "Idea for a Universal History from a Cosmopolitan Perspective" (1784) concerning a world republic that will bring about peaceful relations among nations could better be reconciled with such an unrestricted ethics, although they are presented as solving a problem of law, not of ethics.

Jacques Derrida contested the juridical and formal setting of the question in Kant's essay on *Perpetual Peace*. Inspired by Emmanuel Lévinas, he made a plea for an unrestricted solidarity among humans: "l'hospitalité, c'est la culture même et ce n'est pas une éthique parmi les autres [...] *l'éthique est hospitalité*." Ethics is hospitality, Derrida declares in a work with the telling title, *Cosmopolites de tous les pays, encore un effort!* (1997).[16] According to Derrida, the legal and juridical set-

---

[15] Kant writes: "But here the prohibition that is presupposed in the law of permission concerns only the future manner of acquiring a right (e.g. through inheritance [cf. the second preliminary article]), whereas the exemption from this prohibition, i.e., the permission, concerns the current status of possession. In accordance with the law of permissibility of natural right, the current state of possession can, in the transition from the state of nature into the state of civil society, continue to be preserved as an, although not lawful, nonetheless *honest possession (possessio putativa)*. This obtains for such a putative possession as soon as it has been recognized as such in the state of nature, even though a similar manner of acquisition in the subsequent state of civil society (after the transition) is prohibited. This authorization of continued possession would not exist if such a putative acquisition had occurred in the state of civil society. For in the state of civil society such possession would constitute an injury and have to end immediately after the discovery of its unlawfulness." (Colclasure transl.: 72) (347 note, B 15 f.).

[16] Derrida (1997): 42. "Hospitality is culture itself and not simply one ethic among others. Insofar as it has to do with the *ethos*, that is, the residence, one's home, the familiar place of dwelling, inasmuch as it is a manner of being there, the manner in which we relate to ourselves and to others, to others as our own or as foreigners, *ethics is hospitality*; ethics is so thoroughly coextensive with the experience of hospitality," Derrida (2001): 16 f. According to Derrida, the focus on the *limiting laws* of hospitality makes a perversion possible of what

ting leads to injustice and cruelty. Derrida suspects Kant to be misled by his acceptance of Hobbes' conception of the natural state as a state of war. Therefore he wants to deliver the concept of hospitality from the Kantian concern for the violation of national prerogatives.

However, the cause defended by Kant is interesting and far-reaching. To Kant, *philanthropy (Menschenliebe)* is a duty of imperfect obligation, not an unconditioned duty. In contrast, *respect (Achtung)* for the *rights* of humans is a duty of perfect obligation, an unconditional duty. Therefore the restriction mentioned above on the rights of world-citizenship does not worry Kant ethically. In the quest for a perpetual peace, he sticks to his point. Thus, he conceives the world citizenship in the juridical context of colonialism and imperialism, martial conquest under disguise of legitimacy. He distinguishes between and confronts an unlimited, natural right to have a place and a living on the surface of the limited globe on one hand, and the limited political right to claim citizenship in a particular state on the other. By the energy he spent in making the logical foundation of the distinction clear, Kant has provided models for later discussions of the subject. Importantly, Derrida has pointed out the sophistry in recent distinguishing between being a refugee due to political or to economic reasons (Derrida 1997a: 35, Engl. transl.: 12). We cannot accuse Kant of such a sophistry. His distinction between the natural right to occupy a place where you can be and live and the citizenship within the law of states allows for political reflections concerning the right of visiting in particular cases. However, Derrida refuses to let the political component mentioned in the term 'cosmo*polit*anism' supersede the ethical aspect of hospitality.[17]

We should also recognise that Kant is fully aware of the difference between positive law (as it actually is) and a deeper concept of justice. In the last part of his essay, he demands that politics shall respect what is right. However, that moral claim on politics is of a formal nature. In its claim on politics, it demands that politics shall respect legitimacy. Morality is in this case an instance for critical evaluation, underlining the principle that justice should hold precedence over power, although there is no positive politics determined categorically by morality.

---

he terms as "*the* law of hospitality". Kant's formulation of the law of cosmopolitanism is a problematic instance of that.

[17] Cf. Derrida (1997b, 1999).

V

Kant has two trumps to show that it is not in vain to hope that the vision of perpetual peace on the long view can become reality. Firstly, he assumes that *nature* will force men to act decently in cooperation in spite of their individual concerns and egoism. The devastating effects of war, cultural antagonisms due to differences in languages and religions, and the spirit of trade, compels them to enter into legal relations with one another. Secondly, the thought of peace is reasonable – it is the demand of reason; it is what should be, if someone is asked 'what is right.' Because it is not impossible to fulfill, it is duty. Therefore, Kant spends a lot of effort to show that the politician who does not subdue his morality to political prudence, but assimilates his politics to the demands of morality, is sign of a possible conscious realisation of peace.

However, one may wonder that Kant's reference to such realisation, possible even in "a nation of devils" (366, B 61), seems to give very little space to conscience, education or motivation in his philosophical *'Entwurf'*.[18] However, we know from his pedagogical lessons that his confidence in princes as well as in parents' ability to aim for the far-reaching ends of humankind is rather small. In the book on *Perpetual Peace*, another thing is just as small as his confidence in parents and princes: his expectations to the achievements of opportunistic moralists or lawyers, who take positive law as the highest obtainable expression of justice, i.e. persons whose outlook is limited to the things which exist already.

In fact, Kant's engagement in the *public* sphere of discussion as the locus of Enlightenment is demonstrated in the *'Geheimklausul,'* the co-called "Secret Article" that admits freedom of speech to philosophers. Plato's Philosopher-King is here split up by a clear-cut division of labour: The role of the king is to rule, the work of the philosopher to enlighten the king by expressing his concerns, and among them the worry for consequences of war. Kant assumes that power curbs the ability to assess justly or do justice. Therefore the ruler needs the philosopher, a critical adviser. Philosophy and political prudence do not follow the same rationality; if they contaminate each other, they will be depraved (like the profession of lawyers, cf. 373 f., B 80); but if they are kept separate, the one can supplement the other. Not just absolutistic monarchs, but also what Kant terms as 'royal peoples' (369, B 70), i.e. peoples who rule them-

[18] That lack of confidence in bottom-up development (or in "the universal republicanism") was pointed out by Friedrich Schlegel (1796).

selves, need such advisers to remind them about fundamental principles of justice. Kant admits, however, that the politician makes his decisions under other circumstances than the philosopher.[19] The morally minded politician acts in a responsible way, he is not "as innocent [or false] as the pigeons," although his "executive jurisprudence" (370, B 71 f.) if it is needed has to be as "prudent as serpents."

Although politics, unlike morals, is an art, Kant, in the first part of his 'Appendix,' made an attempt to show that it does not require artful skills to bring politics and morality in harmony:

> True politics can take no steps forward without first paying tribute to morality, and although politics in itself is a difficult art, the union of politics and morality is no art at all. For morality cuts through the Gordian knot that politics is unable to untie whenever the two come into conflict with another. The rights of humankind [*"das Recht der Menschen,"* the human justice] must be held sacred, whatever it may cost those in power. One cannot pursue a half measure here and devise a hybrid, pragmatically conditioned right [*Recht*, justice] (between right and utility). Instead all politics must bend its knee before rights [justice] but can hope to arrive at the point, however gradually, where it can shine perpetually. (Colclasure transl.: 104) (380, B 96.)

There is no real incompatibility; what goes wrong is the subjective egoistic propensity or inclination, which is not based on reason, and therefore does not deserve to be called practise (379, B 94). It is wrong to disavow morality with reference to political concerns, and to take some 'empirical facts' about human nature for granted. If you do this, you can always show examples to point out the mischief of people who make their own decisions. However, Kant says, such theories are co-responsible for the evil they take as an argument (378, B 92). He admits that it is not sufficient for the rise of an authentic general will that individuals wish and will a constitution formulated according to principles of freedom. In that respect it seems that *power* precedes justice, because the creation of a collective unity needs a uniting cause. Therefore, the ruler has no apparent need for laws given by the people. Nevertheless, if *justice* is reduced to power, it means that an unjust condition is made permanent. All constitutional laws, all laws among nations, as well as every cosmopolitan ideal, will have no content if politics simply is the artful skill to use the mechanisms of nature to achieve its goals. The idea of justice itself will

---

[19] Philosophical insight and political prudence do not share the same rationality. According to Volker Gerhardt, this is a very important Modern insight (Gerhardt 1995). However, it might be argued that Plato himself, e.g. in the *Politikos*, started the discussion of the specific form of political rationality, a discussion that has been continued by Aristotle, and later by Machiavelli and Hobbes.

be empty, and sophistic maxims take over. Such as: *"Fax et excusa,"* take your chance and let the result count for legitimacy. *"Sic fecisti, nega,"* if you do injustice, deny you own responsibility. *"Divide et impera,"* divide and rule! These are trivial maxims obstructing the establishment of perpetual peace (374 ff., B 82 ff.).

Thus, Kant assumes that his project for peace cannot be realised without an ideal of justice. Peace is not just a material good. Only recognition of duty can lead to peace. The prudence of government has to be subordinated to the ideal of justice if it is to become wisdom in politics (373 note, B 79). Therefore, peace is promoted by constituting and ordering the state according to principles of justice. In analogy, the relations among states should be ordered according to international law, and the relation between individuals and foreign states according to principles of cosmopolitan justice. Only then can peace be sustainable. The morality respecting politician knows this. Although his political prudence gives him concern about premature reforms (372 f., B 77 f.), he will, in the long view, aim at the ideal of justice (372, B 76 f.; 378 ff., B 91 ff.). Contrary to sophisms crying out the deficiencies of human nature such a politician holds the right of humans to be holy (380, B 97).

Kant's optimistic ideals of enlightenment are expressed in these considerations of how the *aporia* of the relation between politics and morality can be resolved. Kant betrays no mistrust of a rule of law constituted according to principles of freedom (373 note, B 79), just because hitherto there were no perfect examples (378, B 91 f.). In the second part of the 'Appendix,' Kant explains why public justice has to be public. If an act cannot be public, it is a sign of its moral deficiency, and even its illegitimacy (in juridical-legal respect). It cannot be made public because it threatens some other part (381, B 99 f.). It must be kept secret, if it is to succeed.

However, as a guarantee for peacekeeping, it is not sufficient that maxims of action are made public. If the rulers have nothing to fear from public opinion, publicity is insufficient. Kant's objection against a conquering power that takes the role *of "die gesetzgebende Obrigkeit [...], der man gehorchen muss, ohne darüber zu vernünfteln"* (374, B 82) makes a great contrast to his earlier words in *"Was ist Aufklärung"* from 1784 about the great number of soldiers commanded by Frederic the 2nd of Prussia, who was able to hold every public discussion in check with the help of these soldiers. In that text, Kant restricted himself to argue for the (license to) freedom of academic publishing; now the role of publicity has gained a new quality.[20] Kant maintains an affirmative criterion: An action which can only be carried out through a public prescription, i.e. not through coercion alone, is both politically and morally legitimate. It enjoys political legitimacy because it fits with the general objectives of the public, i.e. happiness, and therefore makes the public content. To achieve such harmony is the basic task of politics. Perpetual peace is "a task which, carried out gradually, steadily moves toward its goal (since the periods in which equal advances are made will hopefully grow shorter and shorter" (Colclasure transl.: 109) (386, B 110 ff.).

VI

It has often been held that the effect of Kantian cosmopolitanism is to confuse politics with morality. As has been shown in the above, this is not the case. In fact, Kant distinguished clearly between morality and politics. Without providing a comprehensive political philosophy similar to e.g. the Aristotelian *Politics*, Kant realised that specific political practices and political institutions are essential for international peace. In the past, they were ignored because politics was seen as essentially a question of power. However, if that was the case, (if for instance, Thomas Hobbes was right when he said in Leviathan that covenants without the sword are but words) the key question for peace as a lasting termination of war is: who will enforce such a peace treaty's new international norms of justice? In that perspective, Kant's project would seem naïve or perhaps even dangerous. But in the tract on *Perpetual Peace*, Kant clearly abandoned the idea of a world government, which he a few years earlier had established as the political goal for the history of mankind. In consequence, to assume a cosmopolitan point of view does not require of us that we give up our particular identities or attachments. Kant's thoughts concerning the end of war do entail a perpetual effort, although with a fair, but realistic prospect of success, and not the end of politics or of history in a kind of perpetual sleep.

On the other hand, Kant held that what may seem as realism in ordinary life (making war and injustice the normal situation), is an equally dangerous or even worse kind of perpetual sleep. That kind of realism limits the imagination to stick to a miserable reality. It makes human attempts to provide for loftier answers look like a foolish whimsy. That

---

[20] "Aber auch nur derjenige, der selbst aufgeklärt, sich nicht vor Schatten fürchtet, zugleich aber ein wohldiszipliniertes zahlreiches Heer zum Bürgen der öffentlichen Ruhe zur Hand hat, – kann das sagen, was ein Freistaat nicht wagen darf: *räsonnirt, so viel ihr wollt, und worüber ihr wollt; nur gehorcht!*" "Beantwortung der Frage: Was ist Aufklärung," A 493, cf. A 484.

strand of so-called realism, and the unilateral focus on power, implied that philosophical reason, publicity and morals were disregarded. However, according to Kant they (together with economical and political institutions) are the main tools for a realisation of peace.

Kant does not confound morals and politics. He treats the relations between politics and morals as connecting two distinct fields of practise. Even though morality has an importance of its own in his reasoning, politics has a rationality related to art. However, politics should adjust to morality, not morality to political prudence of a limited, narrow scope. Kant's cosmopolitical reasoning shows that the idea of choice, of being able to choose for oneself, is not at the bottom of our experience of human dignity. Seen in the utmost concrete global perspective, we are not always in a situation to choose how we will live, and under what conditions. This leads to the painful actuality of the demand for recognition of cosmopolitical law, although the perspective of peace makes the limits of cosmopolitical rights clear in pointing out the possibility of some imperialistic or other misuse of the very claims of such rights, misuses that are devastating for the project of peace.

Thus, Kant's limitations on cosmopolitical rights are clear-cut. On the other hand, the focus on indisputable human physical requirements does not discard the cosmopolitan perspectives of Kant's philosophy: the universal human dignity as an end in itself, as an end for a person's duties toward himself and toward others, and an end for the perfection of humankind and of the cultural, political and moral progresses of the human history.

This cosmopolitan idea has the regulative virtue of allowing us to look wider than our particular situation, and to view ourselves in relation to a higher or more general objective. In politics as well as in education, an unempirical, cosmopolitan end should be aimed for, would we not give up critical standards, and understanding of reality. Thus, Kant's book on the necessary and seemingly sufficient conditions for the establishment of a perpetual peace is part of and sharpens his cosmopolitan arguments as well. It does not give them over just to embrace the noble objective of perpetual peace. This is the lesson for cosmopolitan thinking today, often rather unclear in scope, end and means.

REFERENCES

Brandt, R. (1995) "Vom Weltbürgerrecht," in O. Höffe (ed.), *Immanuel Kant: Zum ewigen Frieden*. Berlin: Akademie Verlag: 133-148.

Cavallar, G. (1992) *Pax Kantiana: systematisch-historische Untersuchung des Entwurfs "Zum ewigen Frieden" (1795) von Immanuel Kant*. Wien: Böhlau.

Clausewitz, C. von. (1832-34). *Vom Kriege. Hinterlassenes Werk des Generals Carl von Clausewitz*. Bonn: Ferdinand Dümmlers Verlag (19. Aufl., 1980).

– (1984). *On War*, transl. by M. Howard, P. Paret. Princeton University Press.

Derrida, J. (1997a) *Cosmopolites de tous les pays, encore un effort!* Paris: Éditions Galilée.

– (1997b) *Adieu à Emmanuel Lévinas*. Paris: Éditions Galilée.

– (1999) *Adieu to Emmanuel Lévinas*. Stanford: Stanford University Press.

– (2001, 2002) *On Cosmopolitanism and Forgiveness*, transl. by M. Dooley, M. Hughes. London: Routledge.

Gerhardt, V. (1995) "Der Thronversicht der Philosophie. Über das moderne Verhältnis von Philosophie und Politik bei Kant," in O. Höffe (ed.), *Immanuel Kant: Zum ewigen Frieden*. Berlin: Akademie Verlag: 171-193.

Kant, I. (1793) "Ueber den Gemeinspruch: Das mag in derTheorie richtig sein, taugt aber nicht für die Praxis," in H. F. Klemme (ed.), *Ueber den Gemeinspruch: Das mag in der Theorie richtig sein, taugt aber nicht für die Praxis. Zum ewigen Frieden. Ein philosophischer Entwurf.* Hamburg: Felix Meiner Verlag, 1992.

– (1796) *Ueber den Gemeinspruch: Das mag in der Theorie richtig sein, taugt aber nicht für die Praxis. Zum ewigen Frieden. Ein philosophischer Entwurf*, H. F. Klemme (ed.). Hamburg: Felix Meiner Verlag, 1992.

– (1798) *Die Metaphysik der Sitten*, in Immanuel Kant, *Werke* bd. IV, W. Weischedel (ed.). Darmstadt: Wissenschaftliche Buchgesellschaft, 1998.

– (2006) *Toward Perpetual Peace and Other Writings on Politics, Peace and History*, ed. By P. Kleingeld, & transl. by D. L. Colclasure. New Haven & London: Yale University Press.

Kemp, P. (2005) *Verdensborgeren som pædagogisk ideal*. Copenhagen: Hans Reitzels Forlag: 140 ff.

Lettevall, R. (2001) *En europeisk kosmopolit. En ide'historisk studie av Immanuel Kants 'Om den eviga freden' och dess verkningshistoria*. Stockholm/Stehag: Brutus Östlings Bokförlag Symposion.

Lutz-Bachmann, M. (1997) "Kant's Idea of Peace and the Philosophical Conception of a World Republic," in J. Bohman & M. Lutz-Bachmann (eds), *Perpetual Peace. Essays on Kant's Cosmopolitan Ideal*. Cambridge, Massachusetts: The MIT Press: 59-77.

Ossipow, W. (2008) "Kant's Perpetual Peace and its Hidden Sources: A Textual Approach," in *Swiss Political Science Review*, 14(2): 357-389.

Saner, H. (1995) "Die negativen Bedingungen des Friedens," in O. Höffe (ed.), *Immanuel Kant: Zum ewigen Frieden*. Berlin: Akademie Verlag: 43-67.

Schlegel, F. (1796) "Versuch über den Begriff des Republikanismus veranlasst durch die Kantische Schrift 'Zum ewigen Frieden' (1796)," in W. Hecht (ed.), *Friedrich Schlegel: Werke in zwei Bänden*. Berlin & Weimar: Aufbau-Verlag, 1980, Bd. I: 53-73.

THE ROLE OF PHILOSOPHY IN CITIZENSHIP EDUCATION DURING THE NEOHELLENIC ENLIGHTENMENT

Athanasia GLYCOFRYDI-LEONTSINI

During the Neohellenic Enlightenment, a strong intellectual movement flourished from about 1750 up to 1821, the year of the outbreak of the Greek War of Independence. European Enlightenment's progressive ideas posed an intellectual challenge to Greek educational standards that were, after the fall of Constantinople (1453), associated with a traditional curriculum imposed by the Eastern Orthodox Church, which was left as the only authority in Greek cultural life after the reopening in 1454 of the Patriarchal Academy of Constantinople. In that institution, from the later fifteenth century onwards, the teaching of philosophy – oriented towards the Aristotelian theories – consisted of topics like dialectic, rhetoric, ethics, and natural philosophy. It was only during the eighteenth century that Greek educators (mostly clerics coming from various centers and educated in many foreign universities), eager for the modernization of both secondary and higher education and for the advancement of learning, tried to promote innovative teaching in various institutions, and to modify the curriculum in line with the demands of the Church, the nobility, and the Greek intelligentsia.[1]

The Greek intelligentsia, especially those of the Greek Diaspora (teachers, priests, diplomats, statesmen, bibliophiles, merchants, sailors, and men of letters) encouraged free thought and cultural, social and political change, and exercised a very important role in the formation of Greek educational models and the achievement of social and political innovations and reforms. This freedom allowed them to teach and publish in disciplines like science, history, political economy, government, education, foreign languages, literature, and philosophy in its wider sense. From the remaining syllabi, publications of professors, textbooks and notes produced during classes (most of them still unedited) and from the existing translations of foreign books, it is possible to reconstruct the principal ideas and values promulgated in the Academies (located in Constantinople, Mount Athos, Bucharest, Iași, Moschopolis, and Kydo-

[1] Dimaras, Constantinos T. (1992) 'Greece 1750-1850,' in K. J. Dover (ed.), *Perceptions of the Ancient Greeks*. Blackwell: Oxford UK/Cambridge USA: 203-224.

nies [Ayvalik] in Asia Minor) and in the schools of 'higher education' established in large mercantile centers of the Greek Diaspora, like Venice, Vienna, or the Danubian Municipalities of Wallachia and Moldavia, the Ionian Islands, Ioannina, Thessaly, Northern Greece, the Peloponnese, the islands of the Aegean sea, and on the coast of Asia Minor. These schools, that operated under various names, such as 'academies,' 'lyceums,' 'seminaries,' 'museums' or 'gymnasiums,' a variety that suggests the latitude of their functions,[2] became the focus of the activity of Greek thinkers and teachers who had adopted the general values and ideas of the Enlightenment and were willing to enlighten their countrymen through a new educational programme.

These thinkers and teachers – whilst aiming at educating their countrymen on becoming clerics, administrators, teachers or doctors – developed an educational activity that led to the cultural and national awakening of both Greeks and Balkans through various educational reforms. These reforms were made possible due to the economic boom of Hellenism that flourished abroad and helped the development of Greek education in various ways, particularly through benefactions (money, books, equipment, establishment of institutions and schools).[3] It was actually a group of enlighteners, among which were Eugenios Voulgaris, Iosepos Moisiodax, Benjamin Lesvios, Konstantinos Koumas, Adamantios Korais – to mention only a few – that made possible the inflow of Western ideas to wide audiences through their teachings and writings either in 'Hellenic' or Modern Greek language.[4]

---

[2] Evangelidis, Tryfon (1936) *I paideia epi tourkokratias*, vol. 1. Athens: LXXXI; Glenos, Dimitrios (1945) *I axia ton anthropistikon grammaton stin Ellada.* Athens: 37; Chatzopoulos, Konstantinos (1991) *Ellinika sholeia stin periodo tis othomanikis kyriarchias (1453-1821).* Vanias: Thessaloniki: 226-302.

[3] Henderson, George Patrick (1970) *The Revival of Greek Thought 1620-1830*. Albany: State University of New York Press: 1-11.

[4] I should mention here that the Greek language controversy started when Greek Enlightenment thinkers began to argue on what was the most suitable type of language that should be followed in their educational and scholarly writing. During this period the language they used ranged from the classical Attic of the archaist Eugenios Voulgaris (1716-1806) to the transcription of the spoken tongue by the vernacularist Demetrios Katartzis (c.1730-1807). Ancient Greek was known as 'Hellenic,' while various terms were used to refer to Modern Greek, including 'common language,' 'common *yfos*,' 'simple language' or 'simple *yfos*.' The Greek authors rarely used the word 'modern' to refer to the language of their day, while the term *'yfos'* was commonly used to refer to language variety rather than style. Cf. Mackridge, Peter (2009) *Language and National Identity in Greece, 1766-1976*. Oxford; in particular cf. Mackridge, Peter (2010) 'Korais and the Greek Language Question,' in Paschalis M. Kitromilides (ed.) *Adamantios Korais and the European Enlightenment*. Oxford: Voltaire Foundation, University of Oxford: 128.

The Greek language controversy – part of the debate between 'ancients and moderns' who were either in favour of tradition or of innovation respectively – was actually associated with concerns to introduce politics in education by recognizing educational rights to all social groups. The main advocates of the linguistic controversy agreed that it should be via the Modern European scholars, scientists, and philosophers, and not via the Ancient Greek writers, that the Greek 'nation' should be introduced into the contemporary world of scholarship and learning. In many ways and to a great extent, the Greek enlighteners – from Voulgaris and Moisiodax to Korais – helped in the establishment of a new order that led to the mobilisation of Greek society and contributed to the shaping of both national and social consciousness. Actually, at a crucial time in Greek history, the Greek intelligentsia discovered a host of European scientists, philosophers, novelists, and historians (Locke, Voltaire, Kant, Herder, Fichte, Beccaria, Descartes, Condillac, Condorcet, Montesquieu, Diderot, Rousseau, Muratori, Genovesi, Soave, Wieland, Gibbon, Duhamel, Gravesande, Heinecke, Musschenbroek, *et alia*) and tried to introduce their theories into the Greek speaking world either by incorporating their ideas in their lecture notes or by translating their books into Greek. These translations were published in Europe, mostly in Venice, Vienna, and Leipzig.[5]

The tensions between 'western' and 'classical' influences, the controversies over the modernization of the teaching methods, and the language question were issues variously discussed by Neohellenic Enlightenment scholars, being also relevant to questions related to the organization of Modern Greek education. There is no doubt that the language controversy was highly influential in the development of the Modern Greek written language. At the same time, it also enabled Greeks to understand the importance of language in the transmission of new ideas. In addition, the Greek *literati* advocated the need for the learning of the language of the Ancients as well as that of other European languages. Above all, Ancient Greek meant to them that they were the descendants of the original possessors of a country, having "retained a Right to the Possession of their Ancestors."[6]

---

[5] Staikos, Konstantinos & Sklavenitis, Triantafyllos (2001) *The Publishing Centres of the Greeks from the Renaissance to the Neohellenic Enlightenment (Exhibition Catalogue)*. Athens: EKEBI: 156-165.

[6] This was the opinion of Locke who, in the seventeenth century, pointed out: "Who doubts that the Grecian Christians descendants of the ancient possessors of that Country may justly cast off the Turkish yoke which they have so long groaned under when ever they have a

During the Enlightenment, Greek intellectuals engaged in 'philosophy,' a word adopted by many of the great educators as a signal or watchword. 'Philosophy' was generally conceived as a rationalistic mode of thought, independent of superstitious or dogmatic elements in all fields. The term also extended very frequently to the physical or natural sciences, and even mathematics, covering also theology. It should be pointed out, though, that "for all this generality in the meaning of the term, however, 'philosophy' as introduced and fought over by the Greeks of the seventeenth, eighteenth and nineteenth centuries does include an astonishing amount of philosophy in the conventional, academic sense – astonishing, that is, in relation to the fact that in and through 'philosophy,' broadly speaking, what was being introduced was education, at least higher education, and critical culture as such."[7]

In many cases, Greek scholars associated philosophy with moral philosophy and the Enlightenment idea concerning human rights in citizenship and education. In fact, Greek scholars and teachers always had a special interest in moral education, and moral philosophy was generally perceived by them to be the most suitable academic subject for the regeneration of individuals and society. They sought – through their teachings and publications as well as through their translations and editions of 'the ancients and the moderns' – to render people both 'virtuous' and 'active' citizens and were interested in offering a sound liberal education and 'an archetype of perfection' in promoting traditional and Enlightenment values. At the same time, they were deeply interested in the notions of liberty, democracy, virtue and eudaimonia, and in many ways paved the way to the liberation of their countrymen and to the formation, in 1828, of the Modern Greek nation-state.

Greek intellectuals aimed to educate the youth by teaching the importance of virtue for the pursuit of the good life and the necessity of rules and principles for the conduct of life. They commented on the topic of virtues and vices – having been influenced mostly by Aristotle, the Stoics and Christian ethics – and discussed Enlightenment's promotion of human rights in relation to intellectual and religious freedom and to met-

power to do it?" Cf. Locke, John *Two Treatises of Government*, ed. Peter Laslett. Cambridge, 1960, II, §192 (cited in Evrigenis, Ioannis D. 'Enlightenment, Emancipation, and National Identity: Korais and the Ancients,' in *Adamantios Korais and the European Enlightenment*, *op. cit.*: 91-108.)

[7] Henderson, *The Revival of Greek Thought, 1620-1830*: 3-4.

aphysical, political, and social liberty.[8] Ancient virtue-ethics texts – such as Aristotle's *Nicomachean Ethics*, the *Rhetoric at Alexander*, the pseudo-Aristotelian *De virtutibus and vitiis*, Epictetus' *Handbook*, and the stoic text *Tablet of Cebes* – were used by Greek teachers who commented on them or made paraphrases in Modern Greek for moral purposes and in order to teach philosophy and grammar.

In addition, novels and plays – associating philosophy with literature and ethics with politics – were translated by Greek intellectuals aiming at the political, aesthetic, and moral education of the youth, in an effort to introduce new literary genres and Enlightenment ideas. Novels by Wieland, Voltaire, Rousseau, Ramsay, Fénelon, Barthélemy, Gessner, Marmontel, Restif de la Bretonne and theatrical plays by Molière, Alfieri, and others were translated into Modern Greek during the Neohellenic Enlightenment in order to promote ethical and political teaching. Ancient, Byzantine and European treatises on the subject of educating a king or a prince and general treatises on ethics and statecraft were also translated, paraphrased and taught by Greek educators. These treatises constituted examples of the literary genre that since the thirteen century has been called *specula principum*.[9] Furthermore, Greek intellectuals made new editions of Classical philosophical or literary works for a wider use aiming at the revival of interest in antiquity and the promotion of cultural identity.

During the Enlightenment and the Early Romanticism period, the importance of education *(Bildung)* and culture was particularly emphasized, being connected to the idea of human perfection, excellence or self-realization that every individual could achieve through a humanistic pedagogy. The relationship between education, philosophy and the arts was stressed by both Enlighteners and Romantics who pointed out that art motivates moral action in the same way that philosophical thinking does. The idea of the 'beautiful soul' – i.e. the profound affinity existing between beauty and goodness that makes the unity of aesthetic and ethical values possible – has been a theme in European culture that started with Ancient Greek philosophers' metaphysical speculations and was again introduced during the eighteenth century, through Medieval Christian thought. Several thinkers in England, France and Germany referred to the

---

[8] Glycofrydi-Leontsini, Athanasia (2002) *Neohellenic Philosophy. Political and Moral Questions* (in Greek). Athens: Athens University Press: 17-244.

[9] Glycofrydi-Leontsini, Athanasia "Teaching Princes: A Vehicle of Moral and Political Education during the Neohellenic Enlightenment," *Classical Russia 1700-1825*, 3-5 (2008-2010): 71-90.

moral and aesthetic perfection with terms that were addressed in contemporary discussions of morality. They employed these terms – and especially that of the 'beautiful soul'[10] and the Hellenic ideal of *kalokagathia* – in novels and plays that aimed at moral and aesthetic education.[11] Throughout the nineteenth century the idea of the 'beautiful soul' continued to play a substantial role in many theoretical and popular accounts; according to Schiller's account in *Über Anmut und Würde (On Grace and Dignity)* a person's character is a work of art, because all his or her actions exhibit grace that reveals the spontaneity and harmony of the person's whole character.[12] The figuration of the 'beautiful soul' also appeared in Rousseau's and Wieland's novels; both writers, inspired by Plato, were deeply concerned with the problems of pedagogy and the relationship of arts to morality.

In fact, Christoph Martin Wieland (1733-1813), in his novel *Geschichte des Agathon* (3 vols., 1766-1767),[13] under the guise of a Greek fiction describes his own spiritual and intellectual growth making use of the allegory of the *'schöne Seele'* in order to assert that moral perfection represents the end of human striving. For him education *(Bildung)* meant cultivation towards the very specific goal of *kalokagathia* and the works of art could serve effectively for that goal; in his other works he argues that "ethics in allegorical paintings would be a suitable way to achieve that greater goal."[14] This work, which Lessing recommended as "a novel of classic taste," marks an epoch in the development of the modern psychological novel and is connected with *Bildung*. Wieland deliberately wrote *Agathon* as an allegorical novel having in mind the platonic doctrine according to which certain objects in the visible world (physical beauty) correspond to the invisible sphere of ideas.[15] In his novels Wieland promotes the educational value of art as well as the role of virtues such as justice and wisdom in human life and stresses the importance of concepts such as truth, order, harmony, perfection, and goodness. Above

---

[10] For the myth of the 'beautiful soul,' see Lusius Apuleius, *Metamorphoseon sive lusus Asini XI*, libri IV 28 – VI 24. Venetia: Aldi: 1521; and in particular *Psyche und Cupido. Eine Märchen des Apuleius,* transl. by Julius Breitkopf und Härtel (Leipzig,1872).

[11] Norton, Robert E. (1995) *The Beautiful Soul. Aesthetic Morality in the Eighteenth Century*. Ithaca/London: Cornell University Press: 1-9, 283.

[12] Beiser, Frederick C. (1998) 'A Romantic Education. The Concept of *Bildung* in Early Romanticism,' in A. Oksenberg Rorty (ed.) *Philosophers on Education. New Historical Perspectives*. London/New York: Routledge: 290.

[13] *Geschichte des Agathon* (1979), ed. Fritz Martini. Stuttgart: Reclam.

[14] Norton, Robert E. *The Beautiful Soul*: 135-164.

[15] *Ibid.*: 149 ff.

all, wisdom is for him the main goal of education. His satire against German provinciality, *Die Abderiten, eine sehr wahrscheinliche Geschichte* (1776), is considered as the most attractive of all his prose writings, and stresses also the importance of goodness and wisdom in human life.

Wieland's novels *Agathon* and *Die Abderiten* have been translated into Greek by the Greek scholar Konstantinos Koumas (1777-1836), a man devoted to didactic activity who also carried out the translation and compilation of instructive work in many branches of knowledge. Koumas believed in the scientific element of education, propagated the need for a liberal education, and advocated that natural philosophy can provide material progress. According to him, education should be in gear with reality. Koumas was born in Larissa (Thessaly) and was educated locally and abroad (Vienna, Berlin, and Leipzig). In Germany he had the opportunity to meet scholars such as Wolff, Buttmann, Thiersch, Greuzer, Voss, and philosophers such as Krug and Schelling, and to have some of his scientific books published there. He encouraged the new learning inclusive of mathematics and science and was interested in philosophy, aesthetics, pedagogy, history, and literature. In his four-volume systematic work entitled *Syntagma Filosofias* (Vienna, 1818-20) – a work that could be paraphrased as *Philosophy Drawn up and Constituted,*[16] inspired by W. T. Krug's philosophy – he begins with a sketch of the history of philosophy, and then proceeds to considerations concerning empirical psychology, epistemology, logic, universal grammar, metaphysics, aesthetics, philosophy of law, ethics, and ethical theology; while at the end of that book a long appendix on pedagogy is also included, interesting from the point of view of the history of education. In this work, as well as in the translations of Wieland's novels that Koumas published in the two first decades of the nineteenth century, he indicates the importance of aesthetic education and the relationship of aesthetics to psychology and ethics. It was actually Koumas, headmaster of the Philological Gymnasium in Smyrna and teacher of mathematical sciences and philosophy, who, with his translation of Wieland's novel *Geschichte des Agathon* (3 vols., Vienna, 1814), introduced the idea of moral beauty and the 'beautiful soul' and indicated the importance of the *Bildungsroman* as a mean of moral education for the conduct of life.[17] In his *Foreword* to this translation, Koumas points out the value of Greek mythology and philos-

---

[16] Henderson, George P. *The Revival of Greek Thought, 1620-1830*: 195.

[17] Glycofrydi-Leontsini, Athanasia 'Moral Beauty and Beautiful Soul in the Neohellenic Enlightenment,' in *Neohellenic Philosophy. Political and Moral Questions*: 380-412.

ophy as well as the difficulties an individual faces trying to become virtuous and wise, a theme that he attempts to illustrate further in the *Appendix* which was added with the intention of providing a key of explanation, in his translation of Wieland's *A Very Probable History of the Abderites* (2 vols, Vienna, 1827). In the *Preface* of that translation of Wieland, Koumas characteristically points out that "the acquisition of wisdom makes foolishness to go away."[18] Wieland, through his *Agathon* and his other pedagogical novels, had created the *Bildungsroman*, a new genre linked to the German tradition of self-cultivation.[19] Following Plato, Wieland used in his novels metaphors, allegories, myths and mystical illustrations that combined Platonic and Christian pietistic views with Greek ideals[20] and main aspects of British moral theory.[21] Koumas appreciated the use of myth and allegory in education – an attitude that Winckelmann had also adopted in his *Versuch einer Allegorie* (1766) – and translated Wieland's two novels for pedagogical reasons. Other Greeks before him had also translated similar works such as Abbé Barthélemy's *Voyage du jeune Anacharsis en Grèce vers le milieu du IVe siècle avant l'ère vulgaire* (1788) and A. M. Ramsay's *The Travels of Cyrus* (1727), both translations published in 1783, or Marmontel's *Bélisaire* (Paris: Merlin, 1767), a translation published in Vienna in 1758,[22] all inspired by Greek antiquity that included didactic ideas on government and the role of the king or the governor in the welfare of his subjects. Another significant neoclassical literary work of pedagogical value, that was particularly attuned to the aesthetic and social concerns of seventeenth century France, Fénelon's *Les Aventures de Télémaque* (Paris, 1669), was also translated in Greek and published in Venice by Antonio Bortoli in 1742.[23]

---

[18] Koumas, Konstantinos (1827) *Veilandou Abdiriton I Istoria*, 2 vols. Vienna: Anton von Haykul.

[19] Morgenstern, Karl (1978) 'The Bildungsroman as a Genre,' in Martin Swales (ed.) *The German Bildungsroman from Wieland to Hesse*. Princeton: Princeton University Press; and *Idem*, 'Über das Wesen des Bildungsromans,' in Rolf Selbmann (ed.), *Zur Geschichte des deutschen Bildungsromans*. Darrmstadt: Wissenschaftliche Buchgesellschaft, 1988. Bruford, W. R. (1975) *The German Tradition of Self-Cultivation: 'Bildung' from Humboldt to Thomas Mann*. Cambridge.

[20] Doll, M. (1896) *Wieland und die Antike*.

[21] Eison, Charles (1913) *Wieland and Shaftesbury*. New York: Columbia University.

[22] Tabaki, Anna & Sfini, Athina (1992) 'Typologie des manuels d'éthique et de comportement en langue grecque vers la fin du 18e siècle. L'évolution du genre, reflet du processus de mordenisation du Sud-Est Européen,' *Revue des Études Sud-Est Européennes*, 30, 3-4: 253-268.

[23] *Ibid.*

The many books that were entitled *'Chrestoetheiai'* or *'Cheiragogiai'* should also be mentioned here. These were edited during the eighteenth century, discussing the upbringing of children, the relationship between parents and children, and the initiation of the learner into forms of thought and understanding that should be part of a cultural heritage, aiming to good manners and the advancement of social relations. In particular, *'Chrestoetheia'* by Antonius Byzantius deserves a special mention. Byzantius' *'Chrestoetheia'* was an adaptation of Erasmus' *De civilitate morum puerilium* (1526) written at the beginning of the eighteenth century and taught for a long time in manuscript form at the Patriarchal Academy of Constantinople and also at other schools in a wide geographical area. It was published for the first time in 1780 and is associated with the Italian version of Erasmus' work realized by Giovanni della Casa under the title *Il Galateo* (Venice, 1558).[24] The wide circulation of this book of good manners and Christian ethics is connected with the interest of Greek educators not only in the education of the princes but also in the general education of the youth aiming at the advancement of moral and social virtues and the enforcement of public relations according to the general spirit of that age. This new tension was also apparent in other books published at the end of the eighteenth century especially by Dimitrius Darvaris, a man of German influences who is compared to the German pedagogue J. Campe whose pedagogical works have also been translated into Greek. Darvaris promoted a virtue ethics aiming at common happiness and the tranquility of the soul. Darvaris has written many books, some of them on the education of children, their duties and their guidance towards true human happiness developed within the limits of the civic society, as well as on the need for an organized education and a common teaching method.[25]

---

[24] See Russo, D. (1910) *Studii şi critice*. Bucureşti: 27 ff., and Legrand, Émile *Bibliographie Hellénique ou description raisonnée des ouvrages publiés en grec par des Grecs au XVe et XVIe*, vols I-IV. Paris, 1885-1906, vol. II: 326-327. Byzantius' *'Chrestoetheia'* has been translated in slovenic by the Greek enlightener and educator D. Darvaris (1757-1823) and published in Vienna in 1786.

[25] Darvaris studied philosophy in Halle and Leipzig and has been influenced by the system of education of Franke and Bassedow in the Institut of Dessau, the famous Philanthropinon. Among his books are included *Cheiragogia eis tin kalokagathian* (1790), *Asfalis odigia eis tin gnosin tou anthropou* (1795), *Alithis odos eis tin eudaimonian* (1796), *Cheiragogia ton paidon itoi pragmateia peri chreon tou anthropou* (1810, 1813, 1831), all published in Austria. See Tabaki, Anna (2004) 'Dimitrios Darvaris: Oi peri "ithikis" antilipseis tou', in her *Neohellenic Enlightenment*. Athens: Ergo: 139-165.

In 1750 the pedagogical views of Charles Rollin (1661-1741) – incorporated in his *Traités des Études*, known also as *De la manière d'enseigner et d'étudier les Belles-Lettres par rapport à l'esprit et au cœur* (1727) – were introduced to Greek audiences by a Greek adaptation of Rollin's 'Preliminary Discourse,' in which were exposed his ideas about the importance of character formation and the role of moral and social virtues for the making up of a good Christian and a citizen, along with his liberal views about education, teaching methods, and the education of women.[26] So far, we have seen that Greek intellectuals approved books that emphasized knowledge and critical rationality compatible with religion and spirituality and were particularly interested in virtue ethics and ethics of care involving caring for oneself as well as for the other.[27] At the same time, Greeks had an interest not only in ethics and character education but also in politics; this is apparent in translations like those of the *Theatrum Politicum* by Ambrosio Marliano, the *Education of the Prince* by the French libertine La Mothe le Vayer, *La filosofia morale derivata dall'alto fonte del grande Aristotele* by Emanuele Tesauro, or the *Catéchisme républicain, philosophique et moral* by A. E. X. Poisson de la Chabeaussière. These were produced in an effort to infuse moral and political ideas into Greek cultural tradition and to mold a virtue-centered morality, linking Ancient virtue ethics with Christian ethics, presenting though at the same time a republican education associated with democratic French ideas spread in Europe at the turn of the century.

The interest in themes relating philosophy with literature and aiming at character education was expressed by another Greek eminent philosopher, a man who adapted Western philosophy to Greek philosophical tradition, Eugenios Voulgaris (1716-1806). Voulgaris was educated in Corfu and Italy, was ordained a deacon in 1737 or 1739 and taught various philosophical subjects including natural philosophy and science in

---

[26] The Greek translator, Alexandros Kaggellarios, translated Rollin's *Histoire Ancienne* (Paris, 1731-1738), a translation published in 1750 in 16 volumes. The last volume includes 'Paraggelmata gia tin kalin anatrofin ton paidon' which is the translation of 'Discours préliminaire' of Rollin's *Traité des Études*, a very popular text in eighteenth Europe that has been influenced by Fénelon's *Traité de l'education des filles* and Abbé de Fleury, *Catéchisme historique* (Paris, 1703), a work that has also been translated into Greek (Venice, 1750). See Tabaki, Anna 'Oi paidagogikes antilipseis stin elliniki metafrasi tou ergou tou Charles Rollin: Paraggelmata dia tin kalin anatrofin ton paidon', in her *Neohellenic Enlightenment*: 127-138.

[27] Tabaki, Anna & Sfini, Athina (1992) 'Typologie des manuels d'éthique et de comportement en langue grecque vers la fin du 18e siècle. L'évolution du genre, reflet du processus de modernisation du Sud-Est Européen,' *op.cit.*

different 'internal' institutions, as the Maroutsaian School in Ioannina, the School of Kozani, the Athonite Academy in Mount Athos, and the Patriarchal Academy in Constantinople. After the Patriarchal Academy, his last teaching post, he continued his literary activity and held ecclesiastical positions in Greek communities abroad, meanwhile publishing his own books and translations. He traveled to Saxony (Halle and Leipzig), where he remained for seven years (1763-1771),[28] and had the pleasure to see the publication of some of his books, including his *Logic* (1766) and the translation of Voltaire's *Essai historique et critique sur les dissensions des églises de Pologne* pseudonymously published in 1767, which Voulgaris published in 1768 also anonymously, adding historical and critical notes and an essay on *Religious Toleration*.[29] Voulgaris was the first among the Greek intellectuals to write on toleration which he described as "an attitude of gentleness and clemency in a pious soul," and the tolerant man as a "zealot for piety and not an indifferent one." Voulgaris places toleration between indifference and brutality, believing that it is persuasion, teaching, and good example – and not persecution or physical force or torture – that are consistent with tolerance. He argues that "faith consists in correct and true belief about God; God is one, correct belief about him is one, consequently the faith is one."[30] 'Tolerantismo between the Christian Churches' was advocated by the Venetian theologian Concina in 1754, who talked about freedom of worship and the peaceful coexistence of dissenting Churches alongside each national Church,[31] while the dissensions of Voltaire's concern involved the rights in Poland of both Protestants and Orthodox Christians in relation to Catholics and Catherine's II of Russia efforts to protect the dissidents and prevent civil war. Voulgaris, who discusses in his essay freedom of thought and "freedom to read," is critical to the Roman Church for its confusion of spiritual and temporal jurisdiction, and to Voltaire for his indifference and undefiled faith, recognizes the political and religious rights of the citizens who belong to different religions, like Islam and Judaism, and remains by all means faithful to the Orthodox Church. Voulgaris follows the tradition of religious humanism and maintains that

---

[28] Henrich, Günther S. (2003) *Evgenios Vulgaris und die Neugriechische Aufklärung in Leipzig*. Leipzig: Universitätsverlag: 85-98.

[29] Knapp, Martin (1984) *Evjenios Vulgaris im Einfluss der Aufklärung: Der Begriff der Toleranz bei Vulgaris und Voltaire*. Amsterdam: Bochumer Studien zur Neugriechischen und Byzantinischen Philologie.

[30] Henderson, George P. *The Revival of Greek Thought, 1620-1830*: 69-72.

[31] Israel, Jonathan I. (2002) *Radical Enlightenment, Philosophy and the Making of Modernity 1650-1750*. Oxford: Oxford University Press: 265.

"in the divine and mysterious dogmas of the faith, freedom of thought is brazenness, since it is mere folly to seek reasons for what is beyond reason."[32]

Nevertheless, Voulgaris' attitude to Voltaire is critical but favourable, as he characterizes him as a brilliant and stimulating representative of the Enlightenment. I mention here Voulgaris' interest in Voltaire as I would like to examine his interest in the topic of moral beauty and the 'beautiful soul' as well as in virtue-ethics that is apparent in his choice to translate Voltaire's *Memnon* in verses, a translation through which Voltaire was introduced to Greek audiences in 1766. This translation was added by Voulgaris as a key to a long poem he edited in Leipzig entitled *Vosporomachia* or *Debate between Asia and Europe in Vosporus*.[33] In the edition of this long poem – attributed to Caspar Ludwig Momars, an interpreter serving in the Austrian-Hungarian embassy in Constantinople and having blood relations to noble Greeks of the city, the Phanariotes – Voulgaris, as the editor, had also included in the volume a translation in verse of Voltaire's *Memnon* which is characterized by him as a 'moral poem' and a *clé* to the understanding of another poem he added at the end entitled *Apodosis allegorias: Pseudeis areskeiai kai mataion kallos gynaikos ymnithisetai*. Both these poems had as their purpose to stress the value of the virtues, and especially those of wisdom and goodness, and were aiming at moral education.[34] It is not known whether Voulgaris was the writer of this second ethical poem or the extent of his contribution to *Vosporomachia* beyond his editorial role. Nevertheless, Voulgaris' long-life interest in philosophy and Greek education can be recognized in many instances. When he left Leipzig in 1771, accepting Catherine the Great's invitation, and arrived in Petersburg, in order to become a librarian and advisor to the Russian court, he was ordained a monk and an archbishop of the newly founded archbishopric of Slovinion and Cherson in Ukraine, being involved in the education of the local Greek community.[35] Later, in Petersburg, he devoted himself to reading and writing, and

---

[32] Henderson, George P. *The Revival of Greek Thought, 1620-1830*, 64 ff.

[33] Berger, Albrecht (2005) 'Die Bosporomachia des Senior Momars,' in *Zwischen Polis, Provinz und Peripherie. Beiträge zur byzantinischen Geschichte und Kultur*, hrsg. Von L. M. Hoffmann unter Mitarbeit von A. Monchizadeh. Bisbanden: 749-769 and Henrich, G. S. 'Als Denker Archaist, als Dichter auch Demotizist-zu Vulgaris' Paraphrase des Voltaireschen *Memnon*,' in *Evgenios Vulgaris und die Neugriiechische Aufklärung in Leipzig*: 99-113.

[34] Glycofrydi-Leontsini, Athanasia 'Moral Beauty and the 'Beautiful Soul' in the Neohellenic Enlightenment,' in *Neohellenic Philosophy: Political and Moral Questions*: 381-412.

[35] Batalden, Stephen K. (1982) *Catherine II's Greek Prelate Eugenios Voulgaris in Russia, 1771-1806*. Boulder: East European Monographs.

had a major role in the Greek instruction of the Grand Duke Constantine Pavlovitch. He prepared a Greek translation of Catherine's *Instructions on the Correct Education of the Grand Dukes Alexander and Constantine*,[36] a translation in which the Greek prelate mentioned the role of the Byzantine *specula principum* in the moral and political education of the kings.[37] Voulgaris followed a wide pedagogical program and introduced new philosophical and pedagogical methods in school teaching at home and abroad. He published translations of the most important European philosophers' logical, scientific, and metaphysical works (Duhamel, Locke, Gravesande, Genovesi, Wolff, Tacquet, Segner, Wuckerer, Fortunati, and Tycho Brahe) and was the first scholar to introduce Greek audiences into Locke's thought, having made for educational reasons an abridgement, still unedited, of his *Essay Concerning Human Understanding*.[38] Locke's theories,[39] known among the Greeks mostly via French and Italian translations and abridgements, were introduced even in the Academy of Mount Athos where Voulgaris taught. Voulgaris expressed his esteem for Locke's thought in various occasions in his books, especially in his *Logic*. His students Iosepos Moisiodax and G. Kallonas also published translations of Locke's *Some Thoughts concerning Education*,[40] a text that occupies a central place in Locke's thought and suggests an educational program for the development of the moral person – since it aims at providing parents with an explicit manual on how to guide their children into becoming moral and social persons and on how to acquire those virtues that are necessary for living.[41]

Indeed, Modern Greeks have expressed an early interest in ancient and modern educational texts. This is apparent via the publication of a translation in Venice, in 1544, by N. Sofianos, in vernacular Greek, of

[36] Plavinskaia, Nadejda 'Catherine II et le grand-duc Alexandre Pavlovitch: l'institution du prince russe au siècle des Lumières,' in G. Luciani & C. Volpilhac-Auger (eds.) (2003) *L'Institution du prince au XVIIIe siècle*. Ferney-Voltaire: Centre international d'étude du XVIIIe siècle: 175-180.

[37] Glycofrydi-Leontsini, A. 'Teaching Princes: a Vehicle of Moral and Political Education during the Neohellenic Enlightenment': 71-90.

[38] Batalden, *Voulgaris*: 164.

[39] Kitromilides, P. M. (1994) 'John Locke and the Greek Intellectual Tradition: An Episode in Locke's Reception in South-East Europe,' in G. A. J. Rogers (ed.) *Locke's Philosophy, Content and Context*. Oxford: Clarendon Press: 218-235.

[40] Kriaras, Emmanuel 'I "Paidagogia" tou Moisiodakos kai i schesi tis me to paidagogiko syggramma tou Locke,' *Byzantinisch-Neugriechische jahrbücher* 17 (1939-1943): 135-153, esp. 136, 153.

[41] Yolton, John W. 'Locke: Education for Virtue', in *Philosophers on Education*: 173-189.

Plutarch's *De liberis educandis*.[42] Also, via the anonymous translation of Theophrastus' *Characters*, a sixteenth century text and via the paraphrases for teaching purposes of Isocrates' *Ad Nicoclem* and *Ad Democritum*, by Sevastos Kyminites of Trepizond (1632-1702). Kyminites, who established the Academy in Bucharest (1700), was a teacher who had already been previously active in the Patriarchal Academy in Constantinople and in the School or 'Phrontisterion' in Trebizond. Isocrates' *Discourses* had been translated into Latin by the end of the fifteenth century and later they were translated into other European languages to serve as manuals for the teaching of the Greek language and for pedagogical reasons.[43] In the eighteenth century, with the same purposes, Isocrates' *Discourse to Nicocles* had been translated, in Modern Greek and French, by Iosepos Moisiodax (c.1730-1800).[44] Moisiodax, a pupil of the aforementioned Voulgaris, although a deacon, he was, in educational outlook and practice, a radical, as he was interested in philosophy in a broad sense, including mathematics and 'natural' philosophy. A man – who sought education in many places including Ioannina, the Athonite Academy and the University of Padua – became Head of the official Greek school in Iaşi in 1765, and indicated his-long life interest in modern education and moral philosophy by his own publications. In 1761-62, he published in Venice, in two volumes, the translation of L. A. Muratori, *La filosofia morale esposta e proposta ai giovani* (Verona, 1735)[45] and, in 1779, in Venice again, the *Treatise on the Education of Children, or Pedagogy*, a book that constituted a paraphrase of Locke's *Some Thoughts Concerning Education*, first published in 1693. Moisiodax used for his *Pedagogy* Coste's French version[46] of Locke's *Thoughts* and does not mention his dependence on him or his other influences. In his book, Moisiodax talks about the dangers to noble children from servants and other influences,

---

[42] Legrand, Émile (1874) *Grammaire du grec et traduction en grec vulgaire du traité de Plutarque sur L'Éducation des enfants*. Paris-Athènes: 91-93.

[43] Hofmann, S. F. W. (1961, 2nd ed.) *Bibliographisches Lexicon de Gesammten Literatur der Griechen*, vol. 1-3. Amsterdam: Hannert: 484-485, 487-491.

[44] The French title of Iosepos Moisiodax' *A Version of the Discourse to Nicocles on the Sovereignty or Political Chapters* is *Transformation de l'oraison d'Isocrate sur l'art de régner pour Nicoclés. Faite par Joseph Myssiodax, ou Chapitres Politiques, traduits par le même en français*. Venice, 1779.

[45] Glycofrydi-Leontsini, Athanasia (1994) 'Traduzioni di testi filosofici italiani durante l'illuminismo neogreco (Genovesi, Muratori, Soave),' *Testi italiani tradotti in greco (Dal' 500 ad oggi)*, in cura di Mario Vitti. Rubbettino: 295-316.

[46] *De l'Éducation des Enfans. Traduit de l'Anglois par Pierre Coste*. 1st ed., Amsterdam, 1695; 5th ed., Amsterdam, 1744.

about the cultivation of self-respect, seriousness of mind and the obedient disposition; he also talks about the relations between children and teachers and on how lessons could be rendered attractive to the pupils. Moisiodax considered education to be the root of individual and social reform and a method of directing the temper and the inclinations of children towards virtue and learning.[47] He also believed in the liberating power of knowledge in general, including theological knowledge and considered that a 'sound philosophy' has to be free from dogmatic interference of all sorts and must be taught in 'the simple style' in order to implement the ideas of the Enlightenment.[48]

Many other Greek enlighteners discussed in their books topics belonging to moral or political philosophy. Among them, Benjamin Lesvios (1762-1824) should be mentioned, a man educated in Patmos, Chios, Pisa, and Paris, whose main work as a teacher was conducted in the Academy of Kydonies (or Ayvalik) on the Asia Minor coast, and later in Bucharest, where he went in 1818 in order to reorganize the Greek School there on the model of a 'European Academy.'[49] In his *Metaphysics* (1802), a compendium of epistemology, psychology, gnoseology, ontology, and natural theology, he discusses freedom, under the heading of *liberum arbitrium (autexousion)*[50] while in his *Ethics* freedom is discussed in relation to virtue and morality. Benjamin Lesvios also wrote chapters specially devoted to the subject of natural human rights and was the first scholar to discuss this topic in the Neohellenic Enlightenment period.[51]

The most eager proponent of the regeneration and re-education of Greeks was Adamantios Korais (1748-1833), a physician and a political theorist, a language reformer and mostly a 'philologue,' who gained an international reputation as an editor of classical texts and is considered as a confirmed liberal in his political ideas. Born in Smyrna he had his edu-

---

47 Henderson, George P. *The Revival of Greek Thought, 1620-1830*: 89-91. As I have already mentioned, Gabriel Kallonas (1724-95), a pupil of Voulgaris in the Athonite Academy, has also compiled *Some Thoughts on Education* (Vienna, 1800), inspired by Locke's thoughts on education.

48 For a critical presentation of the Greek enlightener's ideas, see Kitromilides, Paschalis M. (1992) *The Enlightenment as Social Criticism. Iosipos Moisiodax and Greek Culture in the Eighteenth Century*. Princeton: Princeton University Press.

49 This Academy along with the School of Chios and the Evangelical School in Smyrna are connected with the educational life of the Eastern Aegean.

50 Henderson, George P. *The Revival of Greek Thought, 1620-1830*: 127-141.

51 Argyropoulou, Roxanne (2003) *Benjamin Lesbios and the European Thought of the 18th century*. Athens: Centre of Neohellenic Studies, National Institute of Research.

cational experience in his home town in the Evangelical School, which attracted students from far afield, and in 1772 went to Amsterdam as a representative of his father's commercial house where he mingled in the circles of Amsterdam Hellenists. In 1778-1779 he had an extended stay in Trieste and Venice and, after a short stay in Smyrna and in Livorno, he left in 1782 for Montpellier, where he had a medical training and defended his dissertation *Pyretologiae synopsis*. In 1788 he went to revolutionary Paris, where he stayed for the rest of his life, observed the Revolution and the Terror, became a whole-hearted supporter of the Directory, developed close ties with the Idéologues, the new regime's intellectual supporters, and came to the conclusion that liberty should always be combined with justice. Korais devoted himself to scholarly work and political writings and became the first effective neo-classicist among Modern Greeks whose contribution to the Greek educational thought was distinctive and powerful.[52] He urged the need of a systematic study of ancient philosophy, history and literature as well as of a study of the philosophical, literary and aesthetic currents of the Enlightenment in an effort to re-educate his compatriots. At the turn of the century he published his French translations of Theophrastus' *Characters* (1799) and Hippocrates' *Of Airs, Waters, and Places* (1800). He also translated into Greek, from Abbé Morelet's French translation, Beccaria's *On Crimes and Punishments* (1802). He inaugurated his political writings with his famous *Mémoire sur l'état actuel de la civilisation dans la Grèce*, which he read in the 'Société des observateurs de l'homme' on 6 January 1803, a text in which he spoke of a 'moral revolution' and the need for political change that would transform the Greek nation.

Eager to instruct his compatriots in the duties of citizenship and the art of legislation, Korais edited, for political purposes, in the Series of 'Hellenic Library' – his major editorial project designed to make available the Greek classics to the Modern Greeks[53] – Aristotle's *Politics* and *Nicomachean Ethics* in 1821 and 1822, respectively. His 'Prolegomena' to the *Politics* made an important contribution to the ideological prepara-

[52] Kitromilides, Paschalis M. (2010) 'Itineraries in the World of the Enlightenment: Adamantios Korais from Smyrna via Montpellier to Paris,' in Paschalis M. Kitromilides (ed.) *Adamantios Korais and the European Enlightenment*. Voltaire Foundation-University of Oxford: 1-33. For an extensive and substantial entry devoted to him, cf. G. R. L. de Sinner, 'Coray Diamant,' *Biographie universelle, ancienne et modern. Supplement*.

[53] Over a period of twenty years (1805-1827) he made available in his *Hellenic library* sixteen main volumes of Greek classical authors and another nine supplementary volumes in his *Parerga*. In his editions he provided prolegomena that are a source of Korais ideas on cultural, political, religious and moral issues

tion of the Greek Revolution and was an expression of his political thought, having been described by its German translator, in 1823, as 'political exhortations to the Greeks.'[54] Korais, who developed a strategy of cultural change that should be considered in national context, stressed in his 'Prolegomena' the need to select teachers that were educated in 'Enlightened Europe,' and talked continuously about "the enlightened peoples of Europe," considering their philosophical, literary and scientific achievements as a model for the modernization of Greek education.[55] His case illustrates the importance of Diaspora in the promotion of the Enlightenment ideas and his eagerness to teach to the Greeks the value of liberty, democracy and civic virtue, and to demonstrate the importance of their heritage.[56] His discourses on education and language are lengthy, especially his *Improvised Reflections (Autosxedioi stochasmoi)*, a collection of prefaces to some of his editions of the Greek classics during the first decade of the nineteenth century. In these, he complains against the dryness and abstraction in the teaching of Greek and against the 'grammarians' who insisted on the reform of 'grammatical education' and on the teaching methods for the ancient language. Korais aimed at the revival of Ancient Greek as a medium of 'philosophical education,' expressive of practical and theoretical wisdom.[57] He believed in the reforming power of education in general and in the importance of classical studies in particular, and had seen as the most fundamental precondition of the cultural and political regeneration of Greece the language question. His views, although innovative, accommodate lines of thought already developed by eighteenth century Greek educational theorists and had many supporters among the Greek followers of the Enlightenment movement contributing to the establishment of an independent Modern Greek state.

In general, in all philosophical and literary texts of that period, either original or translated, the close relation between personal happiness and moral character is stressed. In addition, it is also stressed the archetype of *'kalos k' agathos'* that the Aristotelian example of the wise and great man puts forward as well as the archetype of the Stoic wise. In these texts, importance is given to notions such as patriotism, duty, love,

---

[54] Cf. Orelli, J. K. von (1823) *Politishe Ermahnungen an die Hellenen*. Zürich, while a second translation by Karl Iken was entitled *Korais' Schrift von alten und neun Hellas*. Leipzig, 1823.

[55] Henderson, George P. *The Revival of Greek Thought*: 142-143.

[56] Korais, Adamantious *Prolegomena,* I: 494-95.

[57] Henderson, George P. *The Revival of Greek Thought*: 142-147.

friendship and philanthropy, and, most important, to the value of prudence acquired via education and moral development.

The most prominent Greek Enlightenment intellectuals were in favour of a liberal education. They regarded education as the highest good, the supreme value in life and a mean for the regeneration of the Greek nation. They placed education in the hierarchy of values together with liberty and justice, considering it in the meaning of the German term *Bildung* that signifies two processes: learning and personal growth. It is well known that the words 'Kultur' and 'Bildung' were extensively used in the eighteenth century along with that of 'enlightenment,' denoting aspects of social life that, according to the German thinker Moses Mendelssohn, were "the outcomes of the efforts and attempts by the people to improve their social position."[58] According to Mendelssohn, *Bildung* produces cultivation which is connected with good manners and the development of the soul – these being the results of social company, art education, and education in general which moulds the individual and arms it with rationality and the will to correct the imperfections of nature and to see with the feelings of compassion and friendship its fellow human beings.[59] The concept of *Bildung*, regarded in early German Romanticism by Friedrich Schlegel as the *summum bonum*,[60] was utilized by the romantics in such a way as to include their hope for the education of humanity and was comprehensible in its social and political context. German romantics had an ideal of education in terms of human perfection or self-realization that can be found in many strands of eighteenth century German thought, as in the classicists (Wieland, Goethe, Herder), the Leibnizian-Wolffian school (Moses Mendelssohn, Baumgarten, Wolff) or the pietists (Spener, Arndt).[61]

During the twentieth century, E. Gombrich in his essay 'The Tradition of General Knowledge' argues that "the humanities […] draw their strength, their nourishment and their *raison d'être* from the traditions and general concerns of the culture. To cut them off from those traditions is to kill them. One wonders, of course, how widely their death would be deplored […] as long as the universities are identified in the public mind not with the passing on of traditions, but with the passing of examina-

---

[58] Mendelssohn, Moses (1974) *Was ist Aufklärung?* Stuttgart: Reclam. I am using the Greek translation by N. M. Skouteropoulos (Athens: Kritiki, 1989): 11 ff.

[59] *Ibid.*

[60] Beiser, F. C. (1998) 'A Romantic Education. The Concept of Bildung in Early Romanticism,': 284-299.

[61] *Ibid.*: 288.

tions, those who have traditions at heart must defend them against bureaucratization".[62] Richard Woodfield in his 'Tradition and *Bildung*' points out that, in thinking about the dissemination of tradition, Gombrich could rely upon an alternative concept of education, *Bildung*, which is what one acquired out of school that is useful for instruction.[63]

In the case of the educational policy followed by the Greek intellectuals during the period of the Neohellenic Enlightenment, it is apparent that philosophy was utilized with the intention to improve pedagogical practices and to enforce moral and civic education. Greek educators tried to combine tradition and *Bildung* and to reform Modern Greek school education by the means of philosophy and the sciences, history and the arts, in order to educate the youth in the right way, to teach them to appreciate their rights and the rights of others, and to develop the set of skills and capacities that would enable them to have a good life in the future and to freely choose for themselves. They insisted that successful learning begins in experience and practice and that education needs reason and social sentiments in order to become a reformer of both individuals and society. They wanted to establish principles of justice and proposed the ideal of a just society that entails the existence of certain institutions which presuposes a certain account of reasonable and free citizens.

[62] Gombrich, E. H. (1979) *Ideals and Idols. Essays on Values in History and Art.* Oxford, Phaidon: 18-19.

[63] Woodfield, Richard (1995) 'Tradition and Bildung,' *Annals for Aesthetics*, 34: 173-182.

CRITIQUE

"CONSCIENTISATION" IN THE PEDAGOGY OF PAULO FREIRE[1]

Enrique DUSSEL

Child development psychologists or psycho-pedagogues are often cognitivists; not only because they are concerned with intelligence and occupied with motivations, emotions, moral judgments, etc., but because they always, and in the end, propose to improve, correct, or unblock the intellectual *performance* (whether theoretical or moral) of the child. Freud, meanwhile, is interested in pedagogically modifying (what is psychoanalysis but a dialogical pedagogy?) the order of the drives when it falls into uncontrollable pathologies. All of them employ the mediation of an experienced pedagogue or psychoanalyst (who is likewise a mediator between the "conscious" and the "pre-" and "un-conscious" through the "super-ego"), that is, they set an *individual* mediator in front of the educands (having some sort of psychological drive-conditioned pathology), who are also generally regarded as *individuals*. All this occurs within a social, cultural, political and economic order, which is treated simply as "given," and whose *transformation* has nothing to do with the task of the pedagogue or psychoanalyst. The stance of Paulo Freire is radically different, since he argues that education is impossible without the educand educating himself in the *process of his liberation*.[2] Freire, therefore, changes their pedagogical purposes – if they really may be named like this, since it concerns something more universal and radical.

In effect, the purpose for Freire is to reach something different than all of the just mentioned, something which has not yet become clear. It is not clear among the "scientific" psycho-pedagogues, who in a certain

[1] About Paulo Freire, see Torres, Carlos Alberto (1992) *La praxis educativa de Paulo Freire*. Mexico: Gernika. I thank Sonia Araújo-Olivera for her help on the bibliography.

[2] Here one ought to compare Freire with the North-American pragmatists. While these rightly affirm that truth is reached within a *communitarian process of verification*, Freire suggests that the critical education process is exclusively realised when the oppressed carries out his own learning process in the proper *process of practical liberation as a transformation of his reality*. It is not only (although also) an intellectual process as in the case of the pragmatists; it is a process fundamental to the *critical praxis*.

manner despise Freire for being like a "politician," but it is still not clear even for those accepting his teachings and seeking to develop the pedagogy of our author. Compared with Freire, the child development psycho-pedagogues or psychoanalysts are, first, *cognitivists* because they are concerned with theoretical or moral intelligence, or with consciousness as a mediation of the pathology; *consciousnesstists* as far as they do not develop a dialogical, linguistic theory; and *individualists* in so far as they are concerned with the relation between an individual pedagogue and single educands. But, they are foremost *naive* as far as they do not try to transform the contextual reality nor promote an *ethical-critical* consciousness in the educator – which is the fundamental purpose in all the educational works of Freire. This means that Freire, unlike the psycho-pedagogues, defines the possible conditions for the emergence of a level of practice for the *political-critical* reason, something which is a condition for an integrative educational process. Therefore, the educand is not only the child but also the adult, and in particular, the oppressed (the culturally illiterate), since the *pedagogical action* is carried out within a dialogical inter-subjective communitarian[3] horizon through a real transformation of the structures that until now have oppressed the educand. He is educated in the very same social process and thanks to the fact that he emerges as a "historical subject." The transformative process of the structures from which the new "social subject" emerges is the central procedure of his progressive education; a freedom that is gradually carried out in the liberating praxis. Therefore, it is not about the theoretical or moral intellect (something which is supposed but is not the primary goal), nor even the unblocking of the drives towards a normal tension of the affective order (*à la* Freud who is also supposed), but something completely different. Freire attempts an education of the victim in the very same historical, communitarian, and real process, that is, an education where one ceases to be a victim:

> Just as the gnoseological circle does not end with the step of the acquisition of existing knowledge, but proceeds to the phase of the creation of new knowledge, so neither may *conscientisation* come to a halt at the stage of the disclosure of reality. Its authenticity is at hand only when the practice of the

[3] Nor is it like the case of the Just Community from Cambridge (it is the example of a primary school as a community; see Hersh, Richard M., Paolitto, Diana P. & Reimer, Joseph (1979) *El crecimiento moral de Piaget a Kohlberg*. Madrid: Narcea: 174-81; English translation: *Promoting Moral Growth: From Piaget to Kohlberg*. Illinois: Waveland Press, 1990), since Freire takes as a point of departure a community of real people, which is authentic and exists.

> disclosure of reality constitutes *a dynamic and dialectical unity with the practice of transformation of reality.*[4]

What in other words would be:

> Reading the world is an *antecedent* act vis-à-vis the reading of the word. The teaching of the reading and writing of the word to a person *missing the critical exercise* [!] of reading and rereading the world *is, scientifically, politically, and pedagogically crippled.*[5]

This is a pedagogical Copernican revolution, which is far from being understood. It is necessary, thus, as Freire writes:

> To criticize the arrogance, the authoritarianism of intellectuals of Left or Right, who are both basically reactionary in an identical way – who judge themselves the proprietors of knowledge, the former, of revolutionary knowledge, the latter, of conservative knowledge – to criticize the behavior of university people who claim to be able to conscientize rural and urban workers without having to be conscientized by them as well; [...] [they] seek to impose the *superiority* of their academic knowledge on the *rude masses.*[6]

Many believe that Freire's pedagogy is not pedagogy, or that it is not scientific; that it only has "social and political purposes." To this he responds:

> As if the existence of a distant, cold, indifferent educational practice when it comes to *social and political purposes* were, or even had ever been, possible in any space-time![7]

Let us briefly see how Freire deals with the pedagogical question. Talking to some friends at the CIDOC (Centro Intercultural de Documentación, or Intercultural Documentation Center) in Cuernavaca (Mexico), where Ivan Illich (who dealt with the pedagogical issue in the same periode) often gathered us, and where Freire met Erich Fromm (who lived in Cuernavaca at that moment), Freire expressed:

> Speaking of conscientisation requires a series of preliminary considerations [...] It is generally thought that I am the author of this strange word by the fact that it is a central notion in my ideas on education [...] It was born out of a series of reflections that a team of teachers developed at the Higher Institute

[4] Freire (1993) *Pedagogía de la Esperanza*. México: Siglo XXI: 98-9; here adopted with modifications from the English translation by Robert R. Barr, *Pedagogy of Hope: Reliving Pedagogy of the Oppressed.* Continuum: New York/London, 2004: 88; author's emphasis.

[5] Freire (1993): 75; translation by Barr: 66; author's emphasis and brackets. Please take in mind, as we shall see, that an analysis in Freire's view is not "scientific" when "*ethical* criticism" is missing.

[6] *Ibid.*: 76; translation by Barr: 66.

[7] *Ibid.*; translation by Barr: 67.

> of Brazilian Studies (ISEB)[8] [...] The word was created by one of the teachers from that period [...] Among others, I remember professor Alvaro Vieira Pinto, a great philosopher who wrote the book entitled *Consciência e Realidade Nacional*[9] [...] When I first heard the word conscientisation, and when hearing it, I immediately perceived the depth of its meaning, and I was absolutely convinced that education as a practice of freedom is an act of knowledge; a critical approach to reality.[10]

I will divide the subject matter into short sections showing the importance Freire has for critical ethics and politics, something so important in a large number of contemporary liberation movements in Latin America and Africa.

1. The "limit situation:" the "point of departure." Inspired by Jaspers, but adding a new meaning, Freire explains:

> Let us for example study the *limit situation*[11] for farmers in the Northeast of Brazil. They have a greatly oppressed consciousness that prevents them from having a structural perception of reality. They are unable to perceive the fact of the limit situation as something that is built in the concrete and objective reality in which man is. But despite this and by the fact of being a man, he needs to explain the reality in which he lives. How is it questioned? What are the reasons he gives? How does his oppressed consciousness analyse this case?[12]

This is a "material" point of departure; analytically economical and political.[13] All possible education starts from the "reality" *in which the educand is*. Here it is the structures of *domination* that constitute the educand as *oppressed*. In his masterpiece from 1969,[14] in exile in Chile, Freire deals with the subject of a foundational contradiction: oppressors-oppressed. Why does Freire depart from the oppressed, the marginalised, the illiterate? Because this person is the "educand" at the limit and as such the one, as no one else, who needs to be educated. Freire, in other words, stands at the *maximum level possible of negativity*:[15] "The criti-

---

[8] In 1963 Freire published an article entitled "Conscientizaçâo e alfabetizaçâo: uma nova visâo do processo," *Revista de Estudios Universitarios* (Recife), 4: 5-23.

[9] See Vieira Pinto, Álvaro (1961) *Consciência e Realidade Nacional*. Rio de Janeiro: ISEB.

[10] "Concientizar para liberar," *Contacto*. Mexico), 8, 1971: 42; citing from Torres (1992): 107.

[11] A chief notion in his vocabulary.

[12] Torres, *ibid.*: 108.

[13] See the chapter "A Sociedade brasileira em transiçâo" in Freire (1980[a]) *Educaçâo como prática da Liberdade*. Río de Janeiro: Paz e Terra: 39ff.

[14] See Freire (1994) *Pedagogía del oprimido*. Mexico: Siglo XXI: 31-67.

[15] Referring to Lucien Goldman who speaks of the "maximum level possible of critical consciousness" ("Acción cultural liberadora" (from 1969), here from Torres, ed., *Entrevistas con Freire*. Mexico: Gernika, 1983: 22).

cism, and the effort to overcome these *negativities* are not only to be recommended, they are indispensable [...] There have been various kinds of negative understanding, and therefore criticism."[16] If Horkheimer tells us that negativity and materiality are the conditions for critical theory, here we not only have a "theory" but a critical practice with much more negativity and materiality. We are no longer speaking about German workers but about the "wretched of the earth" of Frantz Fanon; the farmers without land from Northeast or about forty million of the poorest people on the planet. It is no longer a critical theory for scientists, who *afterwards seek* a historical "subject." It is the "historical subjects" themselves, who in *beforehand seek* someone that may educate them.

2. *"Prise de conscience?"* In relation to Piaget,[17] Freire claims that "conscientisation" (which begins by becoming critical consciousness) is much more than just a *prise de conscience* knowing the world:

> This *prise de conscience* is not yet *conscientisation*. The latter is a further developed *prise de conscience*. It is the *critical development* of the *prise de conscience*. *Conscientisation* implies the transgression of the spontaneous sphere[18] of the apprehension of reality for the benefit of a *critical sphere* in which reality *is now given* as a conceivable object in which man assumes a position [...] that he seeks to know.[19]

To "conscientiate" indicates, as we will see, the *process* where the educand will slowly carry out a complete diachrony from a certain negativity to positivity; a process being a spiral movement with continuous decisions, returns, and assessments. The *pedagogy of the oppressed* is *kath'exokhén* pedagogy, and since it situates itself in the maximum level of negativity it can serve as a model for all other *possible* critical educational processes.

3. *Stage 1: The "naive consciousness,"* the "culture of silence," the "mythification of reality" and so on. Freire describes many determinations as possible negative points of departure, something that is never exceeded by the aforementioned psycho-pedagogues. He is concerned, strictly speaking, with the transition from a "magical consciousness" –

---

[16] Freire (1993): 80-1; translation by Barr: 70-1.

[17] See Piaget, Jean (1985) *The Equilibration of Cognitive Structures: The Central Problem of Intellectual Development*. Chicago: University of Chicago Press.

[18] This is the order of the Heideggerian "world," the Luhmannian "system," the Habermasian "lifeworld *(Lebenswelt)*," the Lévinasian "totality," the fetishised consciousness within the horizon of the "capital" of Marx, in which they are situated but without exceeding it; neither Piaget, Kohlberg, Vigotsky, nor Feuerstein.

[19] Torres (1992): 111.

which is massified or fanatical, still modern and urban, but naive[20] – to a "critical consciousness." In this case, it is all about an "intransitive consciousness"[21] that does not succeed in expressing itself (it is *in-itself* but does not reach the self-consciousness of the *for-it-self*). From the "*naive* consciousness," the "*critical* consciousness" emerges; in front of the "culture of *silence,*" the "being-able-to talk" emerges; in front of the "*mystification* of reality," the "demystification"...

> In his approximation to the world, to reality, in his movement in the world and with the world, man possess a *first moment* in which the world, the objective reality, *is not given to him as a recognisable object* for his critical consciousness [...] it is but a *naive consciousness*.[22]

However, this "*critical* consciousness" is risky; speaking impulsively, the oppressed may not be prepared to face it.

4. "Fear of Freedom." Keeping the drives in mind, and certainly inspired by Fromm, Freire states that the oppressed have a "fear of freedom" – in this respect he is the successor of the first school of Frankfurt, when it comes to negative materiality.[23] Fear of freedom is the "ontological impossibility" for the oppressed to be "subjects" and to face their liberation. The victim, the oppressed, is in a first moment where his drives are "blocked" impeding him to open up to the wide world of critique:

> Not infrequently, training courses participants call attention to "the danger of *conscientization*" in a way that reveals their own fear of freedom. Critical consciousness, they say, is anarchic. Others add that critical consciousness may lead to disorder. Some, however, confess: Why deny it? I was afraid of freedom. I am no longer afraid![24]

Freire constantly refers to this "blocking" of drives, and as Lévinas reminds, the one gaining critical consciousness faces a risky situation of

---

[20] "Education that will put at his disposal the means by which he is able to overcome the naive or magical capture of his reality in favor of a predominantly critical one" (Freire, 1980[a]:106).

[21] See Freire (1980[a]): 59.

[22] Torres (1992): 109.

[23] This is the primary theme always repeated by the young Freire (see Freire, 1980[a]; *Concientizaçâo. Teoría e Prática da Libertaçâo*. Sao Paulo: Moraes, 1980[b]; *Açâo cultural para a Liberdade*. Rio de Janeiro: Paz e Terra, 1978, etc.) "Freedom" for Freire is not the starting point; it is a difficult goal, where obstacles have to be overcome, including immense affective and traditional "blocks" introjected by the punishment, the domination, the torture, which the oppressed people stand. Although referring to Freud, Freire never sufficiently developed these issues concerning drives.

[24] Freire (1994): 21; modified translation from the English translation by Myra Bergman Ramos, *Pedagogy of the Oppressed*, 30th Anniversary Edition. Continuum: New York/London, 2006: 35.

losing his joy, because he now becomes a persecuted "hostage" in and by the oppressing system in the name of the community of victims. Here we find the difficulty in overcoming the utilitarian "happiness," which "enslaves" in a false "vital security,"[25] or overcoming Nietzsche as when he speaks of the "herd" (Zarathustra risks himself jeopardising his "happiness" for the sake of the creative "instinct of pleasure").

5. The participation of the critical educator. This is a very sensitive moment. It is necessary "not [to] separate the act of teaching from the act of learning [...] Experiences cannot be transplanted; they must be reinvented."[26] When Freire arrives to Guinea-Bissau (a country that recently had a revolution at that time), and he had to launch a pedagogical process, he writes:

> It becomes the duty of the educator to search out appropriate paths for the educand to travel and the best assistance that can be offered so that the educand is enabled to exercise the role of subject in relation to learning during the process of literacy education. The educator must constantly create and recreate these paths [...] [T]he most important factor is the development of a critical attitude *in relation to* the object and not a discourse by the educator *about* the object.[27]

The educator must begin educating himself with the "content" given to him by the very same educand:

> What I have said and resaid, untiringly, is that we must not bypass – spurning it as "good for nothing" – that which educands [...] bring with them in the way of an understanding of the world [...] [; t]heir speech, their way of counting and calculating, their ideas about the so-called other world, their religiousness, their knowledge about health, the body, sexuality, life, death, the power of the saints, magic spells, must all be respected.[28]

The educator, then, must "learn" about the world of the educand. Only then, he may intervene:

---

[25] *Ibid.*: 22.

[26] Freire (1977) *Cartas a Guinea-Bissau*. Mexico: Siglo XXI: 16-7; here adapted with modifications from the English translation by Carman St. John Hunter, *Pedagogy in Process: The Letters to Guinea-Bissau*. The Seabury Press: New York, 1978: 9.

[27] *Ibid.*: 18; modified translation from Hunter: 10-1.

[28] Freire (1993): 81; translation by Barr: 71-2. We wrote in *La pedagógica de la liberación (The Latin-American pedagogy)* in 1973: "The future liberating teacher is led by the hand, blind and weak, towards the darkness of the *new* world (the Other is a *reality*), for his son, the youth, and the people. Only the confidence in his word guides him and lets him avoid the error: taking the wrong path away from the one that bears him to the Other [...] The voice of the Other is ex-action, an urgent call for a liberating work," § 53; vol. 3: 190. See: www.enriquedussel.org/Libros.

> The illiterate peasants do not need a theoretical context to become aware of their objective situation of oppression [...] But taking on that consciousness that emerges from being immersed in the daily living conditions does not give them the reasons for their condition of being exploited. This is one of the tasks we [the educators] have to accomplish in the theoretical context.[29]

Freire, then, argues that it is the victim who takes on the critical consciousness. The educator brings him the discovery of his condition of being a victim. In other words, the "consciousness" does not arrive to the victim "from the outside" but "from within;" from his own consciousness elucidated by the educator. The importance of the educator consists in bringing a great criticalness[30] when teaching how to *critically* interpret the objective reality (something that also requires a critical social science). We will return to this subject in the next paragraph.

6. Stage 2: The ethical-critical consciousness. Now we arrive to the moment of crisis *par excellence*. It is the moment in which the oppressed makes the leap into the "critique," which is, as we shall see, communitarian. How is this first level of "critical consciousness" reached? Freire insists that it is reached by a theoretical analysis of the causes behind the oppression of the oppressed: by the means by which the oppressed becomes aware of the *objective* reality that produces his oppression, thus allowing a minimal explicative uptake of an argument that is reflexive, theoretical, and critical in character:[31]

> The critical transitivity at which we arrive through a dialogical and active education that undertakes the social and political responsibility, on the other hand, is characterized by the depth in the interpretation of problems; by the substitution of causal principles for magical explanations [...]; by soundness of argumentation.[32]

---

[29] "Concientización y liberación" (from 1973), in Torres (1983): 86.

[30] "The task of the dialogical teacher in an interdisciplinary team working on the thematic universe revealed by their investigation is to 're-present' that universe to the people from whom she or he first received it – and 're-present' it not as a lecture, but as a problem" (Freire, 1994: 132; translation by Ramos: 109).

[31] This would exactly be an explanation from a Critical Theory. As we shall see, the intervention of the "intellectual" or educator is indispensable here. Otherwise, one would fall into the "spontanism," which obviously opposes "vanguardism."

[32] Freire (1980[a]): 61; modified and extended translation of the English translation by Myra Bergman Ramos, *Education: The Practice of Freedom*. London: Writers and Readers Publishing Cooperative, 1974): 18. "Critical consciousness represents 'things and facts in their causal and circumstantial correlations as they are given in the empirical existence'" (*ibid.*: 105; Freire quoting Álvaro Vieira Pinto; modified translation from Ramos: 44). The opposite is the "magical consciousness," which grasps the facts through mythical causality.

Nothing is further away from Freire than postmodern irrationalism. The oppressed is in need of the theoretical, explanatory reason proceeding from criteria of the economic and political content under the reign of the critical reason. This is the decisive moment in the process of conscientisation in the proper sense of the word: the taking on an explicit, *critical* consciousness. This is where the diagnosis of the "culture of domination" and "banking pedagogy" begins, in which the victims have suffered in the process of domestication and massification, thus forming a "dual consciousness" in man that confuses the true consciousness with the introjection of the consciousness of the dominator (as Memmi taught in *Portrait du colonisé*). This is the result of a pedagogy of domination; the so-called "banking pedagogy" of the system:

> Narration (with the educator [in this case the dominator] as narrator) leads the educand to memorize mechanically the narrated content. Worse yet, it turns them into "containers," into "receptables" to be "filled" by the teacher [...] The more meekly the receptables permit themselves to be filled, the better educands they are.[33]

With this point, Freire calls attention to the psycho-pedagogy of child development that educates the theoretical performance of a child in order to convert him into a disciplined member of a system oppressing him. Without a critical-political consciousness there is no authentic education. And, therefore, the educator must insist, standing next to the educand, "that the social structure is the work of human beings and for this reason, its transformation will equally be a work of human beings."[34]

7. The "historical subject" of the "transformation." Freire often repeats that the "subject" of education is the oppressed one. When the "*critical* consciousness" turns reflectively towards itself thus discovering itself as oppressed in the system, it emerges as a *historical subject*, which is the "pedagogical subject" *par excellence*:

> The *conscientisation* [...] is a critical insertion *in history*. It implies that men assume the role of *creator subjects* of the world; recreators of the world; it calls men to create their existence *with the material that life offers them*.[35]

This is an ethical "material" process. *Life* is the subject matter, the means, the objective, and the obtained joy. It is evident that the *subject* becomes exactly such a subject when it is the very origin of the transformation of reality itself, and it becomes so by situating itself in that "place" from where ethical criticism is possible. It is not a kind of pedagogy that sets

---

[33] Freire (1994), II: 72; modified translation from Ramos: 72-3; author's hard brackets.

[34] Freire (1979) *Educaçâo e Mudança*. Rio de Janeiro: Paz e Terra: 48.

[35] Torres (1992): 111.

up hypothetical examples in order for students of the democratic scholarly community of Cambridge to argue with great ingenuity – by no means. This concerns a *very real* process; at the same time both concrete and objective:

> Uncovering oneself as oppressed only starts being a process of liberation when this uncovering of being oppressed *is transformed into a historical commitment* [...]; a critical insertion in history in order to create it [...] *Conscientisation* implies this critical insertion in the process. It implies a historical commitment to transformation.[36]

The *praxis* of "transformation" is not a place for pedagogical "experience." It is not done in order to learn. It is not something learned in the classroom using a theoretical "consciousness." It happens in the transformative praxis of the "real and historical reality"[37] where the pedagogical process *is gradually effectuated* as a progressive "conscien-tisation" (an "action"-in-which-one-is-taking-on-an-ethical-critical-consciousness: liberation). This presupposes, obviously, a theory of the "social subject," and this especially in a future work on the "fronts of liberation" – where each front has its own distinctive "subjects," which are not "metaphysical" in character, but subjects emerged within a historical conjuncture (although some of these may disappear when the said conjuncture changes.)

8. Communitarian inter-subjectivity: ethical-discursive reason. When Rousseau defined the subject of modern pedagogy, he exposed it in *Émile*: a young male, solipsistic in character, without parents or tradition, and with a bourgeois curriculum. He did so in order to form a technical-industrial spirit that could challenge the old monarchic regime. Freire, however, in his transmodern pedagogy of liberation, relies on a *community* of oppressed victims that are immersed in popular culture, traditions, but still illiterate, miserable... "the wretched of the earth." The grounds for an educator under these circumstances seem desperate; it is the maximum possible negativity. However, Freire believes otherwise. For these reasons, in chapter III of *Pedagogy of the Oppressed,* he is concerned with the theme of "dialoguecity," which is a method that grants the practice of freedom for the non-free: it is the discursive action of the community of subjects aiming at their own liberation.[38] The conscientisation, then, con-

---

[36] *Ibid.*: 112.

[37] Expression by Marx from *Grundrisse*.

[38] This is the indication of the intersubjective formal-moral procedural moment that reaches anti-hegemonic validity in relation to the ethical material contents of the victims, who have become subjects of their own liberation.

tinues its process and is developed as a movement of growing radicalisation.

We might say that Freire, in advance, has "dialogically" subsumed the procedure of discourse ethics, and therefore he cannot agree with the conclusions of Jürgen Habermas where "[d]iscourse ethics does not give any *substantive [inhaltlichen]* orientations. Instead, it establishes a *procedure* based on presuppositions and designed to guarantee the impartiality of the process of judging. Practical discourse is a procedure for testing the validity of hypothetical norms, not for producing justified norm."[39] However, when Habermas draws attention to a possible Stage 4½ in the classification of Kohlberg, he opens up for a solution for Freire:

> At this stage, the perspective is that of an individual standing *outside* of his own society and considering himself as an individual making decisions without a generalized commitment or contract with society.[40]

Are the oppressed of Freire not to be found in the social "exteriority" (as excluded victims)? And whose "dialogue begins by searching for the programmatic *content*"?[41] Does not the entire critical thinking of Freire begin from this "exteriority"? For these reasons, is not the entire participatory democratic process, which creates a new anti-hegemonic validity transformed into a mediation of the "*critical-ethical* consciousness" in order to "transform the world"?[42] The dialogue (the dialogical exercise) has a "content." It contains a demand for overcoming the asymmetry in the dialectics of dominator-dominated:

> Hence, *dialogue cannot* occur between [...] those who deny others the right to speak their word and those whose right to speak has been denied them. Those who have been denied *the primordial right to speak their word* must first reclaim this right and prevent the continuation of this dehumanizing aggression.[43]

The dialogue of the community always has a "content:"

> And since dialogue is the encounter in which the united reflection and action of the dialoguers are addressed to the world which is to be transformed and

---

[39] Habermas, Jürgen (1983) *Moralbewußtsein und kommunikatives Handeln*. Frankfurt am Main: Suhrkamp: 132; translation by Christian Lenhardt and Shierry Weber Nicholsen, *Moral Consciousness and Communicative Action*. Cambridge, UK: Polity Press, 1990: 122; first emphasis by the author; translator's hard brackets.

[40] *Ibid.*: 197; author's emphasis.

[41] Freire (1994), III: 97.

[42] *Ibid.*: 99.

[43] *Ibid.*: 101; translation by Ramos: 88; author's emphasis.

> humanized, this dialogue cannot be reduced to the act of one person's "depositing" ideas in another.[44]

The dialogue is "to speak the word referring *to the world, which has to be transformed* to an encounter between men aiming for this transformation."[45] Freire, then, conceives the dialogue as an "encounter" between subjects revealing to one another the mediations that may transform the world and the *contents* so that everyone may live in the world. Freire departed from a longtime experience from the MEB (Movimiento de Educación de Base, Basic Education Movement); later called Basic Communities. Here, the illiterate, the oppressed, and the poor learned to talk about their misery, about their dreams...

9. "Denounce" and "announce." Freire indicates that there is a negative moment, as when the system is criticised for being the cause of oppression, and also a positive moment; the "utopia" or "untested feasibility:"

> *Utopian* to me is not the unrealisable, it is not idealism. Utopia is the dialectisation in the acts of *denouncing and announcing*. The act of *denouncing* the dehumanising structure and the act of *announcing* the humanising structure [...] What is the future of the oppressor but the preservation of his presence as oppressor? What is the area of denounce that the oppressors have but the denounce of those they denounce? What is the area of announcement of the oppressors but the announcement of their myths, and what may be the hope for those who have no future? [...] Conscientisation is this: an empowerment of reality.[46]

The "denounce" is the fruit from the dialogical community of the oppressed that now have a critical consciousness and are in a dialectic collaboration with educators (intellectual, scientific, in an interdisciplinary position, etc.).[47] Utopia, on the other hand, is the use of the creative imagination of alternatives:

> Once the latter [the oppressed] comes to perceive these situations [the limit situations] as the *frontier between being and being more human*, rather than the *frontier between being and nothingness*, they begin to direct their increasingly critical actions towards achieving the *untested feasibility* implicit in that perception.[48]

---

[44] *Ibid.*: 101; translation by Ramos: 88-9.

[45] *Ibid.* About the dialogue, see Freire (1979): 68ff: "A organizaçâo reflexiva do pensamento" *(A reflexive organisation of the thought)*.

[46] *Ibid.*: 112-4.

[47] Similarly, Marx exercised a (scientific) "denounce" of the capitalistic system in the *Capital*.

[48] Freire (1994): 121; translation by Ramos: 102; author's emphasis.

This "untested feasibility" (the not yet given, but possible) is the project of liberation of the community being subject to transformation.

10. The "praxis of liberation." What sustains the whole process is the actualising, transformative praxis:

> From my point of view, we cannot liberate others; nor can human beings liberate themselves alone, because they liberate themselves *together* by means of that reality, which they must transform.[49]

The "praxis of liberation" is not a final act for Freire but the constant act that relates the subjects to one another in a community transforming the reality that produces the oppressed. It is the water, in which the fish of the critical pedagogy swims. The pedagogical act can only be given *in the process of the praxis of liberation*, which is not only a revolutionary act but a transformative humanising act in favour of the oppressed and for the sake of them in order not to be oppressed anymore.

Inspired by Hegel, Merleau-Ponty, Sartre, Marcel, Mounier, Jaspers, Marx, Lukács, Freud, and many others, Freire develops a genuine discourse from the reality of the victims of the Brazilian Northeast and Latin America. He does so in order to generalise his theory and practical pedagogy, first in Africa[50] and afterwards in other peripheral countries as well as central countries (such as Switzerland). It is a global pedagogy, which sets forth to let an *ethical-critical consciousness* come into existence. Its educational impact, then, not only extends to an improvement of the cognition of the social victims, or of the affective drives, but to the *production of a critical ethical consciousness* that originates in the same victims being the *privileged historical subjects of their own liberation*. The *critical* pedagogical act is exercised in the subject and in his praxis of transformation. Liberation is, in this way, the "place" and "purpose" of this pedagogy.

We would like to end this article with a quote from Freire:

> [I]n the dialogical theory the leaders must dedicate themselves to an untiring effort for unity among the oppressed – and unity of the leaders with the oppressed – in order to achieve liberation. The difficulty is that this category of dialogical action (like the others) cannot occur *apart from praxis*.[51]

Translated from Spanish by Joakim Kromann Rasmussen.

---

[49] "Educación para un despertar la consciencia" (from 1973), in Torres (1983): 43.

[50] See Freire (1977).

[51] Freire (1994): 223; translation by Ramos: 172; author's emphasis.

The Primacy of the Political in Philosophy of Education: A Marxist Perspective

Bhuvan Chandel and Tuktuk Ghosh

> [...] the materialist doctrine that men are products of circumstances and upbringing, and that, therefore, changed men are products of other circumstances and changed upbringing, forgets *that it is men who change circumstances and that it is essential to educate the educator himself*. (Italics ours)(Marx "Third Thesis on Feuerbach")

I. Introduction

The canvas of Education is vast like life itself. It extends from individual subjectivity to beyond the horizons of the Universe. It takes stock of all knowledge ranging from the grounded reality to the most abstract concepts of Mathematics and Natural Sciences. In fact, there is nothing on earth, in heaven or hell, that has not been included within the fold of this attractive discipline!

Yet it has gone through the vicissitudes of the whole range of the moods of human temperament. From the skepticism of Sophists it moved to the wisdom of Socrates, who unlike them refused to abide by any dogmatic trust in conventional morality. Socrates became the harbinger of a new philosophy of education and a true seeker of truth in his search for fundamental principles that explain all reality and value. Knowledge is meaningful if it leads to the pursuit of justice for which the only appropriate method is rational inference. The method of learning is identical with the method of discovering the truth.

Plato shared the conviction of Socrates that virtue can be known and taught and that it is the proper province of education to reform conventional morality. A philosophy of education in Plato's thought means a theory of education – an ethics that justifies the goal which the theory adopts, a metaphysics that explains the psychological and sociological dimensions of the theory of education and an epistemology that explains how the method of teaching and learning could be effective in discovering the truth of any thought.

Marxist thought falls within these parameters. It has a doctrine that explains the foundational realities which are historico-material in character. It has a moral and valuation perspective based on Universal human nature. In this sense it is an all-pervasive knowledge which shapes values and through the creation of awareness educates men to become agents of historical process. In this sense education is synonymous with socialization. As such we can say that politics, education and society walk hand in hand as they move towards the same goal of human perfection and excellence. All political development seeks these ideals and entitles them to become defining characteristic of the foundations of the natural rights of man.

II. Politics and Philosophy: A Synthetic Unity

Marx realized the significance of politics in understanding the nature of social reality and for working out its relationship with the needs and demands of society, including education. Writing about the nature of philosophy, he noted in a letter to Ruge on March 13, 1843:

> The only point where I depart from Feuerbach is when he attributes too much importance, in my opinion, *to nature and not enough to politics. It is only in allying oneself with politics that an actual philosophy can be fully achieved.*[1] (Italics ours)

Marxian socialistic thought has indeed been one of the most dominating influences on the intellectual, moral and political life of our age. Its historical ancestry springs from the 18th century philosophical, cultural and political life of Europe. In fact, it seems to have grown out of a radical interpretation of Christianity which constituted the moral basis of socialism.

The Protestant Christian ethics contributed substantially to the emergence of the political ideology of socialism. Rousseau's assault on privileges and autocracy, the social criticism for reform of Bentham and Mill, and the entire social reform movement was impregnated with the ideal image of an ethical man. In this a radical alternative was emerging in the form of a new ideology which was primarily action-oriented and free from the faults of all hitherto existing ideologies. This was the ideology of socialism as formulated by Marx.

III. Rejection of Metaphysics and Theology

Marx played a significant role in creating awareness about the necessity of bringing philosophy to its completion in action over and above theory. This completion meant the abolition of all speculative philosophy as abstracted from reality and thus full of illusory notions and fetishisms "abounding in metaphysical subtleties and theological niceties"[2] predominantly prevalent in commodity societies. He thus attempted to change

---

[1] Feuerbach, Ludwig (1957) *Essence of Christianity*, Transl. by George Eliot. London: Harper: xxxv.

[2] Marx (1964) *Capital* I. Moscow: Progress Publishers: 71.

moral ideas by first changing the very conditions on which these ideas were based.

This led him to the consideration of social change for the realization of an ideal polity and society. Marx's ideology is in the ultimate analysis the ideology of social change. Philosophy for Marx means a philosophy of action and change. He says in this context, "Philosophers have only *interpreted* the world, in various ways; the point is to *change* it."[3]

He praises Feuerbach for his deduction with regard to man's relation to man and for establishing consciousness of the fact that men in reality do need and have always needed each other. But he criticizes him for being like other theorists in producing merely the correct consciousness about an existing fact "whereas for the real communists, it is a question of overthrowing the existing state of affairs."[4]

In fact, a glance that pierced through the random irregularities of the surface down to the grandiose logic of things historical[5] – made him elbow aside the legends of religious and metaphysical character.

This brought about a paradigm shift in human thinking as it made a clean break from medieval ethics which were characterized by faith in God and were considered the only source of morality and moral beliefs. But with the ascendance of scientific knowledge and secularism, it became possible to consider ideology and ethics entirely within the framework of man and society and to leave the affairs of religion to personal faith. It liberated ideology embedded in social and political values from religion and established it as an autonomous system.

IV. The Contemplative and the Political

In so doing ideology no longer remained contemplative and forged an intimate relationship between the contemplative and the political. As a system of moral and political beliefs, ideology no longer remained *a priori*. It was connected to the essential needs of the society and its welfare within the framework of social, political and moral values.

This socio-political centric approach brought about a shift in the connotation of the term moral responsibility. In addition to moral it became also the social and political responsibility of man to change the

[3] Marx (1964) "XI Thesis on Feuerbach," in Marx-Engels *The German Ideology*. Moscow: Progress Publishers: 647.

[4] *Ibid.*: 54.

[5] Goldway, David (1967) "Appearance and Reality in Marx's Capital," in *Science and Society*, XXXI, 4, Fall, 1967: 439.

conditions which are an impediment to the advancement of man and society. The idea of divine salvation was substituted by the idea of freedom in the social and political nexus. The concept of the moral responsibility of modern man emerged as a protest against the theistic obligation to realize the dream of heaven. It was a reaction against exclusive accent on responsibility towards the self in the traditional ethics wherein salvation and self-realization alone were deemed worthy of realization.

The new concept of moral responsibility in the social and political domain is not confined to an individual's moral excellence alone but also aims at the progress of society. It is in this sense that Marx speaks of the significance of political economy for realizing the freedom of man in society and in history.

As such the new meta-ethical and subjectivist trends in ethical literature would not be adequate accounts of moral reasoning about problems which are social, political and humanistic in character.

V. Feuerbach – The Stream of Fire: Path to Truth and Freedom

Feuerbach is altogether indispensable for a comprehensive understanding of Marxist materialism and humanism. Feuerbach established in the first place the incompatibility of philosophy and religion and of reason and faith. In this context he says:

> The path followed up to now by speculative philosophy – from the abstract to the concrete, from the ideal to the real – is the path that leads to misunderstanding. Being, with which philosophy begins, is not being that is separated from consciousness, nor consciousness that is separated from being.[6]

It is for this reason that Marx said:

> I advise you, you theologians and speculative philosophers, to rid yourselves of the concepts and prejudices of the old speculative philosophy, if you want to deal with things as they are in reality, that is, in truth. *And there is no other road for you towards truth and freedom than this 'stream of fire'* – (Feuerbach). Feuerbach is the purgatory of our time.[7] (Italics ours)

Feuerbach declares that alone to be true philosophy, the high office of which is the true being of man. It was this Feuerbach whom Marx recognized as the enemy of orthodoxies, thus preparing the way for the recovery of man from his alienated condition, through a form of pure natural communion – a kind of universal love of species men – love of "I" and "thou." Marx was not content with this abstract notion of universal love,

[6] Feuerbach, Ludwig (1842) "Provisional Thesis for the Reform of Philosophy," cited in Garaudy, Roger (1967) *Karl Marx*. London: Lawrence & Wirhart: 25.

[7] Marx MEGA, 1, 1: 306, quoted in Garaudy, Roger *op. cit.*: 26.

but drew an insight into the other forms of alienation from Feuerbach's concept of religious alienation.

VI. MATERIALISM, POLITICAL RADICALISM AND PHILOSOPHIC COMMUNISM

It was through this philosophy that Marx and other young Hegelians proceeded to materialism, to political radicalism and to philosophical communism. In this connection Marx said about Feuerbach that he had given to socialism, a philosophical base. On the other hand Engels maintained that of German theoreticians of socialism "Almost none – arrived at communism, otherwise than by way of Feuerbachian dissolution of the Hegelian speculation."[8] In comparison to Hegel, Marx found Feuerbach "extremely poor." He says in this context:

> All the same he was epoch-making after Hegel because he laid stress on certain points which were disagreeable to the Christian Consciousness but important for the progress of criticism and which Hegel had left in mystic semi-obscurity.[9]

Society according to Marx is not characterized by love but by antagonism of classes. Whereas Feuerbach could envisage a perfect humanity resulting from an intellectual deliverance from error, Marx found critical thought rather inadequate.

He sought, in addition, to bring about a radical reconstruction of society in order to establish a truly human society.

Marx criticized Feuerbach for being led to abstract "from the historical process and to presuppose an abstract – *isolated* – human individual"[10] who belongs in reality to a particular form of society.[11] Marx passed much beyond the abstract humanism of Feuerbach to a historical and universal humanism which took the real socio-historical man both for its point of departure and as the end of the moral struggle in the sphere of thought and action.

VII. UNIVERSAL HUMANISM AND UNITY OF MANKIND

Marx as an exponent of humanism sought firm intellectual foundations for his ideology in the concept of man. Humanism, as Adam Schaff holds, is a system of reflections about man recognizing him as the highest

---

[8] Engels (1953) "The Conditions of the Working Class in England," in Marx-Engels *On Britain*. Moscow: Progress: 4.

[9] Marx to J. B. Schweitzer, January 24, 1865, in Marx-Engels (1953) *Selected Correspondence*. Moscow: Foreign Languages: 185

[10] Marx "VI Thesis on Feuerbach," in Marx-Engels *The German Ideology*: 647.

[11] Marx "VII Thesis," in *op. cit.*: 647.

good and is concerned with creating a better world for the welfare of the whole of humanity. The essence of ethical humanism is the idea that all humanity is in each one of us. It is based on the basic reverence for life.[12]

Marx's very concept of philosophy springs from this very image of man. Philosophy for him is thinking about man and his position in the world as a historical being. Since man is a historical being and his situation is constantly changing, the only kind of thinking that can interpret his reality is sociological, political and historical in nature.

In Marx's conception, ethical values do not spring from the heart of the cosmos just as they do not emanate from a transcendental being. Man in his view can experience the eternal life, not in a future heaven or a paradise, but in his transitory existence on earth through the affirmation of his self as a social being, seeking ultimate freedom within the framework of the empirical realities of space and time for himself and for the whole of humanity. There is a boundless concern in his philosophy for the suffering humanity and an endless urge for the unity of mankind and for a symmetric order of society.

And the purpose of man's individual and social existence as envisaged by Marx is the moral elevation of all men and eventually the moral perfection of the whole of mankind.

VIII. Prometheus Unbound: Supremacy of Man

Marxian philosophy of socio-political change, embedded within the framework of concrete history, presupposes the promethean conception of man and rests on the glorification of material achievement. The materialist faith that the world is real is an essential part of the promethean image of man – a man who recognizes obstacles, removes them and creates the possibility for a better, fuller and richer human existence. It is an image of a man who seeks to assert himself through affirmation of his self and recognises a socio-historical and naturalistic framework in lieu of a trans-natural or a trans-social one. As such, Marxian ideology is a promethean ideology of human liberation and of the supremacy of man.[13]

This proclamation of the supremacy of man, embedded within a morality, derived from its socio-political relevance constitutes an integral and significant part of the modern ideology.

---

[12] Schaff, Adam (1967) "Alienation and Social Action," in *Diogenes*, N° 57, Spring 1967.

[13] Chandel, Bhuvan (1979) *Marxian Ethics*. Delhi: Munshiram Manoharlal: 15, 96.

IX. New Concept of Human Happiness

Marx had looked for ideology based on naturalistic rather than supernaturalistic premises. He, like Rousseau, had sought a basis for the moral right of each individual to equality and freedom in the belief that no individual is inherently superior to another. 'Freedom' was usurped for the benefit of a particular class in the name of universal morality, while it was meant for all mankind. Removal of man's misery had to be universal and not class bound. It was therefore an absolute value. His ideology espoused it as an essential condition. Marx thus posited a new concept of human happiness within realizable historico-economic parameters.

X. Bridging the Gulf Between 'Is' and 'Ought'

Profound in valuational insights, Marx also sought to bridge the gulf between fact and value, between "is" and "ought". He rejected the purely conceptual and abstract character of moral beliefs and values for being too far removed from human reality. If ideology with its set moral beliefs and ideas is the theory of good life – then Marx's ideology is conceived within the framework of concrete history.

XI. Moralities of Class Societies

Marx criticized and negated the morality of class societies as he found that they had developed systems of beliefs and values which in the name of universal values subscribed to narrow political interests of dominant classes. He criticized the class morality so that he could transcend narrow selfish interests of classes and propound an ideology for universal humanity irrespective of any class interest, which can be explained in terms of a single moral precept of socio-political significance, namely, 'The freedom and equality of man.'

> The single inscription on the temple of Delphi contained a precept more difficult and more important than is to be found in all the huge volumes that moralists have ever written.[14]

In this context, Engels said, "We are merely saying that this economic fact is in contradiction to our sense of morality."[15]

This evaluative perspective of Marx suggested a radical alternative, i.e. an action-oriented ideology free from the faults of all hitherto existing ideologies for the realization of perfect happiness for mankind. A system

---

[14] Rousseau, Jean-Jacques (1964) *Discourse on the Origin and Foundations of Inequality*, Introd. by Roger D. Masters. New York: St. Martins.

[15] Preface to the first German edition by Friedrich Engels, in Marx *The Poverty of Philosophy*. Moscow: Foreign Languages Pub., n.d.: 11.

of values which aims at this perfection of mankind and its realization is the ideology Marx considered universalistic in character without any class bias as in the past societies.

XII. SECULARISM REDEFINED

Marx explained the kingdom of necessity as one of human bondage. Freedom he equates with creating conditions which are most dignified and adequate to human nature. Only outside and beyond it can that development of human faculties begin which constitutes an end in itself – the true kingdom of freedom.

Marx had criticized the best spokesmen of classical economy for their being hedged in by illusions and thus remaining in a world of half truths and unsolved contradictions. Servitude, Marx described as a kind of perversion of humanity.

> Fanatically bent on making value expand itself, he (capitalist) ruthlessly forces the human race to produce for production sake; […] and creates those material conditions, which alone can form the real basis of a higher form of society, *a society in which the full and free development of every individual forms the ruling principle.*[16] (Italics ours)

The passage from human bondage to human freedom is one from the realm of historical necessity to that of true freedom. History itself is the very realization of freedom.[17] In this context Marx writes:

> In fact, the realm of freedom actually begins only where labour which is determined by necessity and mundane considerations ceases; thus in the very nature of things it lies beyond the sphere of actual material production […] *Freedom in this field can only consist in socialized man the associated* producers, rationally regulating their interchange with nature, bringing it under their common control […]
> But it nonetheless still remains a realm of necessity. *Beyond it begins that development of human energy which is an end in itself, the true realm of freedom, which however, can blossom forth only with this realm of necessity as its basis. The shortening of the working day is its basic pre-requisite.*[18] (Italics ours)

Marx identifies the idea of freedom with the liberation of man from his fragmented and dehumanized state through the transcendence of alienation, whereby man can affirm his individuality as a total man.

---

[16] Marx *Capital* I: 592.
[17] Markus, Gyorgy (1966) "Marxist Humanism," in *Science and Society*, XXX, 3, Summer, 1966: 283.
[18] *Marx Capital* III: 799-800.

XIII. THE FRENCH REVOLUTION AND THE PARIS MANUSCRIPTS

In the history of modern Europe, the French Revolution of 1789 was the greatest attempt to secure liberty, equality and fraternity for the people. It symbolized an endeavour to embody a wholly revolutionary ideology in concrete institutions by a violent and successful seizure of power to assert the intrinsic worth of freedom. Hegel had conceived in it the assertion of the idea of Right whereby the old fabric of injustice broke down. He described it as the most glorious sunrise ever since the sun stood in its firmament.

> […] This was accordingly a glorious mental dawn. All thinking beings shared in the jubilation of this epoch. Emotions of a lofty character stirred men's minds at that time; a spiritual enthusiasm thrilled through the world, as if the reconciliation between the divine and secular was now first accomplished.[19]

It was considered as a landmark in the struggle for social justice.

Eduard Gans spoke about the unmistakable presence of slavery amongst the ill-fed destitute men and women, sacrificing their pleasures of life for the profit of one man in exchange for a meager pittance.

> Is it not pure slavery when man is exploited like a beast when he is left with nothing but the liberty to die of hunger […]? Is it not possible to *awaken in these proletarians their moral consciousness* and lead them to take part in the work they now carry out like machines?[20]

To awaken the consciousness of these proletarians Eduard Gans used the instrumentality of Education in a series of lectures.

A new feeling of passionate indignation and sympathy for the struggle of the dispossessed was deepening in Marx and inspiring a spirit of revolt in him. He says in this context, "[...] the brotherhood of man is no mere phrase with them, but a fact of life, and the nobility of man shines upon us from their work-hardened bodies."[21] And thereafter he fiercely struggled for the freedom and equality of men in the name of social justice, which was the consequence of the great epic of the French Revolution hailed as the sunrise in the life of young Marx. He himself considered his philosophy as a response to the call of history.

The study of French history and the French Revolution secured enough evidence for Marx to prove that class consciousness and class

---

[19] Hegel *Philosophy of History*. Maynard Hutchins Edition: 364.

[20] Cited in Garaudy, Roger (1967) *Karl Marx: The Evolution of his Thoughts*. London: Lawrence and Wishart: 16.

[21] Marx (1967) *Economic and Philosophic Manuscripts of 1844*. Moscow: Foreign Languages: 124-25.

struggles were a part of a very complex set of social realities, which existed in France even before 1789.

Engels has given reasons for Marx's particular preference for French history of which the French Revolution is a significant part. He says in this context:

> France is the land where more than anywhere else the historical struggles were each time fought out to a decision, and where, consequently, the changing political forms within which they were and in which their results are summarized have been stamped in the sharpest outlines […] France demolished feudalism in the Great Revolution and established the unalloyed rule of the bourgeoisie in a classical purity, unequalled by any other European land.[22]

It was in France that the struggle of the upward striving proletariats against the ruling bourgeoisie appeared in an acute form unknown elsewhere. The existence of social classes and the antagonism between them is the motivating force of historical development and is conditioned by the degree of economic development and the mode of their production. Marx says in this context:

> […] we set out from real, active men, and on the basis of their real life process we demonstrate the development of the ideological reflexes and echoes of this life process.[23]

This materialistic conception of history laid bare the fabric of "inner causal connections in the course of development" and made the issues and conflicts of the age intelligible. Marx says in this context:

> The premises from which we begin are not arbitrary ones, not dogmas, but real premises from which abstraction can only be made in the imagination. They are the real individuals, their activity and their material conditions under which they live […][24]

This perception led to a new metaphysics of human progress, the deification of reason and exaltation of human dignity, and gave a new meaning to the concept of humanism. It laid exceptional emphasis upon the natural rights of the individual to attain the ultimate perfection.

XIV. Ideology, Alienation and Education

In fact, the word *"idéologie"* was conceived and coined in 1796 by Destutt de Tracy, who called it the science of ideas. He enunciated the concept so that it may lead to institutional reforms in the system of education, primarily in the schools of France. Ideologists at that time had

---

[22] Engels (1967) "Preface to third German Edition," in *Marx, The Eighteenth Brumaire of Louis Bonaparte*. Moscow: Progress Publishers: 8.

[23] Marx-Engels *The German Ideology*. Moscow: Progress Publishers: 37.

[24] *Ibid.*: 31.

enjoyed key policy-making positions as they had been adept at giving theoretical clarifications in the field of education. Unfortunately their policy decisions could not find favors with Napoleon Bonaparte who thought that they were not practical in their vision and approach and ridiculed them and called them *"idéologues"*. Bonaparte reorganized the Institut National with a view to eliminating the exponents of ideologies and abolished the courses suggested by them for moral and political sciences so that they did not come into conflict with his authoritarian way of running the affairs of his country. The French Revolution of 1789 was a hard lesson to teach all concerned that public interest reigns supreme and the ideology of equality, liberty and brotherhood can play a crucial role when it came to explaining the springs of historical process.

Nevertheless it was in the Napoleonic tradition of contempt for ideology that Marx gave a negative meaning to 'ideology'. But this negative attitude was for class ideologies not for the ideology of universal humankind.

For Marx the mystification to be exposed pertained to the state of alienation, exploitation, dehumanization and oppression which had affected the society as a whole. The masses need to be educated regarding the materialist doctrine that men are products of circumstances and that it is men who change the circumstances and that it is essential to educate the educator himself.[25] It is in this context that Marx's remarks explained in his thesis on Feuerbach have to be seen for their significance for *education* and its relation to ideology and politics.

That entails the knowledge of how a society can recover its lost sense of integrity. This will happen when the state of alienation is transcended and human essence is restored to every human being so that a fulfilled human life can be lived. It is for this reason that salient features of Marx's theory of alienation deserve to be mentioned before we delineate the positive elements of Marx's theory of ideology and its relevance to politics.

The developments which took place during the decades of the 20th century testify to the fact that socialism rose to great heights in most of the countries of the world.

Marx, in his *A Contribution to the Critique of Political Economy*, identified ideology with all forms of social consciousness.

---

[25] Marx, Karl (1964) "Third Thesis on Feuerbach," in *The German Ideology*. Moscow: Progress Publishers: 647.

Marx seems to have postulated the notion of 'false consciousness' in respect to class ideologies. He believed that these were unconscious rationalizations in universal terms of narrow selfish interest into forms of religion and systems of morality in accordance with the interest of the dominant class. To quote Marx:

> The ideas of the ruling classes are in every epoch the ruling ideas, i.e. the class which is the ruling material force of society is at the same time its ruling intellectual force.[26]

For Marx the concept of alienation can be understood in view of the distinction between 'essence' and 'existence.' It is based on the assumption that man's existence is alienated from his essence and from his potentialities. Marx found it to be the essence of Capitalism. He explained the rootedness of alienation in the basic anti-thesis between labour and capital and as a fact of political economy. Alienation is synonymous with forced labour and servitude which result in "crippled monstrosity." Marx says in this context:

> A forcing-up of wages […] would therefore be nothing but better payment for the slave, and would not conquer either for the worker or for labour their *human status and dignity.*[27]

It is the transcendence of alienation and servitude which defines Marxist ideology and in fact it has shaped the educational policies in Russia, China, Eastern Europe and other countries which had come under the sway of communism. The educational content to be imparted in schools, colleges and universities was overwhelmingly full of Marxist-Leninist teachings. It was done that way so that their ideas could penetrate deep into the consciousness of people inhabiting these lands and the banner carrying Marxist ideology could sway far and wide giving a boost to a socialist form of society in contradistinction to a capitalist form of society.

---

[26] Marx, Karl *The German Ideology*. Moscow: Progress Publishers: 60.

[27] Marx (1961) *Economic and Philosophic Manuscripts of 1844*. Moscow: Foreign Languages: 81.

PHILOSOPHY OF EDUCATION AS REFLECTION ON POLITICAL FORMS

Per JEPSEN

I

I shall in the following understand philosophy of education as a part of practical philosophy. Although the 'problems' of a philosophy of education also cover issues that cannot be said to be purely 'practical' – like, for example, the study of the concept of knowledge and the theory of learning – I shall thus claim that the essential concern of educational philosophy is nevertheless a practical concern regarding the values and goals of human action. If the question of practical philosophy in general can be seen as the question of *the good*, alternatively *the better* – a question that is in turn raised with respect to actions, institutions and forms of life –, the knowledge interest of philosophy of education consequently consists in a specific formulation of this question. More precisely, philosophy of education is the part of practical philosophy that investigates the nature, values and ends of educational practice, and is in this investigation guided by the question of *the good,* or *the best possible education.* To answer this question it becomes necessary to develop a theory of the nature of education that implies at the same time a normative picture of its ultimate goal, that is, of the reasons why we educate at all. This picture may turn out to be different whether we consider child education or adult education, pre-school education or school education, and it might also differ with the differentiation of the concept of education that is made in the German distinction between *"Erziehung," "Unterricht"* and *"Bildung."*[1] The key phenomenon of education, however, is in the opinion of this author the same throughout these distinctions and differentiations, namely, what might be called *the facilitation of possibilities of human self-expression and action through the widening of knowledge and reflection.* I will in this essay take the validity of this definition of educational philosophy more or less for granted.

[1] As is well known, a similar distinction cannot be made in English. Since the words refer to genuinely different areas of the theory and practice of education, I therefore prefer to keep the German formulation.

As a part of practical philosophy that investigates the norms and values of a certain practice – namely the practice of education – educational philosophy shares with practical philosophy as such the premise of individual autonomy. Obviously, the question of what I or we have to do only makes sense if there is indeed an alternative; if there are in fact different options for the action, institution or form of life in question. Practical philosophy therefore is dependent on the actuality of human freedom in the sense that it must necessarily presuppose the ability of the individual to determine his or her own actions. Without the premise of individual autonomy – here understood in a non-differentiated sense as freedom of action as well as freedom of the will – practical philosophy empties itself of any possible meaning.[2]

The assumption of the autonomous or self-determined individual can, however – at least this is the assertion I will try to defend here – only be made as a *problematical assumption*. As a consequence of this, practical philosophy itself becomes in its traditional form problematical. Because the autonomy of the individual is under the actual circumstances at best problematically given, the positive project of practical philosophy can in other words not be realized. Instead, what is actually left for practical philosophy is the reflection on the conditions of its own failure. As we shall see these conditions are essentially political.

The above assumptions regarding the form and possibility of practical philosophy are all defended in detail elsewhere.[3] They will therefore not be presented in their full systematic context in this essay. What I will on the other hand do here is to discuss some aspects of the way in which the thesis of the problematical character of practical philosophy can be said to affect the philosophy of education. As already mentioned, educational philosophy in its traditional form must, like practical philosophy in general, presuppose the possibility of individual autonomy. Whereas the other areas of practical reasoning might be characterized as concerning the right use of human freedom, philosophy of education is defined through the concern for *the cultivation of freedom*. This understanding of educational practice can be traced back to an early point in the history of European philosophy and is already at stake in Aristotle's emphasis on

---

[2] For a further discussion of this cf. Jepsen, Per (2012) *Adornos kritische Theorie der Selbstbestimmung*. Würzburg: Königshausen & Neumann: 34-37. See also Tugendhat, Ernst (1979) *Selbstbewusstsein und Selbstbestimmung: Sprachanalytische Interpretationen*. Frankfurt a. M.: Suhrkamp Verlag: 194ff.

[3] Cf. Jepsen, *Adornos kritische Theorie der Selbstbestimmung*.

the importance of child education for the acquisition of character virtue.[4] Manifestly, the characterization of education through the idea of a cultivation of freedom can be found in Kant's lectures on education.[5]

If there is under the given societal circumstances no such thing as unrestricted human freedom, also the ideal of education as a facilitation of the autonomous individual is, however, referred to insoluble inner contradictions. As the German philosopher and educational theorist Andreas Gruschka observes, the point of departure for educational theory must thus be the fact that education in practice necessarily fails in realizing its own aims.[6] Consequently, it becomes the goal of the theory of education to clear up the conditions of "the necessary failure of educational practice" instead of theoretically legitimizing its false self-understanding.[7]

The reflections put forth in this essay correspond to a large degree with the basic assumptions of Gruschka's negative theory of education. I will, however, in the following independent of Gruschka try to explicate the assertion that educational theory must under the present circumstances be a theory of the failure of educational practice. Since what inhibits a realization of unrestricted individual autonomy – and thereby a realization of education – is in the end a specific organization of society, the negative philosophy of education presented in the following can in a certain sense be characterized as a *reflection on political forms*.

As a historical model to put the more general philosophical considerations in concrete terms, I will choose the German philosopher and sociologist Theodor W. Adorno's discussion of the concept of education as *"Bildung"* in his essay *"Theorie der Halbbildung"* ("Theory of Half Education") from 1959.[8] As we shall see, the phenomenon of 'Half Education' in Adorno at the same time designates the failure of educational practice and traces this failure back to a certain *political form*: To the failure of the emancipatory project of the enlightenment.

II

In the following, Adorno's essay on the "Theory of Half Education" will serve as a model for a certain type of philosophical reflection on the prac-

---

[4] Cf. Aristotle *Nicomachean Ethics*, 1103b, cited after Aristotle, *Selections*, transl. Terence Irwin & Gail Fine. Indianapolis/Cambridge: Hackett Publishing Company, 1995: 366-367.

[5] See Kant, Immanuel *Über Pädagogik*. Langensalza: Hermann Beyer & Söhne: 77.

[6] Cf. Gruschka, Andreas (2004) *Negative Pädagogik*. Wetzlar: Büchse der Pandora: 15ff.

[7] *Ibid.*, 38.

[8] Adorno, Theodor W. "Theorie der Halbbildung," in Adorno, Theodor W. (1972) *Gesammelte Schriften*, vol. 8. Frankfurt a. M.: Suhrkamp Verlag: 93-121.

tice of education. More precisely, Adorno's concept of half education will be seen as representing a form of educational reflection that, instead of presupposing the possibility of a successful cultivation of freedom, shows why this cultivation must under the current societal conditions necessarily fail. Moreover, Adorno's essay shows how the absence of genuine human autonomy – an autonomy that according to Adorno could only be realized through political action – affects the conceptual structure of philosophy of education itself.

The concept of half education – in German, *'Halbbildung'* – is in Adorno developed to explain the crisis of education as *"Bildung"* after the Second World War. This crisis, according to Adorno, cannot be reduced to a crisis of the educational system but reflects a much more fundamental political and cultural crisis.[9] Thus the crisis of education as *"Bildung"* expresses what Adorno in *Negative Dialectics* and elsewhere formulates as "the failure of culture" *("das Mißlingen der Kultur")*[10] respectively as "the dialectics between culture and barbarity" *("Dialektik von Kultur und Barbarei".)*[11] As we shall see, the failure of culture must in the end be explained as a consequence of the failure of the modern political project of a common will that, rather than relying on a repression of its members, emerges from the free association of all individuals.

The thesis of a dialectics of culture and barbarity in Adorno goes back to the *Dialectics of Enlightenment (Dialektik der Aufklärung)* which he published together with Max Horkheimer in 1944, 1947 and again in 1969.[12] Horkheimer and Adorno in this book identify the project of enlightenment in a broad sense with the project of occidental culture as such and define both as the ambition to free human beings from their slavery to nature, "installing them" instead as "masters" over inner and outer nature.[13] In its final consequence, though, enlightenment culture with the mastery over inner nature reproduces the barbarity it tried to escape and establishes itself as a new 'force of nature' at which the individuals have

---

[9] Cf. *Ibid.*: 92.

[10] Cf. Adorno, Theodor W. *Negative Dialectics*, in Adorno, Theodor W. (1970) *Gesammelte Schriften*, vol. 6. Frankfurt a. M.: Suhrkamp Verlag: 359.

[11] Adorno, Theodor W., "Kulturkritik und Gesellschaft," in Adorno, Theodor W. (1977) *Gesammelte Schriften*, vol. 10.1. Frankfurt a. M.: Suhrkamp Verlag: 30.

[12] The title of the 1944 edition was, however, the later subtitle, *Philosophical Fragments (Philosophische Fragmente)*. With the exception of a series of terminological adjustments and the last of the seven paragraphs in "Elements of Antisemitism" *("Elemente des Antisemitismus")* that was not published before the 1947 ed., the three editions are largely identical.

[13] Adorno, Theodor W. & Horkheimer, Max (2002) *Dialectics of Enlightenment. Philosophical Fragments*, transl. Edmund Jephcott. Palo Alto: Stanford University Press: 1.

to adapt themselves in order of their self-preservation. Horkheimer and Adorno in the book formulate this thesis as the thesis of a "dialectics of myth and enlightenment"[14] as well as that of a "self-destruction of enlightenment."[15] As the historical prism through which the self-destruction of enlightenment lets itself be seen, Horkheimer and Adorno in the book give a historical-philosophical analysis of the social and intellectual roots of fascism and anti-semitism in Europe in the 1930s and 1940s. The rise and triumph of European fascism is thus seen as undoubtful evidence for the relapse of culture into barbarism.[16]

The phenomenon of half education must, according to Adorno, be explained in context with the above-mentioned dialectics of culture and barbarity. Thus the concrete point of departure for Adorno's discussion of the concept of education as *"Bildung"* seems to be the affinity between the self-destruction of enlightenment and what might be termed *the self-destruction of education as "Bildung."* As evidence for the tendency towards the latter, Adorno in *"Theorie der Halbbildung"* mentions the seeming paradox that people who on the one hand "participated passionately and with great understanding in the so called cultural properties *(Kulturgüter)*," on the other hand voluntarily joined "the murder practice of National Socialism."[17] The participation of culturally educated people in the political system of the Nazis *seems* a paradox because, according to the very concepts of 'culture' and 'education,' the possession of culture should in itself be antidotal to a totalitarian and inhumane ideology like that of National Socialism. Not at least it should be antidotal to the practical execution of this ideology in the form of a racialist mass murder like the genocide against the European Jews.

That culture and education should *in themselves* have prevented the genocide against the Jews is, of course, a normative statement. That they *did not* actually prevent it is, however, as we all know a historical fact. What Adorno attempts in *"Theorie der Halbbildung"* – and what he and Horkheimer aim at in *Dialectics of Enlightenment* – is exactly to explain this contradiction between *normativity* and *reality*, between on the one hand the normative self-understanding of Western European culture and on the other hand the fact that these cultures could "produce" such a thing as anti-semitism and thereby give rise to the historical mass murder of the Jews.

---

[14] *Ibid.*: xviii.
[15] *Ibid.*: xvi.
[16] Cf. once again Adorno, *Negative Dialectics*: 359.
[17] Adorno, "Theorie der Halbbildung": 94.

In the first place, what Adorno wants to emphasize is that the emergence of the fascist regimes in Western Europe in the 1930s and 1940s cannot leave the cultural – philosophical, political and educational – ideals of this part of the world untouched. Applied to the field of the philosophy of education, the very concept of education can after its historical affiliation with fascist ideology no longer be the same. The meaning of culture, Adorno insists – and thereby also the meaning of education – "cannot be separated from the organization of human affairs."[18] The breakthrough of political totalitarianism on the grounds of classical European culture therefore necessarily affects the way in which we are to view the fundamental categories and ideals of this culture. It is as such a 'categorical' change in the inner structure of educational theory and practice that Adorno views the concept of 'Half Education' *(Halbbildung)*.

Second, the new way of looking at the political and educational ideals of enlightenment culture that becomes necessary in light of its relapse into barbarism at the same time provides the framework for a deeper understanding of this relapse. Thus, the concept of half education intends to help us further in understanding why the presence of educational culture *did not* keep the individuals from being mobilized by fascism and National Socialism. To make a long story short, the answer to this question is that educational culture was not – or no longer – present. Instead of education there was half education. But what exactly does this mean?

What was once *the promise of education (Bildung)* has in the course of its own history changed into what Adorno terms "socialized half education" *("sozialisierte Halbbildung")*.[19] That half education is 'socialized' means that it is not internalized through conscious individual reflection and decision-making but unconsciously through the media of socialization, first and foremost through mass media or the so-called 'culture industry.'[20] That half education is 'half' on the other hand indicates a loss of substance compared with the classical bourgeois ideal of education. This loss of substance can for the sake of clarity be divided into the following aspects:

– a loss of the subjective capacity for experience, respectively for the "concrete sensitivity for ideas" *("leibhafte Fühlung mit Ideen")*[21]

– the loss of the possibility of a subjective identification with society[22]

---

[18] Adorno, "Theorie der Halbbildung": 95.

[19] *Ibid.*: 93.

[20] Cf. *Ibid.*: 110-114. For the theory of 'culture industry' in Horkheimer & Adorno, cf. Adorno/Horkheimer, *Dialectics of Enlightenment*: 94-136.

[21] Adorno, "Theorie der Halbbildung": 105. Cf. *ibid.*: 118.

– the loss of the individual capacity for critique and resistance[23]
– the transformation of the contents of educational culture to status symbols and "cultural assets."[24]

Half education implies as well a reification of the "contents of education" *("Sachgehalte von Bildung")*[25] as an alienation of individual consciousness: It is "the omnipresence of alienated consciousness."[26]

What exactly, according to Adorno, is responsible for the transformation of education into half education? In answering this question we will return to the topic of the previous paragraph of this essay, namely the thesis of the *problematical* character of individual autonomy. Thus, Adorno, when he has to explain the social philosophical dynamics of half education, again and again recurs to the absence of individual autonomy:

> [Education] has as its precondition freedom and autonomy. At the same time it refers until this day the individual to the structures of a [...] fixed, in a certain sense heteronomous and therefore frail *(hinfällig)* order by the adaptation to which he is alone able to form himself. Therefore, education *(Bildung)* actually from the moment of its emergence no longer exists. The disintegration of education is teleologically implied already in its origin.[27]

Education has become half education because its own precondition – the actuality of human freedom – has not been fulfilled. In this sense – and only in this – the development of half education is "teleologically implied" in the phenomenon of education.[28] The assertion of a teleological implication does not mean that the regression of education into half education was necessarily given with the very idea of education. What it does mean is that this idea has not been realized because its *"a priori"* – autonomy – "has not had the time to form itself."[29]

That the autonomy of the individuals – contrary to the ambition of the classical educational project – is still absent must according to Adorno be explained through the absence of a free and rational society. It was the end *(Zweck)* of classical education to "qualify the individuals to behave rationally in a rational society, to behave freely in a free society."[30] The bourgeois tradition of educational thought thereby presupposed that

---

[22] *Ibid.*: 103.
[23] Cf. *Ibid.*: 106 and 115.
[24] *Ibid.*: 110. Cf. *ibid.*: 115.
[25] *Ibid.*: 103.
[26] *Ibid.*: 93.
[27] *Ibid.*: 104.
[28] *Ibid.*
[29] *Ibid.*: 99.
[30] *Ibid.*: 98.

the intellectual enlightenment in itself would lead to the enlightenment of the social whole.[31] This presupposition can, as intellectual and social history shows us, not be made. As Adorno puts it, it is thus the "wound" of the classical tradition of *"Bildung"* that "education *(Bildung)* alone does not guarantee a rational society *(die vernünftige Gesellschaft)*."[32] This is, of course, another way of stating the fact that educational culture did not prevent National Socialism. Only in a free and rational society, however, would individual autonomy get the time to 'form itself'. This means at the same time that the healing of education from 'half education' would only be possible through political emancipation.

III

The tradition of education, Adorno insists, has failed in realizing its own aims because the modern political project of an emancipation of society did not succeed. *The failure of education as "Bildung"* must be regarded as an effect of the self-refutation of emancipatory thought and practice. The concrete realization of autonomous individuality that constitutes the *sine qua non* of education is referred to the realization of a genuinely free society. The means to such a realization is what is traditionally termed *politics*. Only by the means of political organization can there be any hope of a realization of freedom in society. I have shown elsewhere that the theory of politics marks a blank space in Adorno's critical theory, since there is in this theory no specification of the way to an attainment of societal autonomy.[33] Adorno repeatedly suggests that the form of an autonomous society is to be imagined after the model of a 'common subject of society' *(gesellschaftliches Gesamtsubjekt,)* thereby appealing as well to Marx as to the concept of a common will in bourgeois philosophy.[34] But even though the constitution of a common subject of society is without doubt thought as resulting from the free organization of all individuals, there is in Adorno no *theory* of the political and institutional means to such an organization. Adorno himself seems to defend this lack through

---

[31] Cf. *ibid.*: 97.

[32] *Ibid.*: 98.

[33] Jepsen, Per (2012) *Adornos kritische Theorie der Selbstbestimmung*. Würzburg: Königshausen & Neumann, chapter 7.

[34] Cf. for an example Adorno, Theodor W. "Fortschritt," in Adorno, Theodor W. (1977) *Gesammelte Schriften*, vol. 10.2. Frankfurt a. M.: Suhrkamp Verlag: 617-638. Cf. too the essays collected in Becker, Jens & Brakemeier, Heinz (eds) (2004) *Vereinigung freier Individuen: Kritik der Tauschgesellschaft und gesellschaftliches Gesamtsubjekt bei Theodor W. Adorno*. Hamburg: VSA-Verlag.

the thesis of a temporary obstruction of political practice.[35] On the other hand, apparently only true political practice would be able to lead contemporary society out of this dead end.[36]

In my concluding remarks I will, however, not dwell on the deficits of political theory in Adorno – a deficit that can just as well be interpreted as a manifestation of the real contradictions to which political practice is today exposed –, but instead recapitulate the picture of educational philosophical reflection that is implicated in Adorno's analysis of half education. This picture corresponds to the description of the challenges of philosophy of education in the first paragraph and can be summarized as the concept of *philosophy of education as reflection on political forms.*

Adorno at the end of his essay states the current challenges of educational philosophy as follows: "It is," he writes, "time for the anachronism: to hold on to education *(Bildung)* after the society has deprived it of its basis. It [education, PJ] has no other way to survive than as the critical reflection on the half education which it necessarily became."[37] To hold on to its own promise of a cultivation of freedom, in other words, the philosophy of education must continually criticize what in the history of Western European culture became of this promise. What is left for the philosophy of education is, to repeat a formulation from the first paragraph of this essay, the reflection on the conditions of its own failure. Adorno's concept of half education in this context exemplifies how this failure affects the very categories of educational theory.

The conditions of the failure of education – as well as those of its possible future realization – are essentially political. That philosophy of education must take shape of a political reflection means that it must integrate the question of these conditions into its understanding of the normative dimensions of educational practice. Adorno's "Theory of Half Education" was in this essay chosen as a model not at least because of the conciseness with which it shows the necessity of an inclusion of 'material' culture in the normative reflections of practical philosophy. As a reflection on political forms, educational philosophy must give up the idea of its own autonomy and instead accept that the realization of education is not – only – up to education.

---

[35] Cf. for an example Adorno, Theodor W. "Marginalien zu Theorie und Praxis," in Adorno, Theodor W. (1977) *Gesammelte Schriften*, vol. 10.2. Frankfurt a. M.: Suhrkamp Verlag: 759-782.

[36] Cf. Adorno "Marginalien zu Theorie und Praxis": 764.

[37] Adorno "Theorie der Halbbildung": 121.

LITERATURE

Adorno, Theodor W. "Fortschritt," in Adorno, Theodor W. (1977) *Gesammelte Schriften*, vol. 10.2. Frankfurt a. M.: Suhrkamp Verlag: 617-638.

–, "Kulturkritik und Gesellschaft," in Adorno, Theodor W. (1977) *Gesammelte Schriften*, vol. 10.1. Frankfurt a. M.: Suhrkamp Verlag: 11-30.

–, "Marginalien zu Theorie und Praxis," in Adorno, Theodor W. (1977) *Gesammelte Schriften*, vol. 10.2. Frankfurt a. M.: Suhrkamp Verlag: 759-782.

–, *Negative Dialectics*, in Adorno, Theodor W. (1970) *Gesammelte Schriften*, vol. 6. Frankfurt a. M.: Suhrkamp Verlag: 7-412.

–, "Theorie der Halbbildung," in Adorno, Theodor W. (1972) *Gesammelte Schriften*, vol. 8. Frankfurt a. M.: Suhrkamp Verlag: 93-121.

Adorno, Theodor W. & Horkheimer, Max (2002) *Dialectics of Enlightenment. Philosophical Fragments*, transl. Edmund Jephcott. Palo Alto: Stanford University Press.

Aristotle (1995) *Selections*, transl. Terence Irwin & Gail Fine. Indianapolis/Cambridge: Hackett Publishing Company.

Becker, Jens & Brakemeier, Heinz (eds) (2004) *Vereinigung freier Individuen: Kritik der Tauschgesellschaft und gesellschaftliches Gesamtsubjekt bei Theodor W. Adorno*. Hamburg: VSA-Verlag.

Gruschka, Andreas (2004) *Negative Pädagogik*. Wetzlar: Büchse der Pandora.

Jepsen, Per (2012) *Adornos kritische Theorie der Selbstbestimmung*. Würzburg: Königshausen und Neumann.

Kant, Immanuel (1883) *Über Pädagogik*. Langensalza: Hermann Beyer & Söhne.

Tugendhat, Ernst (1979) *Selbstbewusstsein und Selbstbestimmung: Sprachanalytische Interpretationen*. Frankfurt a. M.: Suhrkamp Verlag.

UNIVERSITY

THE STORM BREAKING ON THE UNIVERSITY: UK POLITICS AND HIGHER EDUCATION SINCE 1979[1]

Gordon FINLAYSON

1. INTRODUCTION

In one form or another, universities have been around for centuries. Universities existed long before what is now known as the Westphalian world of sovereign states came into being. They survived through a remarkable shift in the intellectual and epistemic climate. They witnessed the gradual decline in the power and influence of Church, the fall of the Aristotelian and Scholastic world view, the rise of modern science, and the invention of modern academic disciplines. They lived through the mathematicization of science in the early modern period, and saw out the rise to prominence of the scientific ideals of mechanical and structural objectivity. They survived and flourished in the 19th Century which saw the Industrial Revolution, military expansion, and the conceptual invention and gradual actualisation of ethnically homogenous monolinguistic nations. They lived through the emergence of democracy, the expansion of the franchise, and the outbreak of communist revolution. They survived the abhorrent 20th Century with its two World Wars, followed by the rebuilding of the European economies in the shadow of the Cold War. They saw the emergence of the Welfare State compromise, of free education, and the rise of the modern multicultural, liberal democratic state. They witnessed the shrinking of the state's reach and the relentless expansion of global capitalist economy.

No doubt the historical resilience of the university is partly to do with its capacity to adapt to the changing historical, political, cultural and intellectual landscape. But it also has to do with its being well fitted to one of the more enduring facts of human life, namely that human beings are social animals who educate their young, and also rational animals,

---

[1] This is a much revised version of an article I initially co-wrote with Daniel Hayward entitled "Education Toward Heternomy: A Critical Analysis of the Reform of UK Universities since 1978", in Mark Fisher (ed.) (2011) *The University is not a Factory: Resisting the Neo-Liberal Academy*. Zer0 Books. The section on the Thatcher era is mainly Daniel's.

who are capable of learning, and who hand their acquired knowledge down from generation to generation.

Now is the time to remind ourselves of the enduring value of the university, because, to borrow a phrase from Cardinal Newman, which is not overdramatic in the circumstances, in the 21st Century a storm has broken on the university in Britain (and in Europe), an ideological storm from the West of such severity that it threatens to undermine and possibly destroy an institution that has so far withstood the stern test that history has thrown at it.[2]

2. THE PURPOSE OF THE UNIVERSITY

I want to begin with what I hope is a near platitude about the purpose of the university. A university is an educational institution and its primary purpose is to educate well. In its task of education we can still say, as Cardinal John Henry Newman did in 1858, that the university aims at "the perfection or virtue of the intellect." That is to say "[its] function is intellectual culture […] and it has done its work when it has done as much as this. It educates the intellect to reason well in all matters, to reach out towards truth, and to grasp it."[3] There are two thoughts here, and the first concerns the intellectual formation of the individual, the second concerns the development and transmission of culture, in all its dimensions. The first of these is captured nicely by the Homeric motto of my alma mater, St Andrews University, "aien aristeuein," always to be the best, or always strive for excellence. Transplanted from the context of the warrior ethos in the *Iliad*, to the context of the university, the motto has great relevance today. Some might think that this aim, though once admirable, is now merely quaint, if not entirely obsolete. That would be wrong. As a matter of fact all modern universities do aim at excellence in education, and this is just as it should be.

It is, however, also true that the term 'excellence' has now been integrated into the economistic, pseudo-technical management speak that has become the lingua franca of Government and university administrators, a language which has been imported, as Stefan Collini points out, from the sphere of "management schools, business consultants and financial journalism."[4] But this does not mean that the idea that universities

---

[2] Newman, J. H. (1907) "Discourse 7," in *The Idea of a University*. London: Longman, Green & C°.

[3] *Ibid.*, "Discourse 6."

[4] Collini, S. (2011) "From Robbins to McKinsey." *London Review of Books*, vol. 33, n° 16, August.

aim at excellence is as shallow and (nowadays literally) bankrupt as the ideology that hijacked it, as for example, Bill Readings claims in *The University in Ruins*. Readings maintains that the very idea of 'excellence' is ideologically contaminated, and utterly vacuous. "All departments of the University can be urged to strive for excellence since the general applicability of the idea is in proportion to its emptiness."[5]

He takes an example due to Jonathan Culler that Cornell University Parking Services received an award for excellence in parking. However, this example does not bear out Readings' worry. Any practice that takes some skill can be done well or badly. So it is just as appropriate that a parking service should aim for excellence in parking, as that a university should aim for excellence in education. Besides, the fact that an evaluative ideal can be integrated into a prevailing ideology does not mean that it should be rejected, along with the ideology. On the contrary, the fact that an ideal has been hijacked by a prevailing ideology offers opportunities to the social critic to hold the society to the very ideals to which it says it aspires, as for example with the bourgeois ideals of freedom and equality that are endemic to Western capitalist society.

Cardinal Newman considered universities primarily as teaching institutions, distinct from academies, whereas nowadays universities are also research institutions. This does not detract from their aim, which is to educate, rather it enhances it. In most subjects good teaching and good research are mutually beneficial. It would odd if someone only taught philosophy, but did not pursue his or her own philosophical inquiry, or if a piano teacher only taught people to play the piano, but did not play it herself. There may be such people, but in my experience they are unlikely to excel at teaching.

If this is true our initial platitude can help us throw light on what a good university should be: a good university aims at and reaches excellence in teaching and research. And this conclusion can be put to work as a criterion of good Higher Education policy: good policy will encourage universities to fulfil their proper aim, and a bad policy will detract from this aim.

Although Universities nowadays still have as their primary aim excellence in teaching and research, it is true that the modern university is different from the university about which Newman wrote in 1858, and we need to bring his analysis more up to date. In 1967 Jürgen Habermas

---

[5] Readings, B. (1996) *The University in Ruins*. Cambridge: Harvard University Press: 23-25.

identified four different functions of the university in a democracy, each of which is still relevant today.

1. The first is that the university should transmit and produce technically exploitable knowledge, which means that through its "teaching and research the university is immediately connected with the functions of the economic process." This pithy statement needs unpacking. Technically exploitable knowledge does not just mean scientific or technical knowledge. Nor does it only or even primarily refer to the kind of know-how that is close to market, such as accountancy or business management skills. All knowledge can be technically exploitable, and it is very difficult to predict which knowledge will be in practice. No-one could have predicted that work in philosophical logic and mathematics would ultimately have led to the birth of the discipline of informatics and the invention of computers. No-one could have known that the discovery by a Soviet chemist in 1952 of carbon nanotubes would eventually lead to breakthroughs in solar cell technology.

The other thing to note is that what Habermas means by the economy cannot be reduced to the narrow goal of increasing Gross Domestic Product per capita, it should be defined more broadly in terms of social well-being. It would be well to say that universities should produce specialized technically exploitable knowledge that is social beneficial. Of course, it is extremely difficult to know in advance which kinds of knowledge in the medium to long term will be socially beneficial, and which will not. In this case we can see that, in the light of this function universities are well advised to aim at excellence in teaching and research across a broad range of disciplines.

2. The second function Habermas identifies is that Universities should equip students with professional knowledge and with extra-functional abilities.

In virtue of their skills and capacities graduating students form what is known as human capital. In this respect university education produces a social and economic benefit. One should not make the mistake of thinking that in order that students gain such skills the subjects they study have to be directly vocational. In many respects the opposite is the case. Knowledge dates fast. However, the general and discipline specific skills that one acquires in studying whatever subject, whether French, Mathematics or Philosophy, remain valuable in a rapidly changing world. In learning any subject to a high level students develop reflexive learning capacities, which make them adaptable. They learn how to learn. These reflexive learning capacities will be the better, where the students are not spoon-fed, but encouraged to be self-organising and self-reliant.

3. The third function of the modern university is *the transmission and development of culture*. This function is properly fulfilled in the domains of both teaching and of research. Readings is suspicious of this idea because he associates cultural with national culture, and this idea with the now outdated Humboldtian project of the 19th Century.[6] Though it is true that this function came to prominence in the 19th Century, it has by no means become outdated. For one thing, culture, along with the need to transmit it, has been around in one form or another before the rise of the nation-state, and will continue to be around whatever the effects of globalization on national culture turn out to be. For another, reports of the demise of the state have tended to be greatly exaggerated. States may be increasingly in hock to the global economy, but it is not as if anything else has come close to replacing them on the political level.

4. Finally there is what Habermas calls "the formation of political consciousness," and which I would call education towards democratic citizenship. Of course Habermas was writing in the context of the Federal Republic of Germany in 1967, and as one of the first and second generation of citizens brought up in a democratic constitutional state after the fall of the National Socialist regime, was extremely aware of the fragility of democracy. Still it would be very wrong to think of this function of the university as particular to Germany, and not generally applicable. Rather we should, as Martha Nussbaum is only the latest to remind us, be very conscious that democracy is not a stable and robust administrative machine, which once set up will likely continue normal functioning into the long term.[7] Democracy, as a meaningful, healthy and actual political ideal, requires a democratic culture. Moreover if actual democracy is to be resilient, it requires an electorate who can make significant, informed choices based on an assessment of and commitment to the common good. Democracy requires educated citizens, not just educated leaders.

Since this has been very broad brush account we should draw the various strands together. We began with Newman's suggestion that the purpose of the university is to educate well, and defended the relevance of the idea of excellence. We brought this idea more up to date by looking at the university as a research institution: *the aim of the modern university is to excel at teaching and research across a broad range of dis-*

---

[6] Readings, *The University in Ruins*, ch. 5.

[7] Nussbaum, M. C. (2010) *Not For Profit: Why Democracy Needs the Humanities*. Princeton: Princeton University Press.

ciplines. Finally, we tried to unpack the significance and the relevance of this aim to the technical, social, economic, cultural and political functions of the modern university. If we assume that the account given so far is broadly correct, it provides an illuminating foil for the assessment and criticism of recent UK government policy, to which I now turn.

3. UK Government Policy from Thatcher to Brown

I will here offer a necessarily abbreviated account of successive Higher Education and university reforms in the UK over the last four decades. Of primary interest here is not the detail but the overall direction. This will help us make sense of the sweeping changes which are being ushered in at breakneck pace throughout the UK and university sector. These changes have not come out of nowhere. Nor are they just the unplanned, quasi-natural consequences of broader social and historical changes: they are the effects of specific policies aimed at repositioning the UK in respect to the global economy, and of the various mechanisms, particularly audits, put in place to monitor their performance.

3.1 The Thatcher Legacy: Self-Incurred Efficiencies

The rapid and radical changes in UK Higher Education since 1997 are virtually all due to New Labour, but it was Conservative policy in the 1980s and 1990s that prepared the ground for New Labour policy in the following two decades. This fact helps explain the remarkable ease with which such radical changes were made and the indecent speed of their implementation.

Margaret Thatcher's government was elected in 1979 with a "mandate" to attack public services. The Conservative manifesto of 1979 included a pledge to reduce "waste, bureaucracy and over-management" at the state level.[8] An "efficiency review" of the Civil Service, conducted by Derek Rayner, chief executive of Marks and Spencer, led to over 100,000 staff cuts in the Civil Service by April 1984. The Thatcher Government tended to use financiers, industrialists, as advisors rather than academics. They reinforced the view of Government ministers that business created wealth and that educational institutions (and social services) consumed it, and that the job of universities was to supply business and industry with skilled employees.

Although there was no direct Government intervention in universities but nonetheless an internal restructuring of the universities took

[8] Metcalfe, L. & Richards, S. "The efficiency strategy in central government: An impoverished concept of management." *Public Money & Management*, Vol. 7, N° 1, June 1987: 27.

place. What was then called the Committee of Vice Chancellors and Principles (CVCP) judged that by cutting themselves they could avoid major government surgery.[9] In 1985 the Chancellor of the University of Birmingham, and former chief executive of Reed International, industrialist Alex Jarratt, was commissioned to conduct an efficiency review whose findings were published in the 1985 'Report of the Steering Committee for Efficiency Studies in Universities.' Under its rubric of efficiency the Jarratt report of 1985 recommended a fundamental change in managerial structure in the universities.

Hitherto the UK university system had been run on traditional college lines. Positions of administrative authority were assigned to academics on a rotating basis. Heads of Departments and even Vice-Chancellors were research active academics still sensitised to the needs and interests of their academic staff. According to Jarratt these management structures had to make way. From now on VCs should act more like Chief Executives, implementing their strategic visions in partnership with Business. Budget control should be devolved to the department level and greater emphasis should be placed on corporate governance.

In effect this meant abolishing self-governance by committees of academics radically scaling down the size of Senates and reducing their powers. Senates were the bodies that oversaw university policy. They were populated chiefly with academics often elected by the departments. Their members espoused academic values and they provided an important link between university management and the academic.

These were effectively replaced with chains of command from the centre. Significantly, Jarratt advocated increased "lay" membership of Councils, the executive administrative bodies.[10] Revealingly, The Education Reform Act of 1988 defined lay members as persons with experience in "industrial, commercial or employment matters, or the practice of any profession."[11] University Councils effectively became Boards of Directors with a token academic membership, run by professional managers or businessmen.

It is worth noting that the deliberate corporatisation of universities by Government does not set them free from political control. On the contrary, as Derek Rayner was quick to note, where authority in an institu-

---

[9] Since 2000 the organisation has operated under the name 'Universities UK.'

[10] *Report of the Steering Committee for Efficiency Studies,* March 1985: 36, 23. Hereafter to be referred to as the "Jarratt Report."

[11] Dearlove, J. "A Continuing Role For Academics," *Higher Education Quarterly*, Vol. 56, N° 3, July 2002: 261.

tion is invested in a "top manager," direct *government* influence can be far more effectively exerted. Corporate universities are much more amenable to direct government control than colleges.

The Thatcher Government effectively used this control to exact value for money. One of its means of doing this was to hugely expand the numbers of students entering Higher Education, while restricting the per capita expenditure. The Higher Education Reform Act freed polytechnics from the administrative control of the Local Education Authorities. (Part of the rationale here was to destroy local government, which Thatcher saw as offering a challenge to central Government authority, and applying a brake to her radical reforms.) Four years later the Further and Higher Education Act of 1992 allowed polytechnics to attain university status. This led to a very rapid and unplanned expansion of student numbers and a decline in the "unit of resource" per-student. At the same time the government introduced various measures to create more competition between the Universities for available resources.

The developments in the sector during the Thatcher period can summed up as follows:
(1) an expansion of the university system, leading to resource scarcity;
(2) the deliberate imposition of resource competition between institutions;
(3) an adoption by all but the élite institutions of a corporate management structure;
appropriate to these conditions.

3.2 Universities, Governance and the Power of Audits

In the 1980s and the 1990s the phenomenon of audit, which originated in accounting and finance, spilled outwards into management, law, medicine. The Conservative Government oversaw the introduction of audits into Higher Education, although, once again, the universities, rather than waiting for controls to be externally imposed, established their own body tasked with implementing audits on research and then teaching for quality assurance purposes.

Audits, as Michael Power explains, arise because of the breakdown of trust and the consequent need to check that a certain practice is going ahead as it should. The function of an audit is to verify that a practice is proceeding properly.[12]

Generally speaking practices such as accounting, medicine, music, and education can only be evaluated by experts, because only experts

---

[12] Power, M. (1997) *The Audit Society*. Oxford: Oxford University Press.

really know the relevant criteria for good and bad accounting, music, education, etc. An experienced physician can monitor the performance of an inexperienced physician. What characterises self-regulation and monitoring is a kind of feed-back mechanism between practitioners. On the one hand there is a hierarchy between the evaluator and the evaluated, while on the other hand there is an essential equality between them, for they are both practitioners of the same practice.

Audits are different from evaluations. Audits arise when the results of the evaluation or monitoring of a certain practice are presented to external agents, who themselves are not practitioners of, and experts in, the evaluated practice. In this case performance measures have to be devised which are open to verification by lay persons, or public verification.

This feature of audits gives rise to a curious phenomenon. For the imposition of performance measures leads to the production of auditable performances that differ from the original practice. This is because practices which stand in need of verification or monitoring are complex and fine grained, and are difficult to capture in terms of simple, verifiable performance measures or criteria. The audit will overlay a structure of behavioural incentives on the original practice, which will attract behaviour that conforms to audit requirements.

Consequently the audit practice percolates into the audited practice and distorts it. If hospitals are penalized for keeping patients waiting, one response is to segment the administrative procedure, and move patients around so they wait in several smaller queues for shorter periods. The overall waiting time may be the same, but the strategy now conforms to the audit requirement.

However, as Power also shows, audits of institutions or practices easily morph into a means of exerting administrative control over them. This is because even if audits begin merely as a means of keeping accounts, or of verification, they can have the unforeseen consequence of reconstituting the practice which they are designed to monitor. Because of this effect audits are a very powerful, but also unpredictable tool of corporate governance.

This is in effect what happened in Britain with the introduction of the Research Assessment Exercises by the Higher Education Funding Councils that were carried out in 1989, 1992, 1996, 2001 and 2008. Their aim was to evaluate the quality of research undertaken by British Universities. The RAE is a kind of self-evaluation of university research by a panel of experts. However, it is also an audit, since its results are transmitted to non-experts in the form of quantitative assessments, which are made public and on which basis research funds are allocated. In the most recent exercise of 2008, performance was measured on a scale of five quality levels. The RAE submissions from each subject area were ranked by a subject specialist peer review panel, whose rankings were then used to allocate the quality-related research funding (QR) each institution received from their national funding council.

The RAE was brought into being as a means of providing assurance to Government that it was getting value for money, by verifying that high quality research was taking place. On the face of it, the RAE only stimulated academics to perform better in one of the activities they were supposed to doing anyway: producing high quality research, which was no bad thing. But as with many audits its effects were multiple and far reaching. One consequence of the RAE is to have incentivised departments and individual academics to prioritise research over teaching: to teach less and to write more. It tilted the balance of university activity toward research, because individual promotions depended mainly on research outputs, and departmental success depended heavily upon RAE performance. Hence it quickly led to a culture of good enough teaching and excellent research. The RAE was a classic case of an audit percolating into the very practice it was supposed to monitor and changing it. This effect was intensified by other powerful pressures. In an era where student numbers increased rapidly, the RAE encouraged Universities to deliver more efficient modes of tuition, and consequently to abandon small group teaching as "inefficient." In turn this led to the demise of face to face tuition and small group teaching in all but the élite institutions of Oxford and Cambridge.[13]

To be sure, audits of teaching quality and subject review undertaken by the Quality Assurance Agency (QAA) for Higher Education have documented a general rise in standards of teaching across the sector since 1997. However, given that, as we have seen, audits create the auditable performances they are designed to measure, this may in part have been a documentation of the rise in the standards of those auditable performances. That is, the improvement in scores might reflect an improvement in the ability of academic institutions to play the audit game. Certainly, the fact that the QAA audits indicate not a decline but an improvement in the standard of teaching is one that suited all concerned: Government, university administrations and academics.

---

[13] For a recent study on the importance of this kind of teaching for democratic citizenship, see Nussbaum, M. C. (2010) *Not for Profit: Why Democracy Needs Universities*. Princeton: Princeton University Press.

Whether the improved scores reflected a genuine rise in teaching quality across the sector is hard to judge. The practice of getting good scores from teaching evaluations is not the same as the practice of good teaching. Indeed, excellent teaching is dependent on teachers whose motivation is other than that of getting high teaching evaluations. As soon as teachers begin to aim for good scores, it becomes an exercise in satisfying consumer expectations. One effect of audits of teaching quality might have been to lower the level of demandingness of undergraduate courses. Another was increasingly to spoon-feed students – providing extensive handouts, smaller amounts of directed reading, etc. In fine, it is quite possible that the RAE, along with the rapid, unplanned and under-resourced increase in student numbers in the period, contributed to a general decline in teaching quality and a diminishment of the learning experience, even despite the demonstrable, i.e. auditable, increase in teaching quality and student satisfaction.[14]

Another interesting effect of the RAE was that it led many Universities to close down what they saw as poorly performing departments, and to focus on their "areas of strength," i.e. their high scoring departments.[15] Third, the RAE led to the creation of an academic transfer market in the mid to latter part of the RAE cycle. Universities poached highly performing researchers from rival institutions prior to the assessment period in order to boost their own RAE scores. This quickly drove up the salaries of star performers, leading to an overall increase in cost for the sector, and thus undermined the aim of value for money which was one of the main reasons for the audit process. A fourth unforeseen consequence of the RAE was that any activity for which performance indicators were not invented – reviewing and editing for journals, pastoral roles, conference organisation, or whatever – was relegated in importance and increasingly delegated to junior faculty, graduate students and teaching assistants.

---

[14] Apart from the general need for assurance arising from the breakdown in Government's trust of the professions, one rationale for teaching audits was a general anxiety that the *under-resourced* expansion (or 'democratisation') of Higher Education, as well as the privileging of research inculcated by the RAE, was pushing teaching standards downwards.

[15] One of the more mind-boggling examples of this management folly is the fate of The Centre for Contemporary Cultural Studies, at the University of Birmingham. Founded in 1964 by Richard Hoggart, with Stuart Hall becoming Director in 1968, it gained world-renown in the emerging field of cultural studies. However, the Centre closed in 1991 and was superseded by a new Department of Cultural Studies and Sociology. This department was in turn closed by the University in 2002, because of its poor performance in RAE 2001. In its place a new Department of Sociology was opened in 2004. This new department was subsequently closed again in 2010, due to its performance in RAE 2008.

4. New Labour's Neo-liberal Romance

In a speech to the Labour Party conference of 1996, Tony Blair famously declaimed: "Ask me my three main priorities for government, and I tell you: education, education, education." One might have thought that the outlook for UK Universities under Labour would be considerably rosier than it was in the Thatcher-Major years. The truth is that New Labour's increasing investment in education was accompanied by an intensification of the attack on the integrity and autonomy of British Universities, and that higher education policy in the period was marked by a giant leap forward in the path toward marketization that Margaret Thatcher had originally charted.

The Lisbon Agenda of 2000 proclaimed that the Union was to become "the most competitive and dynamic knowledge driven economy by 2010." In this schedule for new growth, the UK represented the avant-garde. Other members of the Union struggled to bring about an "Anglo-American" standardisation of their variegated and antiquated degree programmes.[16] By contrast British higher education had already been thoroughly primed for market-integration. Labour's enthusiasm for the central principles of the Lisbon agenda was forged in the conviction that, first, the organisational and academic structure of its universities were ready for (and were by now accustomed to) change, and that, second, a "knowledge economy" could become not a supplement, but a *substitute* for the British manufacturing base that had been eviscerated by a sustained programme of privatisation, reduction in public subsidy and strong fiscal policy. The result was that an enormous weight of responsibility for economic growth was rolled on to the shoulders of the UK universities.

However, with New Labour a fundamental shift in the conception of higher education had taken place. The Thatcherite vocabulary of "value for money" and "efficiency" in public services, including the universities and polytechnics, was now supplanted by a new, more radical, but also more one-dimensional understanding of the university as the UK's primary locus of economic "dynamism." Whereas Conservative policy was to reduce the economic *input* to Universities, Labour policies aimed to increase their economic *output*, and to change the nature of that output.

The relevant government policy documents of the Labour era, the White Paper, 'The Future of Higher Education' (2003), the 'Lambert

---

[16] For a case study in the great tribulations faced by European governments attempting to implement unpopular "Bologna" reforms, see Dietrich Lemke's articles on the situation in Germany, especially *Mourning Bologna*, available online at: http://www.e-flux.com/journal/view/123.

Review of Business-University Cooperation' (2003), and the 'Science and Innovation Investment Framework' (2004-14), make clear that the most important, if not the sole purpose, of university education is the economic goal of increasing GDP per capita. Mere lip service is paid to any other aim that university education might have. Moreover, New Labour did not have any Conservative or Liberal scruples about avoiding regulation and 'big Government.' On the contrary, they liked to micro-manage from the centre, "consulting" quickly, generally with their own appointed "tsars" or individual advisors, and then rushing through legislation. True to form, Blair's Government commissioned Richard Lambert, a member of the Bank of England's Monetary Policy Committee (and educated, like Blair, at Fettes and Oxford) to conduct a review of University-Business collaboration. The Lambert Review is less a review than a programme for change. And the programme is not confined to the question of how to facilitate interaction between Universities and Business for the benefit of the regional and national economy; it challenges the very idea of the university.

Noting that on the one hand UK business lags behind its international competitors in Research and Development, but on the other, that there is a strong research base in UK Universities, Lambert's solution is "knowledge transfer" (from UK Universities to Business.) This looks like a scarcely concealed attempt to offset the high business costs of R&D onto the university sector. Soon however it becomes clear that Lambert's Review has an even wider remit: it is a highly prescriptive blueprint for transforming universities from autonomous educational institutions into mere providers of research and skilled labour. To facilitate cooperation with Business, it is necessary for universities to become not just business-like, but to become businesses.

This applies not just to the services that they provide, accommodation, food and so forth, but to the academic structure. "Business is critical of what it sees as the slow-moving, bureaucratic and risk-averse style of university management."[17] Doing business with Business requires dismantling what remains of their academic committee structures and replacing their participatory governance models with streamlined management systems. Senates should be downsized and universities run by a small council with a "majority of lay members" and small senior management executive.[18] Universities depend above all for their success, in

[17] *Lambert Review of Business University Collaboration*, December 4 2003: 6. http://www.hm-treasury.gov.uk/lambert_review_business_university_collab.htm.
[18] To see what 'lay member' means in this context see note 10 above.

Lambert's view, not on their academic staff, nor even their Professoriat, but on the management skills of their senior managers, especially of their Vice-Chancellors.

Lambert's proposals go much further than those of his predecessor, Alex Jarratt. He insists that there must be three major changes in research funding. First, he recommended that larger amounts of money go to fewer projects, at fewer Universities, allocated by cheaper, dirtier methods. To this end he calls for the creation of "a basket of metrics that might in the future provide the basis for a predictable way of allocating funds."[19] Metrics of excellence, assuming such can be found, would relieve the academic community of the expensive and time consuming task of expert evaluation and peer review of research proposals. They would also enable the allocation of research funds to be determined by non-experts, such as government officials and business people, rather than by their academic peers.

Second he stated that universities must be encouraged to be more risk taking and entrepreneurial. University managers need to be trained in entrepreneurship by professional development agencies such as the Leadership Foundation. Lambert chides universities for being inward looking and conservative, and recommends using professional Recruitment Consultancies to make appointments from the private sector, rather than promoting University Managers from within the academic community.

Third, since the purpose of universities is to feed the economy with market ready employees, and to transfer knowledge to it, Government and Business should exert a much greater "influence over university courses and curricula" and there must be "significantly more business input into the priority setting, decision making and assessment panels of both of the peer review processes."[20]

Three comments are in order here. First, it entirely escapes Lambert's notice that "peer" review should be conducted by *peers*, and that by definition business people and politicians cannot "peer" review academic research, which as non-experts they are not in a position to judge. They can assess it against external criteria, or "audit" it, but that is an entirely different matter.

Second, this marks a complete break with the "so-called" Haldane Principle, of which there is no mention in the Lambert Review. This is roughly the principle first formulated by the Conservative Lord Hailsham

[19] To see what 'lay member' means in this context see the reference to the Dearing report above.

[20] Recommendation 6.1. *Lambert Review*: 125.

(Quintin Hogg), who had been in charge of the research councils from 1957 to 1964, that decisions about what to spend research funds on should be made by researchers rather than politicians, "and not directly by a Government Department itself."[21] It informed Higher Education Funding policy and research funding in Britain from 1904 onward and which was one of the main guardians of academic freedom in the period.

Third, compare Lambert's recommendations with Jonathan R. Cole's analysis of the reasons that propelled the Great American University to success. Cole, Professor of Sociology, who went on to be Provost and Dean of Columbia University, writes: "research universities should not attempt to imitate corporations in their organizational structure. The hierarchical culture of the corporate world would not further the other important aims of the university."[22]

5. FROM RESEARCH ASSESSMENT TO RESEARCH EXCELLENCE?

In 2007 the Higher Education Funding Council of England (HEFCE) announced a new framework for auditing research quality. Universities would replace the RAE, originally scheduled for 2012, with the Research Excellence Framework (REF).[23] The REF reflects New Labour's dissemination agenda – the idea that research should be made available to non-academic audiences; the importance of "knowledge transfer" which somewhere along the line was rebranded "knowledge exchange" (as if someone suspected it looked too one-sided); and the impact agenda, the idea that research should be demonstrated to be socially beneficial and economically useful.

It is clear from the 2003 White Paper and the 2007 Annual Review of the Science and Innovation Investment Framework that, in spite of lip service paid to the diverse values of education, the Government's overriding concern is to harness and increase the *economic impact* of research. Lambert makes no bones about this. In fact, all the policy documents of the last Labour Government are primarily about how to make Higher Education serve the needs of the knowledge economy. No Government research was commissioned into what the non-economic social, cultural and political functions of universities and higher education are

---

[21] Edgerton, D. "The Haldane Principle and other invented traditions in science policy," in *History and Policy*. July 2009, viewed on 10 September 2011, http://www.historyandpolicy.org/papers/policy-paper-88.html.

[22] Cole, J. R. (2009) *The Great American University: Its Rise To Pre-eminence; Its Indispensable National Role; Why It Must Be Protected.* New York: Public Affairs: 67.

[23] "Research Excellence Framework," in *Higher Education Funding Council for England.* Viewed on 21 August 2011, http://www.hefce.ac.uk/research/ref/.

and have been, and how these might be best maintained. Even the recently created AHRC appears to submit to this view: their most recent report, *Leading the World: The Economic Impact of UK Arts and Humanities Research*, a document which tries cautiously to widen the definition of impact, still advertises prominently in its subtitle the Government's central priority.[24] It is indicative that none of these government documents, prepared and presumably also written by university educated politicians and civil servants, have much to say about any other values of education besides economic impact. It is indicative of the one-dimensionality of party politics in the 21st Century, in which governments ignore issues of the value and quality of human life and focus almost exclusively on strategically adapting everything to the demands of a global capitalist economy, with the narrow aim of increasing GDP per capita and seeking re-election for themselves.

This is the neo-liberal economic rationale that lies behind the REF, which, building on Lambert's recommendations, will ensure that research in the humanities and the sciences be assessed partly on the basis of its impact, which is to be defined in terms of its consequences external to the academic community (e.g. benefit to economy, society, culture, and so on). According to the REF, 25% of the rating of a unit of assessment will be determined by a measure of its impact.

What, one might think, can be wrong with the Government trying to reap more social and economic reward from its investment in university research? One problem, as we have noted, is that it is extremely difficult to predict what research will have 'impact.' Academics working in the philosophy of mathematics and logic did not know that their research would give birth to the discipline of informatics and to the invention of computing. The route from research to impact is highly diffuse and uncertain. Researchers themselves have little privileged insight into such eventualities, and experts on peer review panels are unlikely to fare better. Certainly businessmen and politicians are not well placed to make such difficult predictions. As a consequence, enforcing the impact agenda will almost certainly mean that resources will tend to be diverted to projects with the best impact statements, rather than those that will end up having most impact. But awarding grants to proposals on the basis of the plausibility of their 'impact statements' is not a reliable way to pick winners, i.e. social and economically useful research. An impact statement is

---

[24] "Leading the Word: new report reveals international pre-eminence of UK arts and humanities," in *Arts and Humanities Research Council*, 16 June 2009, viewed on 08 September 2011, http://www.ahrc.ac.uk/News/Latest/Pages/leadingtheworld.aspx.

just an auditable account of the usefulness of a project, which may not correlate with its actual social and economic benefit to the nation. Factor in the 'concentration' of research funds on fewer, bigger projects, and fewer bigger universities, that Lambert recommended and that successive Governments have been implementing, and the effect is multiplied. The Government is behaving like a bank, which instead of diversifying its portfolio of investments and spreading it risks, puts all its money on the winners it misguidedly thinks it can pick.

The strategy is not just pointless, it may well be self-defeating. 'Impact,' i.e. social and economic benefit, is achieved (when it is achieved) largely as a by-product of research. It cannot be made into the goal of research. Incentivising academics to do high-impact research is like Sir Alex Ferguson's instructing his players to go out on the pitch and deliver increased revenue to shareholders. The economic success of the club depends on footballers focusing on playing football well on the pitch, not on making money off it. This is the point that escaped Lambert. He noticed that universities were good, and British business poor, at Research and Development, but forgot to ask why that was. It had in all probability a lot to do with the fact that the pressure within business and industry to get an economic pay off in the short to medium term, did not weigh so heavily on publicly funded university researchers, who were more or less free to pursue their inquiries wherever they took them. The moral of this story is that if the Government were really interested in impact, rather merely than justifying its expenditure to itself and to the voting and tax paying public, it would be cheaper and better for it to back off, not to enforce the impact agenda.

Second, the goal of research impact, however broadly defined, may well pull in a different direction than the goal of research excellence, so it is not obvious that they can both be pursued simultaneously. Consequently, a "Research Excellence Framework" that attempts to assess research proposals on the basis of impact may end up incentivising academics to pursue something other than excellent research, namely whatever they think will be deemed a "high-impact" activity. What is important to bear in mind here is the tendency for audits over time to colonise and transfigure the audited practice. It is likely that the REF will have a far more distorting effect on academic practice than the RAE ever did. The cultivation of impact, which is supposed to complement or to run alongside the pursuit of excellence, may well end up competing with, and eventually detracting from or supplanting the goal of excellence in teaching and research.

Third, it may well be the case that research excellence is the most reliable indicator of the economic impact of research, in terms of the publications it generates, the overseas students it attracts to Universities, and so forth. But research excellence can only be judged by peer review. So establishing the reliability of a metric of research excellence requires peer review anyway. Therefore, if excellence is the aim, the search for a metric with which to allocate funds on the basis of it is self-defeating. If (non-academic) impact becomes the aim, or if the impact tail wags the excellence dog when it comes to making funding decisions, then we are landed back with the problem that the impact audit will inevitably change the kind of research being done.

Fourth, it is obvious that one cannot measure anything accurately if one does not know what is to be measured. If impact is defined narrowly, in merely economic terms, one at least knows what is supposed to be measured. That said, finding reliable metrics to quantify the economic benefit to the nation may well outstrip the abilities of even the most skilled economists. Current metrics for assessing the merely economic impact of research have not yet been demonstrated to be reliable. If, on the other hand, impact is defined broadly, the difficulties of measuring it are multiplied.

6. Brief Assessment of the Politics of Higher Education since 1979

The moral of the story is that while governments pay lip service to academic independence, they rarely cede control of matters they can interfere with, once they have taken it. Since 1997 successive Governments have taken firm control of universities, directly interfering in their mode or of organisation, and attempting to influence university curricula and their research activities by both direct and indirect means. The recent "clarification" of the Haldane principle in a BIS document signed by David Willetts and Vince Cable, is a case in point. In the words of Peter Mandler, Vice President of the Royal Historical Society, it has been interpreted so narrowly that it has been "neutered."[25] Ironically, as Lord Haldane, a Liberal peer, and Lord Hailsham, a Conservative minister, well knew, this hands-on tendency offends against a principle that both parties claim to cherish, the principle of the limitation of government. And the principle is a good one in the domain of university teaching and

[25] Mandler, P. "While you were looking elsewhere…The Haldane Principle and the Government's Research Agenda for the Arts and Humanities," in *Humanities Matter*, 30 January 2011, viewed 08 September 2011, http://humanitiesmatter.com/?p=159.

research, since Government interference in this sector generally leads to mediocrity.

No single party is to blame for this gradual but appreciable erosion of the autonomy of academic institutions that began in the last quintile of the 20th Century. Rather it has been a Continental Drift, observable in the series of policy innovations by both Conservative and Labour regimes since 1979. There is all the more reason, then, to evaluate these political changes, in the light of the purpose of the modern university, which we begin by identifying, namely *excellence in teaching and research across a broad range of disciplines*. After all, all of the various regimes whose policies we have just sketched, have claimed to be promoting the end of excellence in teaching and research, and none of them would readily admit to having undermined this end.

Three conclusions can be drawn.

1. It is not as clear as it should be that the various measures introduced in order to assure the Government that the ends of excellence in teaching and research were being met, actually promote those ends. For example we saw that the RAE imposed incentives that undermined the aim of excellence in teaching, led to a reduction in the number of subjects taught and to an increase the size of departments. Even the audits of teaching quality may have had some adverse effects on the level at which courses were pitched. It is also highly probably that research and teaching have been adversely affected by the almost constant restructuring of universities that has taken place in the last 15 years.

2. The story of the last 40 years of Higher Education Policy in Britain is one of serial attempts to bring universities into line with the ideals of "value for money," efficiency, and economic and social benefit. There can be little doubt that the pursuit of these aims is in tension with that of excellence in teaching and research across a range of disciplines. The huge and largely unplanned expansion in student numbers, the reduction of the unit of resource per student, and the introduction of competition for scarce resources has not helped British universities realise the aim of excellence in teaching and research. The rationale behind the restructuring of university management along corporate lines is largely ideologically driven, and has little to do with the aim of excellence in teaching and research. While it has demonstrably had the effect of making universities more vulnerable to economic forces, and open to direct and indirect political manipulation, it is wholly unclear whether it has made them better universities. The fact that in increasing number the decision makers in universities are not academics, and that consequently academic values are

no longer the overriding factor in their decisions, does not bode well for the aim of excellence in teaching and research. Finally, as we have seen, the UK Government's impact agenda may have a tendency to undermine and even to supplant the aim of excellence in research.

3. Although British Government Higher Education policy over the last four decades has transformed universities, there is little evidence that it has improved them by promoting the aims of excellence in teaching and research. The jury is still out. The greater irony is that Government policy over the period may not even have facilitated the ideals of efficiency, value for money, and social and economic benefit. As we have seen, the RAE led directly to an academic transfer market that increased the wages of high flying academics. The use of management consultancies and recruitment agencies from the private sector (as recommended by Lambert) and the introduction of a cadre of highly paid managers in key positions have enormously increased the wage bill of modern universities, which is probably their biggest cost.

Again it is not clear that the measures introduced in order to maximise the economic and social benefits of university research, will actually do so. The impact component of the Research Excellence Framework is, in the opinion of most academics, another piece of ill thought out and rushed legislation, the ins and outs of which academics and universities will have to work around as and when they come to light. It remains to be seen whether the UK Government's latest attempt to make universities directly serve what it sees as its economic and social purpose (without sacrificing the ideas of excellence in teaching and research) is an improbable success, or a costly mistake.

Politics and Education in the Spanish University
Neoliberalism, Bureaucratization, and Society of Control

María José Guerra Palmero

> Bologna is the end of the university as we knew it [...] The university we knew was that which was made for learning, where one studied to get rid of prejudices and which confirmed that reason ruled. Nowadays, the university is conceived for doing and offering productivity, in conformity with the three gods of capitalism: productivity, competitiveness, and innovation. Universities were made for thinking. Today we speak of the need for freedom of expression, but what thoughts are you going to express? Freedom of thought is essential to think for oneself and get away from dogmatic thinking.
>
> José Luis Sampedro.

> [...] the university is being confronted with strong questions for which it has so far provided only weak answers. Strong questions are those questions that go to the roots of the historical identity and vocation of the university in order to question not so much the details of the future of the university but rather whether the university, as we know it, has indeed a future. They are, therefore, questions that arouse a particular kind of perplexity.
>
> Boaventura de Sousa Santos.

The voices of José Luis Sampedro, a point of reference for critical thinking in Spain, and of Boaventura de Sousa Santos[1], one of the most creative thinkers in current social theory, will accompany me in this attempt to reflect on the transformations experienced by the Spanish university in a juncture marked not only by Bologna, the creation of a European higher education environment, and the shift of the learning methodology towards a more prominent role for the students, but also by the deep economic crisis of the last three years, which, through cuts in public spending on education and research, is seriously jeopardizing both the quality and the survival of the Spanish university system.

Through this text, I hope to share what many professors, lecturers and researchers think about the institutional and organizational changes that have recently taken place in the Spanish university. For this purpose, I will highlight the teaching perspective, but will also refer to research, since both of these are inextricably linked in the demands and conflicting pressures that professors are subjected to. There has been an upheaval both in teaching and research over the last decade, the reasons being not only the spirit of Bologna and its ensuing competitive model for higher

---

[1] *The University at the Crossroads, Human The University at the Crossroads Architecture: Journal of the Sociology of Self-Knowledge*, IX, special issue, 2011: 7-16.

education institutions reflected in highly publicized rankings – themselves the result of the new discipline of "scientometrics" whereby everything must be indexed and referenced; in addition, the competitive logic of a "university stock market" has discriminated between first-rate and second-rate universities. I believe that in Spain, this has resulted in organizational inefficiency, bureaucratic complexity, loss of autonomy and sovereignty of professors and researchers with respect to their work, misunderstood monitoring and control, extremely confusing technocratic conceptualizations of the quality of teaching services and research "products," and of the researchers themselves, who are constantly being assessed and reassessed in conformity with the refinement and sophistication of the above-mentioned discipline of "scientometrics."

Research has ceased to be "free" and is being forced to respond directly to the demands, objectives, priorities, and strategic plans of the market and of public agencies. Research must be committed to innovation and knowledge transfer since the so-called "knowledge economy" – an expression that masks the privatization of publicly funded knowledge – imposes its competitive rules. In teaching, the magic word is "employability." The word employability does not appear in the *Dictionary of the Spanish Royal Academy of Spanish Language*;[2] it is a neologism imported as a *trending topic* by neoliberalism. Likewise, research follows a model of innovation transfer that is only interested in patents and *spin-off* enterprises. The objective is for researchers to become part of entrepreneurial structures and to change their motivation, from the search for knowledge and basic research, to financial interest and entrepreneurially-oriented applied research.[3] "Knowledge economy" and innovation are the mantra of the dominant model, in which the university subsidizes the private sector by providing "human capital" and profitability. We could call it "the Garmendia Model," after the Minister who has promoted it in Spain. The university-enterprise synergies and the funds allocated to this connection caused the Ministry of Science and Innovation of Spain to have to return a quarter of its budget in 2010 because the enterprises, already in the midst of the crisis, had not requested the corre-

[2] *Diccionario de la Real Academia de la Lengua Española*. Vigésima segunda edición, 2001. http://buscon.rae.es/draeI/SrvltConsulta?LEMA=cultura

[3] López Facal, Javier "¡Socorro! La destitución fulminante del director general responsable del Plan Nacional de I+D aumenta el riesgo de desbaratar en una legislatura el sistema de ciencia construido desde 1986," *El País*, 29/10/2010. http://www.elpais.com/articulo/sociedad/Socorro/elpepusoc/20101029elpepusoc 7Tes

sponding grants and subsidies.[4] If the public university has any meaning at all in the neoliberal state model which proceeds unchecked, it is that of preventing enterprises from financing training programs for workers and human resources, and from appropriating, with the minimum possible cost, the results of R+D+i. The *Joint-Venture* masquerade – taking risks together – masks the transfer from public to private.[5] The university humiliates itself, forgets its autonomy and its essential academic, social, and civic goals, and surrenders to the logic of the market. The students, on the other hand, have absorbed the basic elements of the neoliberal ideology; and since it pays off, especially at the graduate studies level, and, I am afraid, will pay off even more in the future, they want a degree in exchange for their investment. With very few exceptions, professors no longer receive any acknowledgement from their students, who do not value their scientific competence at all, and are starting to treat them as mere suppliers of a service for which they must have full availability, facilitated by virtual classrooms and e-mail messages that must be answered immediately. Unfortunately, Habermas's idea of the colonization of the lifeworld – university life in this case – by the establishment (market and bureaucracy) has taken place in the harshest way possible in Spain. Neoliberal ideology, masked by the popularity of misleading terms such as flexibility, competitiveness, or innovation, has become entrenched in the authoritarian routines of monitoring and control of the Spanish universities and is giving birth to an inefficient, poor model that renounces the goals of the university as an autonomous and critical institution. Like a stupid institution, the university magnifies and hypertrophies means by turning them into ends, forgetting its mission regarding comprehensive education and the pursuit of knowledge, while at the same time forgetting, to a great extent, its civic and political function regarding citizen education. Neoliberal imperatives and bureaucratic inertia bordering on irrationality triumph. And in the midst of all this, the big crisis came.

---

[4] Rivera, Alicia "Ciencia dejó sin gastar uno de cada cuatro euros de su presupuesto. Las subvenciones a la I+D disminuyeron en 635 millones el año pasado respecto a 2009 – Del dinero previsto para los préstamos solo se dio el 60%," *El País*, 2/04/2011.
http://www.elpais.com/articulo/sociedad/Ciencia/dejo/gastar/euros/presupuesto/elpepisoc/20110402elpepisoc_3/Tes

[5] Criado, Emilio & Durán, Alicia "La nueva Ley de la Ciencia, entre la frustración y el estado de excepción laboral," *El País*, 26/04/2011.
http://www.elpais.com/articulo/sociedad/nueva/Ley/Ciencia/frustracion/estado/excepcion/laboral/elpepusoc/20110426elpepusoc_7/Tes

***

In what follows I will focus on two of the many issues that could be addressed in relation to the diagnosis outlined: first, the impact of the crisis on the institutional educational design created by those who have implemented the Bologna plan in Spain. The second topic, which will be considered at the teaching practices level, will focus on unraveling the pragmatic uses of a device called the "teaching guide,"[6] a pedagogical artifact that, when analyzed in the light of the methodology and the active learning that it supposedly serves, shows numerous contradictions. The objective of such a device is to equate studies with work, to pattern study according to a work schedule, thus stripping the task of learning and knowing of any interest. It is a device intended to deactivate passion and curiosity by focusing on the exacerbated quantification (which is ridiculous most of the time, especially in the case of Humanities) of *ad hoc* indicators that insist on planning educational actions, with excessive zeal, down to the last detail.

Iron cage, colonization of the lifeworld by the system, reinforced combination of the old model of a disciplinary society with that of the society of control... Weber, Habermas, Foucault, and Deleuze give us critical keys to interpret the new institutional design sponsored by the reforms. Nevertheless, I do not want to turn this text into an erudite dissertation, but to foster an analysis of how, in the field of teaching, the neoliberal model strangles the university *ethos*, especially its dimension related to autonomy and critique, and of how the same neoliberalism transforms scientific research radically by making it just another link in the knowledge economy chain, a radically unenlightened program which has important consequences. For example, it obstructs the development of the countries of the South via the strengthening of patents and intellectual property. There are alternatives to these models, but the pressure exerted by political decisions concerning education and their implementation at the service of neoliberalism does not leave much room for the self-reflexiveness of the academic community. De Sousa Santos summarizes what the university has been for many of us in our experience as students and teachers:

> At its best, the modern university has been a locus of free and independent thinking and of celebration of diversity, even if subjected to the narrow boundaries of the disciplines, whether in the sciences or the humanities. Bear-

---

[6] Models of teaching guides could be found in the web pages of all Spanish Universities. One of the first documents could be found in http://www.recursoseees.uji.es/guia/g20061010.pdf, another example in http://www.aqu.cat/doc/doc_52850666_1.pdf

> ing in mind that for the past 30 years the tendency to transform the truth value of knowledge into the 'market truth' value of knowledge has become increasingly strong, could there be any future for nonconformist, critical, heterodox, nonmarketable knowledge, and for professors, researchers and students pursuing it? If yes, what will be its impact upon the criteria of excellence and inter-university competitiveness? If not, can we still call university an institution that only produces competent conformists and never competent rebels, and that only regards knowledge as a commodity and never as a public good?[7]

My experience, on which this is based, is that of the teaching activity of a Philosophy professor. This has allowed me to read about and assimilate a critical view of teaching and to foster a practice committed to enlightened values and aware of systemic contradictions. Philosophy has the privilege of asking questions, of reactivating them and reformulating them once and again, but also that of experimenting with new conceptualizations of reality. I have been able to live my professional activity with pride and dignity. However, today the systemic pressure that we identify with the Bologna constellation casts a shadow and poses distressing questions for those who make up the Spanish university.

BOLOGNA'S UNCERTAIN FUTURE: AN IRRESPONSIBLE INSTITUTIONAL DESIGN

The intertwining of totally conflicting demands has ruined the self-esteem of university professors and demoralized them, especially when they have to dedicate most of their time to filling out forms and dealing with forever changing computer applications, on account of innovations established for the mere sake of change – without proposing observable improvements –, writing complicated and unintelligible teaching guides (what we used to call syllabi), attending committee meetings that have to respond to conflicting institutional demands and changing criteria deriving from quality or innovation units created *ex nihilo* and in an impromptu manner. Changes in internal regulations following the new institutionalization are constant and prevent the university from achieving the minimum stability needed to concentrate on its very purposes: teaching and doing research. The institutional change has not made good use of the teachers' potential for self-reflection; on the contrary, it has been imposed from above with unusual haste and speed – since we came to Bologna late. That which is urgent and imperative keeps us from dealing with that which is necessary and important. Hyper-bureaucratization not only makes the working hours endless; it also generates distress by taking

[7] *The University at the Crossroads*: 9.

time needed for class preparation and research. At this point, I must clarify two things for our European colleagues. The aging of the Spanish university faculty and the lack of teaching assistants, on the one hand, are characteristics to be considered. On the other hand, administrative and service personnel have tightly defined tasks and hierarchies, and in most cases the idea of supporting teachers and research activities is alien to them. Like the faculty, administrative personnel have not benefited from the generational replacement and that has a high cost in an era of technological acceleration. Speaking of costs, the premise for implementing the new Bologna system was zero cost, but now the budget cuts make it impossible to reduce the number of students to ensure the personalized attention that was intended. The crisis itself and the excessive unemployment that plagues Spanish youth in particular have caused the number of students enrolled in universities to rise. For example, enrollment in Master's and other graduate programs increased by 73,500 students in the last term. Continuing education, attention to diversity, and individualized tutoring become impossible for professors who have to serve about 400 students per semester in programs such as social sciences and health sciences, which have high demand. The work overload becomes dramatic, given that the institutional design has opted for hyper-bureaucratization and for subjecting professors to all sorts of demands without diagnosing and estimating their needs and demands. The pressure to be innovative and use cutting-edge ICTs, the demands imposed by continuous evaluation, and the number of unpaid hours spent correcting tests, essays, and papers have increased, calling into question the outmoded social privilege that university teachers assumed they had. In fact, I believe that their loss of autonomy and control over their work correlates to the proletarianization to which neoliberalism degrades public professions. A similar phenomenon has affected the healthcare professionals who are part of the public health system.

The most serious problem, however, is that the competences model, applied to courses and consistent with the restrictive professional profile included in the degree documents, has short-circuited the possibility of thinking about teaching as an open forum for deliberation, critique and experimentation – basic activities of the academic environment – by forcing the equation between studies and work. We will see how this operation, when applied to teaching practices, is pierced by tensions and ambivalences. The competence model seems to promote the students' *know-how,* practices, and participation, but the bureaucratic, authoritarian bias introduced by the Spanish pedagogical technocracy has set up a model in which the rigid planning of the syllabi and their development in time contradict the supposed flexibility and creativity assumed by the system.

That is, the disciplinary device known as the "teaching guide" eliminates the playful and passionate sense of learning collectively and individually, of researching and questioning reality. Just when neuroscience gives value to the emotions tied to meaningful learning, the technocratic and neoliberal interpretation of how to train individuals for a professional profile for employability impoverishes the conception of undergraduate and postgraduate studies, by conceiving them from the perspective of competences, in a purely utilitarian manner. The passion for learning is excluded from the assumptions of the system. Training professionals is its only goal. In Spain, with an indecent unemployment rate and extremely high levels of job instability and temporary jobs, together with the practice called "mileurismo," that is, paying young people salaries that almost never exceed a thousand euros, the promise of a bright future sounds like a mockery. Research fellows and young researchers are forced to migrate if they want to get jobs that are consistent with their professional and research hyper-qualifications because the labor market does not offer opportunities to even the very best. Meritocracy has entered a phase of profound crisis of legitimacy.

University autonomy stipulates that each one can create its own organizational chart and operation scheme; however, the general trend is to build quality units, virtual teaching units, research support units, etc., all of which require that teachers and researchers incessantly produce data and papers, innovation projects, justifications and reports – using changing and variable formats – and in most cases do not help them meet needs that are pressing for this collectivity.[8] Given these changes, de Sousa Santos wonders:

> Is the Bologna Process a break with the negative aspects of the traditional university, or is it a brilliant exercise in reshuffling inertias and recycling old vices? Is it possible to standardize procedures and criteria across such different university cultures without killing diversity and innovation? Is it possible to develop transparency, mobility and reciprocal recognition while preserving institutional and cultural diversity? Why are bureaucrats taking control of the good ideas and noble ideals so easily?[9]

---

[8] A case that has provoked a protest has been the affair of the *Curriculum Vitae*. In the various calls for proposals related to teaching and research, presentation forms of the most varied types are requested, and candidates have to spend hours and hours typing data on poorly designed application forms. Finally, after countless complaints, a standard and hopefully definitive *Curriculum Vitae* Form has been produced.

[9] *The University at the Crossroads*: 10.

My opinion regarding the last question is that the exacerbated and hypertrophied bureaucracy strongly hampers the effectiveness of the Spanish University and promotes demoralization by overlooking the human factor and the teachers' need for time and autonomy.

PEDAGOGICAL DEVICES: THE STANDARDIZATION OF A TEACHING GUIDE

The multiplication of endless bureaucratic procedures, in line with the educational reform mandated by Bologna, is imposed by new organizational structures allegedly linked to Quality, a concept that no one can explain clearly and which is concerned with merely quantitative indicators. Technocratic hegemony outlaws the qualitative dimension, with the consequent damage to the study of the Humanities and other programs. An interesting system of devices and protocols that critical pedagogy should analyze and criticize is taking shape in Spain. Foucault and Bourdieu, authors in the best tradition of the critical institutional analysis of education, would swiftly return to their grave if they saw the Kafkian scenario of today's Spanish higher education, which results from the hegemony of a technocratic conception of education.

Bologna, we have repeated *ad nauseam*, is a document that includes the minimum requirements that ensure the convertibility of degrees at the European level, which promised a greater sensitivity towards the horizontal cooperation between professors and students since it chose to give the latter an authentically prominent role through an active and participative methodology of continuous work involving a major change in the practice of teaching. This, which sounded so promising, has become an unattainable ideal in the Spanish university. The resulting ill feeling is heightened by the combination of the neoliberal rhetoric of the reform – competitiveness, individual initiative, innovation, flexibility, etc. – and the authoritarian bias of our national bureaucracies. This fateful combination has generated a model of Commissions and Coordinators, "Quality" ombudsmen, who impose, for example, "teaching guides" with rigid models for professors to adapt to whether they like it or not. Any dissent is settled by denying approval to the guide in question.

A guide, as the dictionary defines it, is a set of orienting guidelines. The meanings provided by the *Dictionary of the Spanish Royal Academy of Language* that are applicable here are the following: "*Guía* 1. f. That which directs or routes... 3. f. Treaty providing precepts to route or direct in spiritual or abstract matters, or in purely mechanical ones: *Fishermen's Guide*, *Farmers' Guide*. 4. f. Printed list of data or information concerning a particular matter: *Traveler's Guide*, *Railways Guide*." But there are other meanings of interest that could be used to characterize teaching and, what professors literally do. For example: "24. com. Person who directs, leads, and teaches others the way. 25. com. Person who teaches and directs another to do or achieve what is intended." Needless to say, the notion of education draws on these meanings. The fact is that in the context of bureaucratized teaching praxis, words no longer mean what they mean in the *Dictionary of the Royal Academy*. It is not a question of subjecting the hidden meaning of the teaching guide to a superficial psychoanalysis. However, the spiritual guides of the Catholic tradition, which prevailed as official educational documents during Franco's dictatorship, were dogmatic and far from flexible. Some of this and of the technocracy imposed by the *Opus Dei* at the end of the Franco regime must remain in the subconscious of the new champions of the bureaucratic pedagogy.

In short, the teaching guide (formerly called "syllabus") frames and organizes the teaching plan for a subject. This guide has become a control and subjugation "device" in the praxis of most universities. To begin with, the newly created Quality Commissions usually understand it as a "Contract" – we have even been forced to sign them, though we have not come to the point of having to do so before a notary – that must be strictly complied with by the teachers. This is the predominant exhortation whether or not the circumstances of the student groups – especially for those of us who give basic training to students in the first years – allow it, or a review of the plan is required. Everything is closed, sealed and published on the web, in the manner of a notarized document. As we will see, the guide firmly establishes unheard-of details that turn it into a new literary gender: pedagogy fiction.

When the model was sold as an instance of openness to and opportunity for reflecting on our own teaching commitment, many of us welcomed this shift in educational orientation. In the end, the course of events has shown us that we can do nothing but disagree with a model that I will diagnose as toxic from the point of view of the ethical and pedagogical quality of its artifacts.

I will put some issues on the table to show not only the self-contradictory nature of such documents but also their "toxicity," which is clearly counterproductive in the sense that it ruins not only the professors' autonomy but also the substrate of confidence that must govern the relationship between professors and students:

a. The first issue is the intelligibility of the document, for the students and often for the professors themselves. The attention given to details, indicators, and quantification in terms of percentages is exceedingly baffling. The exegesis of said guide entangles the first few classes because you have to take time to unravel its cryptic codes, almost as it had to be done with the Rosetta stone.

b. The urge to establish a "work schedule" for the students – which results in contact hours, virtual classroom activities and personal study – really disconcerts them and they immediately point out that that model or prototype of student does not exist, since it will take some of them more time, and others less, to meet the objectives. The promise of personalized teaching and attention to diversity is shattered. The guide encourages and seals "normalization."

c. When we read the quantitative system broken down into hours of study, by way of simulation of a work schedule, we understand the hidden intent of the guide: to prepare students for the discipline of the job market. This makes professors comparable to foremen and overseers of their dedication and performance.

d. The section on Evaluation and Grading has taken a peculiar direction; it has gone from informing students about the evaluation method itself to being a document of what I will call "Defensive Education," by analogy with the expression "Defensive Medicine." The latter, characterized by the extreme zeal in treating the patient (even if it is a futile effort) in order to avoid any legal action, helps us judge what is happening with the section on evaluation. The intention in this section, as Deans, Coordinators, and Technicians voiced it, is literally to ensure that students have no opportunity to make any claims. Everything must appear in extreme detail, quantified and converted into percentages.

e. The passion for the quantification of the intangible is another of the key ideas of this bureaucratic pedagogy obsessed with indicators. The wording of sections like the one shown below makes it clear that the substrate on which the Coordinating Committee for Quality or the corresponding Coordinator are based is the distrust of the students – potential plaintiffs and claimants in the making – in line with the assimilation of students to users and clients. This manic detail regarding evaluation and grading dynamites the old proverbial ethical quality of the relationship between students and professors, which is based precisely on trust. Professors become links in a control and monitoring system that relegates to a second place "the adventure of knowledge" or "the love of wisdom," to say it in the old terminology.

f. The teaching guide as we know it in Spanish universities treats students as children. The emphasis on the casuistry of what students should and should not do to pass makes it clear that their dedication has to be continuous, that they cannot neglect anything, and that they must then sprint to cover the distance that others have walked. It privileges, therefore, discipline and work habits, but leaves out the talents of those who choose alternative routes or have a higher degree of maturity. It does not allow for the existential crises usual at that age and requires strict compliance. A continuous, mediocre performance is rewarded; creativity and alternative thinking, if they occur periodically, are not.

g. To corroborate that the disciplinary model has become entrenched in the competence rhetoric of degrees and qualifications, let us examine the following: one of the consequences of the obsession with detail in the preparation of assessment procedures is the implementation in the higher education system of something that was alien to Spanish universities until now: the control of class attendance. Values such as student autonomy and responsibility are affected in this operation that, clearly, "normalizes" and "assimilates" college education, which we must not forget is voluntary and targeted at adults, while the previous levels are designed for young people.

h. The resulting effect (whether deliberate or not) is the aforementioned permanent treatment of students as children. That is, if the result sought was to promote autonomy and personal initiative, the contradictory situation is that now students are being subjected to a hardened disciplinary system, adorned with a false rhetoric of flexibility, innovation and personalization, which forces them to continue to have a disciplinary and supervisory relationship. The continuous tutorship that the model promotes has the perverse effect of intensifying the Peter Pan syndrome, that of the child who did not want to grow up, in students who are overprotected by family and teachers, and whose process of autonomy is impeded.

i. There is a final aspect left to deal with. Initially, the famous teaching guides included a section called "Guiding Schedule," in which a projection of the evolution of work in the course was recorded and some tentative timeframes for the development of course topics were provided. We do not know why the adjective "guiding," which is the only one that befits a guide, as the concrete semantics of the word shows us, was lost and the schedule became "mandatory," and, in short, the object of inspection and control. This triggers a brutal contradiction between a competence model and what is reproduced here with the allocation of weeks per topic. The return of repression, through this section, turns classes into the delivery of a rigid program, similar to the lessons private academies use to prepare teachers for the official tests required for certification. This is yet another example of how the supposedly well-intentioned educational rhetoric gives way to the iron cage of bureaucratic irrationality.

The above is meant to show that the rhetoric of Bologna is betrayed by devices and/or artifacts aimed at standardizing and normalizing teaching at the university. The critical sociology of education is a good tradition to exercise the hermeneutics of suspicion when confronted with new practices and devices. Faced with the avalanche of educational reforms that we have had to bear in the last decades, Deleuze said the following in the 1990s:

> The administrations in charge never cease announcing supposedly necessary reforms: to reform schools, to reform industries, hospitals, the armed forces, prisons. But everyone knows that these institutions are finished, whatever the length of their expiration periods. It's only a matter of administering their last rites and of keeping people employed until the installation of the new forces knocking at the door. These are the *societies of control*, which are in the process of replacing disciplinary societies.[10]

The new forces are those of neoliberal capitalism, which sets up corporations as a model, a model that devours the old educational model and becomes hegemonic:

> [...] in a society of control, the corporation has replaced the factory, and the corporation is a spirit, a gas. Of course the factory was already familiar with the system of bonuses, but the corporation works more deeply to impose a modulation of each salary, in states of perpetual metastability that operate through challenges, contests, and highly comic group sessions. If the most idiotic television game shows are so successful, it's because they express the corporate situation with great precision. The factory constituted individuals as a single body to the double advantage of the boss who surveyed each element within the mass and the unions who mobilized a mass resistance; but the corporation constantly presents the brashest rivalry as a healthy form of emulation, an excellent motivational force that opposes individuals against one another and runs through each, dividing each within. The modulating principle of "salary according to merit" has not failed to tempt national education itself. Indeed, just as the corporation replaces the factory, *perpetual training* tends to replace the *school*, and continuous control to replace the examination. Which is the surest way of delivering the school over to the corporation.[11]

Constant monitoring and the glorified continuing education replace exams, that old disciplinary device which is now masked and reduplicated by various activities and tests. The transitions between patterns and

---

[10] Deleuze, G. "Postscript on the Societies of Control", http://www.n5m.org/n5m2/media/texts/deleuze.htm

[11] *Ibid.*

modulations are not clear. In fact, the Spanish university has not abandoned the disciplinary model, but it has added the model of control. The pressure is stifling.

Students should be consulted, but not through surveys, which they consider silly because they focus on the teachers' fulfillment of their duty and include questions such as whether they believe that teachers know enough about their subject matter. Such surveys suddenly promote students to members of professor selection panels. Discussion groups and qualitative analysis are preferable to surveys that resemble those used to ask about the quality of hotel or airline services.

Teachers cannot bear the workload and stress of continuously monitoring the performance of childlike and dependent students who seem entrenched in the "you do it all, Prof" mentality. Some anecdotes that come to my mind are that of a student who expected me to give him photocopies of my revised class notes, or of another who asked me for the test questions since at the institute they used to give him questions and answers. Faced with an active process of research, documentation, and processing newly arrived students suffer unspeakable vertigo. They wish to receive a service, not to have to make an effort to carry out a collective and individual learning task. The word "motivation" has become a pedagogical mantra that masks the force of social and economic trends which override the spaces open to creativity and critical thinking that at least a minority of professors, myself included, could implement in the classroom.

AN EDUCATIONAL AND SOCIAL STEP BACKWARDS

Finally, the convertibility of credits, (its acronym in English is ECTS) was required because of the insistence on the function of preparing professionals and experts for the common labor market. The magic word was "employability." This concept, a neologism in Spanish, would benefit from a pedagogical model based on the development of basic and specific skills, which redefined the role of the professor as an advisor, motivator, guide and evaluator, in a personalized learning process that would encourage the students' capacity to learn how to learn. All of this is aimed at a labor market where flexibility, mobility and innovation are the three fetish words which have ideologically masked what they really mean: instability, uprooting, and adaptability to the worsening of working conditions. Sociologically speaking, in Spanish universities this neoliberal rhetoric fits perfectly with the effort to mask the aforementioned "mileurismo." The best prepared generations in the history of Spain, resulting from the democracy, well-being and development of the previous decades, enter a labor market characterized by temporary contracts and the lack of recognition of professional worth. The punk slogan of the late seventies, another decade of crisis, comes to life again: No Future. Nevertheless, the possible indignation of a young generation that rebels against the frustration of its expectations allows us to hold a faint hope.

Ideas of University in China: A Critical Review

Tong Shijun

In last decades Chinese universities have been developing tremendously in material, technical and professional terms. During this period there has been another change that is perhaps more important, though less prominent, one I would like to call a "cultural turn" of Chinese universities, which is expressed most clearly in the fact that many people, especially university leaders, are talking about the idea of the university in general and the ideas guiding particular universities. In this chapter I try to describe this phenomenon and explain its backgrounds and implications.

1. Scholar, Space and Spirit: Growing Interests in "The Idea of the University" in China

Although in 1983 a book in Chinese with the title of *The Idea of the University*[1] was already published by Jin Yaoji, then the vice chancellor of the Chinese University of Hong Kong, and similar discourse was started in Taiwan slightly later,[2] when I proposed to a young editor of a journal in Shanghai towards the end of 1999 that it might be interesting to write something on the idea of the university, the phrase "the idea of the university" seemed to impress her very much as something quite new in the Mainland. I was too busy to write on it after I proposed this title, so the young editor pushed me again and again, and the strongest argument was that she had invited several scholars to write on this topic and Professor Xie Xide, the former President of Fudan University, was one of them, and although she was too ill to write herself, she had agreed to publish her interviews with that editor in which she expressed her last views on the university. Xie died one month before that issue of the journal[3] was published in April 2000.

---

[1] Jin Yaoji (1983) *The Idea of the University* [da xue zhi li lian.] Taibei: Times Cultural Publishing Company [shi bao wen hua chu ban gong si.] This book was later reprinted many times in Hong Kong and Beijing.

[2] See for example Huang Junjie (1999) *The Idea of the University and the Selection of the University President*. Tabei: Society of the General Education in Republic of China.

[3] *New Knowledge of the Ocean of Words* [ci hai xin zhi,] N° 5, April 2000, Shanghai. On this issue my paper is titled "The Idea of the University," and Xie Xide's interview is titled "Last Talk on Education."

Just a dozen of years later, the expression "the idea of the university," or *da xue de li nian*, is not only frequently used in writings by scholars and journalists on college education,[4] but also frequently talked about by university leaders. This cannot be better illustrated by a book published earlier this year with the title of *Voices from Universities*. This book is composed of interviews with leaders of 24 best universities in China, conducted by Huang Daren, the former president of Sun Yat-sen University. In his Introduction to this book, Huang said that the most important lesson he got both from his own personal experience as a university president and from his interviews with other university leaders is that "As a university president you must have your own idea *[li nian]* of your university." (Huang *et al.*: 7) "In my interviews," he said, "I was most impressed by the fact that everybody I talked to emphasized the spiritual dimension of a university. Many university presidents regarded 'forming an idea that is widely accepted by the staff on the campus' as the most important work that he or she had done to give a print on his university." (Huang *et al.*: 7)

How should we understand this phenomenon, the phenomenon that university leaders in China show growing interest in talking about the idea of the university?

In Xie Xide's last talk on the university mentioned above, she discussed four phenomena that characterized the situation of higher education in China at that time, and I think it is at least partly as a reaction to these phenomena that university leaders have more or less reached the consensus on the importance of the idea of the university. These phenomena are: the expansion of enrollment of college students, the merging of several colleges even universities into larger ones, the reform of the way how college students are enrolled, and the tendency that the higher education could be turned into an profitable industry. (Xie Xide: 15-19) Yang Wei, the president of Zhejiang University, said in his interview with Huang Daren that "the three most important things about a university are '3ss' in English: Scholar, Space, Spirit." (Huang *et al.*: 295) The growing interest in the idea of the university in China, therefore, can be explained with regard to the relation between the "spirit" and the "space" on the one hand, and with regard to the relation between the "spirit" and the "scholar" on the other.

---

[4] See, for example, Gan Yang (1999) *Civilization, Nation and University* [wen ming, guo jia, da xue.] Beijing: SDX Joint Press.

In the past ten years or so, the "space" of Chinese universities has been tremendously expanded. In 1979 there were only 633 higher education institutions. In 2010, however, there are altogether 2723 higher education institutions. The "space" of Chinese universities in the literal sense also greatly expanded. There are approximately 60 "university cities" in China, home of many new universities or new campuses of existing universities. My university, East China Normal University in Shanghai, for example, got a new campus in suburb area in 2004, which is two times as large as the original one in downtown.

At the same time when the number of universities and university campuses were increased, the number of students has also grown tremendously. In 1979 there were only 1,002,000 registered students, in 2010 the number is 31,050,000, with 6,000,000 graduates, and the gross rate of enrollment to higher education is 26.5%. China surpassed the USA around 2005 as the country that ranks first in this respect.

The space of universities not only grew domestically, but also internationally. From 1978 to 2011 there were 2, 245,100 overseas students and scholars, and 818,400 of them came back home to work. At the same time in 2011 we have 292,611 students from 194 countries and regions all over the world. And we have established 350 Confucius institutes in 105 countries and regions in the world. In addition to these, more substantial progresses have been made in sharing of courses, mutually recognizing of student credits between Chinese universities and their overseas counterparts, and even in jointly running higher education institutions. ECNU, for example, is building up a brand new university in Shanghai together with New York University, and this new university is going to enrol its first students in 2013.

In terms of "scholar," there have also been great improvements. First I should mention the "Project 211," a project initiated in 1995 by the Ministry of Education of China with the aim of raising the standards of research and teaching of a group of selected universities. The name for the project comes from an abbreviation of the 21st century and approximately 100 participating universities. Then I should mention the "Project 985," a project aimed to promote the development and reputation of an even more selective group of Chinese universities. This project was announced by then Chinese President Jiang Zemin at the 100th anniversary Peking University on May 4, 1998, and hence its codenaming. In addition to these large scale projects supporting universities, there have been many projects aimed to attract talents from abroad and support scientists and professors at home, such as the "Changjiang Scholars Program" and

"China National Funds for Distinguished Young Scientists," both involving billions of funding.

Against these developments of "space" and "scholar" universities, many problems have occurred that suggest the lack of "spirit" of the university might be a possible key cause of them.

First is the problem of the imbalance between the quality and the quantity of scientific research. According to an article published on *Science and Development Network* on November 25, 2005, Chinese research "is plentiful but not original," for although the number of the papers published by Chinese scientists continues to grow, they are rarely cited in later studies.[5] The situation has been gradually improved since then, but compared with our achievements in the economic field, the situation in the scientific field is far from being satisfactory.

Second is the problem of the imbalance between the mission of research and the mission of teaching. Many students and their parents complained that professors, especially those leading ones, are busy in conducting scientific research and lobbying for funding, but neglect teaching and tutoring students, especially undergraduate students.

Third is the problem of the imbalance between the growth of higher education and the growth of the people's expectation for higher education. According to the plan of the State Council, by 2020 the total number of registered college students will be 35,500,000, with a gross rate of enrolment of 40%, and the percentage of those who have received higher education among the labour population from 20 to 50 years old will be 20%. So "going to colleges" will less and less be a problem in China. The central government has decided in its budget that government spending on education will account for 4 per cent of the country's GDP this year, and this does not only mean larger government budget for universities, but also mean higher expectation of the ordinary families for "going to good colleges" or for better quality of higher education.

In order to solve these problems and to compete with each other for better students and better scholars, university leaders in China are eager to improve their universities' public images and to increase their appeal to prospective students and their parents by talking about the "idea" of the university in general and about the ideas of their own universities in particular on occasions like commencements and freshmen greetings. Their speeches on these occasions, especially those by presidents of pres-

[5] See the website:
http://www.scidev.net/en/news/chinese-research-is-plentiful-but-not-original.html.

tigious universities, frequently attract wide attentions and incur various comments on mass media and websites.

The growing interest in the idea of the university has both contributed to and been encouraged by the anniversary celebrations widely held by universities all over the country in the last decades. On the occasions when Peking University celebrated its 100th anniversary in 1998, and Tsinghua University celebrated its 100th anniversary in 2011, for example, the ideas and efforts of Cai Yuanpei, the most famous one of presidents of Peking University, and Mei Yiqi, the most famous one of presidents of Tsinghua University, were recalled with great interests and admirations both by university leaders and education officials, on the one hand, and by university professors and education commentators on the other. Most frequently quoted are Cai's remark that "what is called a university is an institution for higher and deeper learning" (See Yang: 324), and Mei's remark that "a university is an institution of great learning not for great buildings in it but for great scholars in it." (See Yang: 353)

During these anniversary celebrations university leaders tend to emphasize the importance of the "mottos" of their universities. For Peking University, for example, the motto is "Patriotism, Advancement, Democracy and Science;" for Tsinghua University, the motto is "Self-discipline and Social Commitment." For Fudan University, the motto is "Rich in Knowledge and Tenacious of Purpose; Inquiring with Earnestness and Reflecting with Self-practice," and for East China Normal University, the motto is "Seek Truth and Creativity, Live up to the Name of Teacher." All these mottos are regarded as expressions of the "spirit" of these universities.

2. CREATIVITY, CHARACTER AND COMMUNITY: MAJOR ELEMENTS IN THE IDEA OF THE UNIVERSITY

The "spirit" of a particular university is related to, but not the same thing as, the "idea of the university." We should differentiate the constitutive idea of the modern institution of higher education called "university" from the distinctive idea guiding the practices of a particular university such as ECNU. The idea of the university in general, in my view, provides a standard by which we judge the value of the guiding ideas of particular universities. These two types of "ideas" are very often mixed up; when Huang Daren said that in the 12 years in SYSU when he was its president, he was most proud of the fact that together with his colleagues he had developed some core ideas of the university, and these ideas in my view are important especially because of their relevance to SYSU. These ideas are: "a university is an academic community," "a university is nothing but its professors," and "taking good care of our students." (Huang *et al.*: 7)

The best presentation of the idea of the university, in my view, was given by Meng Xiancheng, the founding president of East China Normal University. In 1932 he published a book with the title of *University Education*, in which he gave a presentation of the idea of a university that is still very valuable even now in my view: "The university is an academic institution of highest level, and this is so not only because as an institution of education it reaches the highest level of them; it is so especially because in the university human beings show their upmost efforts in searching for the true, the good and the beautiful by means of their wisdom, and in promoting the upward development of culture and society by means of what they have achieved thereby." (Meng: 1)

University is important, according to Meng, because of three ideals embodied in it.

First is the ideal of "creation of Knowledge:" "Conservation of knowledge is important, and the scholars in medieval times have done their best in fulfilling their mission in preserving and sticking to ancient classics. But the totality of the systematic knowledge of modern mankind has suddenly enlarged and grown purely as a result of the scholars' efforts in discovering and inventing, rather than their conservative and perfunctory efforts. The establishment of the University of Berlin in 1809 is the earliest manifestation of this new ideal." (Meng: 2)

Second is the ideal of "cultivation of characters:" "A university is a school, and teachers and their students there should have their school-like group life. Teachers and their students are traditionally regarded as the intellectual elites of the society, they are supposed to embody the most beautiful ideal of morality in the society." (Meng: 3) It is noteworthy that here Meng refers to the tradition of education in China: "Just as what was said by the ancient educator of our nation: 'In the system of teaching at the Great college, every season had its appropriate subject; and when the pupils withdrew and gave up their lessons (for the day), they were required to continue their study at home […] Therefore a student of talents and virtue pursues his studies withdrawn in college from all besides, and devoted to their cultivation, or occupied with them when retired from it, and enjoying himself. Having attained to this he rests quietly in his studies and seeks the company of his teachers; he finds pleasure in his friends, and has all confidence in their course'." (Meng: 3)

The third is the ideal of contribution to the "development of the nation and the community:" "A university's contribution to the society lies in its research and teaching. But there has also been a movement of 'university for the people' in which universities, following the demands of democracy, make efforts to extend their knowledge to the world outside the ivy tower. " (Meng: 7)

During the celebration of the 60th anniversary of East China Normal University, these three ideals were summarized into "3Cs": Creativity, Character and Community. Yu Lizhong, ECNU's current president, quoted Meng's words in his keynote speech at the celebration assembly and said that they expressed "not only a commission from our predecessors, but also a call from our times." (Yu 2011)

The discourse of the idea of university in contemporary China can be discussed in more detail with regards to these three "ideals of university."

With regards to the ideal of "creativity," I should mention the debate triggered by a question posed by Qian Xuesen, the founding scientist of China's Space industry, to Wen Jiabao, when the Premier paid a visit to the national scientific hero in 2005: "Why does China produce so many clever people, but so few geniuses?" Shortly after Qian died on October 31, 2009 at the age of 98, 11 professors in Anhui province published an open letter to the Minister of Education Yuan Guireng and the professional educators in general, in which they are appealed to seriously think over the "Qian Xuesen Question." This appeal received wide and enthusiastic responses, including from the Ministry of Education in Beijing.[6]

With regard to the ideal of "character," I should mention the recent efforts in providing a general education in Chinese universities. Since early 1990s there has been a growing movement critical of what is called a "test-oriented education" and in favor of "personality-oriented education," and the efforts from the above and those from the below were then converged into what I would call a "movement of general education" or a "movement of liberal arts education" on university campuses in China. In Fudan University, for example, the curriculum of general education is composed of six categories of courses, 300 in total according to the plan: literature and history classics and cultural heritage, philosophical wisdom and critical thinking, dialogues among civilizations and the world-wide vision, scientific progresses and the scientific spirit, ecology, environ-

[6] See http://news.xinhuanet.com/politics/2010-05/05/c_1273985.htm.

ment and the concern for life. Almost all the general education programs would include a course called "Introduction to Philosophy." When I started to teach this course in 1991, I was probably among the first ones to teach this kind of course in the Mainland China after 1949, when Marxist philosophy started to be regarded as the only possibly true form of philosophy. But now this course is not only part of the standard curriculum at every department of philosophy, but also a popular course provided to non-major students in all major universities.

With regard to the ideal of "community," I want not only to mention the continuity between the past call to "rescue the nation with science and education" in the first half of the 20th century and the current mission of "reviving the nation with science and education" widely publicized since mid 1990s, but also to emphasize the social and cultural mission of universities and their professors and students. Since the New Culture Movement started in 1915 and resulted in the May 4 Movement in 1919, university professors and students are typically expected both by themselves and by the society at large to become forerunners of the general public, and the university campus is very often regarded as a place for experiments of societal progress at large. In the words of the "motto" of Renmin University, a major part of the university education in China is to produce "Examples to the Citizens and Pillars of the Society." Considering this dimension of the idea of the university in China, the following remark made by Xie Heping, the president of Sichuan University in his interview with Huang Daren, is of special significance: "I'm always of the view that the most important condition for a school's deserving the name of a university is it has the spirit of the university and the culture of the university, and the core values of the culture and spirit of the university is the unlimited pursuit for freedom, truth, democracy and justice." (Huang *et al.*: 254)

It is because of the social and political mission of Chinese universities in this sense that the issue discussed in the next and last section of this paper deserves special attention.

3. PARTY, PRESIDENT AND PROFESSOR: PURSUIT FOR AN INSTITUTIONAL FRAMEWORK CONSISTENT WITH THE IDEA OF UNIVERSITY

When people are talking about the "spirit" or the "idea" of the university, especially when people are reflecting upon the history of prestigious universities like Peking University, Tsinghua University, Nankai University and the university composed of these three universities during the war time, the Southwest United University [xi nan lian da], many of them, especially higher education scholars, journalists and public intellectuals, tend to be highly critical of the current practices and achievements of the Chinese universities not only after 1949 in general, but also Chinese universities at present in particular. But many university leaders expressed their disagreement. Gong Ke, the president of Nankai University, for example, said in his interview with Huang Daren: "When you think of the opportunities that the ordinary people now have got to send their kids to colleges, when you think of the contributions that universities have made to the economic and social progresses of China, when you think of the level of the teaching and scientific research as well as their contributions to the progress of science in the world, and when you think of the national projects of higher education and the conditions for the development of universities themselves, it is hard to understand that some people would say that the universities now are inferior to those in the period of the Republic of China." (Huang *et al.*: 309) Huang Daren echoed by saying that "in the field of higher education, we do not need 'to speak nothing without Greek,' because in today's China we do not lack great educators, and they have contributed their best to the development of their universities, and to the higher education in China in general. Engaged in a great cause, they represent the main stream of the higher education in China, and they have deep understanding of the development of the higher education." (Huang *et al.*: 309)

The fact that Chinese university leaders are self-confident about the Chinese higher education, especially about its future if not its current situation, shows that they do not accept the frequently-heard complaining that there is a fundamental contradiction between the idea of the university on the one hand, and the Chinese university system "under which the presidents take over-all responsibility under the leadership of the primary committees of the Communist Party of China (CCP) in higher education institutions," as prescribed by the article 39 of the Law of Higher Education of the People's Republic of China, on the other.[7]

I do not think there is no tension between the idea of the university that is basically dated back to Western educators and thinkers like W. Humboldt, Cardinal John Newman, K. Jaspers and J. Habermas, on the one hand, and the law-guaranteed leadership of the CCP in contemporary China, on the other, and neither do I think this tension can be easily re-

[7] http://www.lawinfochina.com/display.aspx?lib=law&id=987.

solved. But I want to clear three possible misunderstandings concerning the governance structure of Chinese universities.

Firstly, we should not mistake the system of the "President-Responsibility under the Leadership of the Party Committee" as the system of "President-Responsibility under the Leadership of the Secretary of the Party Committee." The dual leadership system in Chinese universities is not composed of the president of the university and the party secretary of the university, but composed of the university's president and its party committee, and the party committee can well function in the way the board of trustees function in universities in other parts of the world, i.e. as an agent of collective leadership.

Secondly, we should not mistake the system of "President-Responsibility under the Leadership of the Party Committee" as the system of "President-Responsibility under the Leadership of the Standing Commission of the Party Committee." I emphasize this point because of the importance of the representative leadership as well as the importance of collective leadership in Chinese universities. The leadership of the party committee in Chinese universities embodies the principle of the collective leadership, which means that the party committee, of which the president is almost always one of the most important members, makes any decision on the basis of collective deliberation, and by voting if necessary. But for the sake of efficiency, in most sizable universities the everyday decision-making activities are commissioned by the party committee, whose members are usually around 20 or even more, to a standing commission under it, whose members are usually no more than 10. Since the standing commission is usually composed of the party secretary, two or three deputy secretaries, the president, and four to five of his deputies, its functioning is not based on the principle of representative leadership. That is why in recent years some universities are making experiments to make it possible for the plenary of their party committees not only to supervise more substantially the function of their standing commissions, but also to function by themselves on a more routine basis.

Thirdly, we should not mistake the system of the "President-Responsibility under the Leadership of the Party Committee" as the system of the "President-Responsibility under the Leadership of a Party Committee that is against the 'idea of the university'." It is quite possible, and in many cases it is a reality, that the party committee of a particular university is very serious about realizing in China an idea of the university that is widely acceptable across national boundaries. This can be clearly seen in the fact that almost all the party secretaries interviewed by

Huang Daren agreed that we should give a much more important role to the academic part of the university leadership in Chinese universities. It is because of this consensus that the otherwise politically sensitive call for the so-called "de-administrativization" of higher education management is quite popular in recent years in China.

In addition to pointing out the three possible misunderstandings concerning the Chinese university system of the "President-Responsibility under the Leadership of the Party Committee," I want to refer to a remark by Li Yanbao, the former party secretary of Sun Yat-sen University, which explains quite well the rationale behind this system. "The system under which the presidents take over-all responsibility under the leadership of the Party committees is adopted," said Li, "because it is suitable to the organizational structure of the modern universities with Chinese characteristics, characterized on the one hand by its 'huge size' and on the other hand by its double management function of 'school plus community'." (Huang *et al.*: 348) Then he explained: "School and community as social groups or organizations belong to two different categories. A 'school' is oriented to academic growth, with the higher quality of student education as its goal, therefore it is run mainly by 'favoring what is best,' or the so-called 'policy in favor of elites,' according to which you have to prefer something to something else, whereas to a community the most important consideration is its stability, with a harmonious community as the goal, so the policy is to pay attention to 'disadvantaged' groups, and adhere to the principles of equity, justice and fairness, taking equal accounts of everybody." (Huang *et al.*: 348) Put in another way, universities in China should pursue both the value of "excellence" and that of "harmony," and the best institutional arrangement in Chinese universities should make it possible to have an positive interaction between the efforts for both values, rather than to pursue one value at the cost of the other.

Seen from the perspective of a top-down institutional design, according to Li, two problems should be addressed with great efforts. On the one hand, we should appropriately deal with the relation among the three "power systems:" the political power (responsible for what kind of university we want to have), the administrative power (responsible for by what means we run our universities), and the academic power (responsible for by whom our universities are to be operated). On the other hand, we should appropriately deal with the relation between the two "decision-making systems," i.e. the system of administrative decision-making and the system of the academic decision-making. Li admits that many problems remain to be solved, such as problems concerning the relationships between the government and the university, between the party committee and the administration, between the president and the party secretary, problems concerning the way the party secretary is elected and appointed, including the way that administrative roles that a party secretary is commissioned by the government such as the university council chairperson, chairperson of the board of trustees or of the board of directors of a university, the way a university president is searched for and appointed, the way the academic committee is constituted and its rights are defined, and problems concerning those affairs that are related to the university charter, especially the specification of the tenet of a university and its basic idea, and so on. But the existence of these problems does not mean that we should definitely in principle give up the system of the "President-Responsibility under the Leadership of the Party Committee."

It should be noted that a university governance structure that is both in agreement with the idea of the university and applicable to the reality of Chinese society is a goal encouraged by the central government of China as well. In the "Outline of China's National Plan for Medium and Long-term Education Reform and Development (2010-2020)" promulgated in 2010, for example, it is stated that "All kinds of higher educational institutions should draft their constitutions according to law, act on such constitutions in governance and operation, respect academic freedom and furnish a friendly and relaxed academic environment, and carry out systems for appointment, teaching and work post management in an all-round way. They should establish scientifically assessment frameworks and incentive mechanisms."[8] The Ministry of Education in Beijing then encourages individual universities to make experiments in this general direction, and my university is one of the universities that are making experiments in reforming the internal governance structure in order to endow it with a higher level of legitimacy and efficiency.

In conclusion I want to make three points in this paper.

Firstly, in the growing interest in the idea of the university among university leaders and other people we can see that there has been a "cultural turn" in Chinese universities during a period in which they were (and still are) undergoing a tremendous growth in material, technical and professional terms. This cultural turn can be regarded as part of what Fei Xiaotong, the most important Chinese sociologist in the 20th century, called "cultural self-awareness" in his last days. And in a sense this turn

[8] https://www.aei.gov.au/news/newsarchive/2010/documents/china_education_reform_pdf.pdf.

can also be evidenced by a widely quoted remark by President Hu Jintao on the 100th anniversary celebration of Tsinghua University in last April: "In order to raise the quality of higher education, we must energetically advance the work of cultural transition and cultural creation, and let the higher education play the role of an important vehicle to carry forward the fine traditions of the Chinese culture and important sources of ideals and thoughts."

Secondly, within this cultural turn there have been several versions of "two cultures" debates, concerning not only the relation between the scientific culture and the humanistic culture, but also the relation between the academic culture and the utilitarian (economic and administrative) culture, and the relation between the national culture and the international culture. Considering the fact the whole discourse on the "idea of a university" or "die Idee der Universitaet" was introduced from the West when China entered the modern epoch in the world history under the pressure of the Western powers, the relation between the national or the local dimension and the international or the global dimension of the idea of the university in China deserves special attention.

Thirdly, the idea of the university is important not only because it helps university leaders to run their schools in a more self-reflective way, but also because it makes it possible for all those who care about the higher education of China both to have an immanent critique and to have an immanent justification of it. To those who criticize Chinese universities without proper respect for their historical and cultural conditions, we should pay special attention to the role of the idea of the university in the immanent justification of Chinese universities, and to those who defend Chinese universities without sufficient self-reflection, we should pay special attention to the role of the idea of the university in the immanent critique of Chinese universities.

REFERENCES

Huang Daren *et al.* (2012) *Voices from Universities* [da xue de sheng yin]. Beijing: Commercial Press.

Meng Xiancheng (2010) *University Education* [da xue jiao yu]. Shanghai: East China Normal University Press.

Xie Xide (2000) "Last Talk on Education," in *New Knowledge of the Ocean of Words* [ci hai xin zhi], N° 5, April 2000.

Yang Dongping (ed.) (2000) *The Spirit of the University*. Shenyang: Liaohai Press.

Yu Lizhong (2011) "A Speech at the Celebration of the 60th Anniversary of East China Normal University," in *East China Normal University Weekly*, N° 1504, published on November 1, 2011.

HOPE

POLITICS, EDUCATION AND NATIONAL DEVELOPMENT: A PROLOGUE TO PHILOSOPHY OF EDUCATION

D. P. CHATTOPADHYAYA

I. PHILOSOPHY FOR HUMANISTIC EDUCATION

It is, indeed, a categorical necessity of the intellectual life of each country that there should be amongst us men who can rightfully claim to be our guardian philosophers – philosophers sensitive to philosophic change and connected with political and social relationships at a particular stage of the emergence of societies so that social and political events can be reviewed and re-evaluated in the context of conclusions of thoughts and methods prevailing at that time. This is all the more important so that the tradition of philosophic reflection on historical events along with their socio-political significance can be kept alive and rejuvenated.

It is true that due to circumstances beyond our control, i.e. the politics of the 20th century and the horrific occurrences of world wars, this 'political obligation' got disrupted and our great thinkers of the 20th century could not address themselves to problems of political significance and therefore it was believed that political philosophy has not been able to survive in the 20th century.

Marxists are being held responsible for this situation as it is observed that they erected a system in which sociological descriptions and determinations tended to fill the function of philosophical analysis. But it may be argued that a political philosophy having its moorings in traditional thought could be built up around Marxian sociology and the debate between the Marxists and their critics has been carried on within the conventions of traditional political philosophy. This criticism needs to be debated which will be one of the intentions of the present paper.

Neither Marxist thought nor 20th century philosophers, who gave a call to withdraw unto themselves for a time to re-examine their logical and linguistic apparatus, perhaps intended that a traditional area of philosophic enquiry regarding the relationship of politics with society and such rational instrumentalities as education should be delinked from the process of philosophic reflection. Appropriately, therefore, in recent years there have been signs that our philosophers are preparing to take up their responsibilities towards 'politics' once more and this gives hope for the revival and rebirth of traditional political philosophy – be it in the form of reformulation or rejuvenation of inherited positions in the political realm or in the form of new and fresh ideas regarding political ends and institutions to be established in order to achieve desired ends.

The present attempt seeks to join the efforts of such political thinkers who wish to restore a philosophy of all humanity which represents not the extinction of political philosophy but its metamorphosis. It will take into account the realities of sovereign nation-states and the educational policies and parameters employed for their development after due reflection upon the principles of progress for the same.

In the context of countries, having gone through the civilizational crisis of colonisation, the question of national development is extremely crucial. And equally crucial is the instrumental rationality of education which facilitates this highly desirable development.[1]

In this context, the statesmen, the citizens and the political thinkers expect unequivocal answers to certain questions regarding the meaningfulness of life. What is the notion of a good life? How can this be achieved? Is it through politics we can attain it? Or is education the proper instrumentality to have access to it? Is there such a thing as a socialist morality? If so, on what grounds should I adopt it? To these normative, analytic, prescriptive and predictive questions they expect philosophic answers. Does it require a reconsideration of how an Aristotle or a Plato answered these questions by taking into account a complete and coherent view of all knowledge and experience? This will be the new identity of a political philosopher who answers these questions in the process of a long and respectable lineage going back to the roots of tradition.[2]

In this context Paul Ricœur's reflections on politics, justice identity, human agency and recognition of responsibility are illuminating. He says the Science of argument in the broadest sense leading to the nature of the 'Sovereign Good' is "politics," the "most authoritative art." Ricœur discusses the sciences necessary in states and cities and the subordination of ethics to politics in so far as the end of nations is considered to be higher than that of the individual. He quotes Aristotle in this context:

---

[1] Laslett, Peter (1975) *Philosophy, Politics & Society*. Oxford: Basil Blackwell: 19-20.

[2] Hurka, Thomas (1987) "The Well Rounded Life," in *The Journal of Philosophy*, Vol. LXXXIV, N° 12, December, 1987: 727. – See also, Tagore, Rabindranath (1957) *Sadhana*. London: Macmillan: 147.

> For even if the end is the same for the single man and for a state, that of the state seems at all events something greater and complete both to attain and to preserve; for though it is worthwhile to attain the end merely for one man, it *is finer and more godlike to attain it for a nation or for a city state.*[3] (Italics mine)

II. National Development and Educational Policy

Education is important for the development of all societies but it is particularly so for developing societies which have emerged from the dark shadows of alien rule. My own country is an example for making a plea for national development through the instrumentality of education. We needed an educational policy which could contain an inbuilt flexibility so that it could adjust to changing circumstances. The alien rule had its own compulsions of meeting its own requirements; so education was designed to serve the cause of continuous servility of our nation to the rulers from beyond. Hence for good reasons the educational system of yesteryear no longer was desirable to a young liberated nation seething with the passionate impulse to catch up with the standards of life already accomplished by other nation states.[4] In a science-based world, the policies for education and research called for new parameters so that the development process of the country could accomplish welfare, progress and security like that existing in other nation states.

A purposeful deliberation on education is a political priority of a nation state in the phase of its infanthood as the political leaders are entrusted with the task of building the nation, preparing its citizens to perform their political obligations of contributing to the welfare of the community of which they are members. In other words the task is stupendous as nothing short of an educational revolution is required.

The salient features of a new educational policy included stress on moral education for inculcation of a sense of social responsibility and political obligation. It was necessary to equip the minds of a younger generation passing out from the level of school education to institutions of higher education and/or vocational and secondary education or for making a transition to the world of work and life. It was a challenging task to strengthen the centers of advanced study at par with other similar institutions the world over with the highest international standards and to establish new centers of higher learning and research either in the form of universities or research organizations in the applied fields like agriculture

---

3 Ricœur, Paul (2005) *The Course of Recognition*, Transl. by David Pellauer. London/Cambridge (USA): Harvard University Press: 162.

4 Ray, Niharranjan (1973) *Nationalism in India*. Aligarh: Aligarh Muslim University: 27-41.

in a country which was predominantly agricultural in nature and production.

Educational reconstruction also needed to give high priority to the domains of the allied sciences, both natural and social, besides taking imaginative steps for preserving and enhancing 'quality' in education and taking steps to encourage 'talent' in the country.

To quote an instance to substantiate my preceding argument it is relevant to mention that politics got directly linked to education when in India, the Government duly elected by the people of India asserted its political will be by appointing an education commission to advise the government on the National Pattern of Education. The Commission was assigned the responsibility of formulating the General Principles and Policies for the development of education at all stages and in all aspects.

The Commission expressed the political will of the nation in stating the following purpose:

> *No task in our views could be more challenging, more vital and relevant to India's progress and development – economic*, cultural and spiritual. In facing a task of such a colossal magnitude and complexity, there is always a danger that the approach and recommendations may not be sufficiently radical.[5] (Italics mine)

If further expressed a fear:

> There is also the other possibility that the recommendation may go beyond the capacity and resources of the nation.[6]

This fear was expressed because difficulties could be accentuated on account of plans being long term, i.e. twenty years. Also projections of needs and resources during the two decades could vary and face serious uncertainties.

Education, science based and in coherence with Indian culture and values, was deemed fit to provide the foundation – as also the instrument – for the nation's progress, security and welfare. The segments chosen for recommendations included the following: (1) School Education, (2) Higher Education, (3) Technical Education, (4) Agricultural Education, (5) Adult Education, (6) Science Education and Research, (7) Teacher Training and Teacher Status, (8) Manpower, (9) Educational Administration and (10) Educational Finance.

The recommendations for policy plans also covered (a) Women's education (b) Education of backward classes (c) School-community rela-

---

[5] Kothari, D. S. (1971) *Education and National Development: Report of the Education Commission 1964-66*. Delhi: NCERT.

[6] *Ibid.*

tionship (d) Pre-primary Education (e) School curriculum besides structural designing of school buildings.

It was emphasized that urgent action was called for with respect to each one of the above *mentioned stages and sectors of education.* The inputs of other countries like the UK, France, Germany and the USSR and international organizations like UNESCO, the British Council and USAID were availed through their consultants. UNESCO International Institute of Educational Planning facilitated interaction with educational institutions located within their countries.

It was believed that the experience of other countries with respect to their economic and cultural development, national integration and realization of the ideal of democratic and socialistic patterns of society would provide significant data for our own transformation of the system and for linking it closely to the life of our people. This would enable us to expand educational opportunities, increase the sustained and intensive effort necessary to raise the quality of education at all stages, emphasize the development of science and technology and the cultivation of moral and social values.

These interactions were envisaged as capable of enabling the educational system to produce young men and women of character and ability, committed to national service and development. Such an informed system of education could play its vital role in promoting national progress, creating a sense of common citizenship and culture as well as strengthening national integration. This was necessary if the country sought its rightful place at par with other nations, in conformity with its great cultural heritage and unique potentialities.

The principles adopted by the government included the following:

1. *Free and Compulsory Education*: In fulfillment of the Directive Principle under article 45, the Constitution sought to provide free and compulsory education for all children up to the age of 14.

2. *Status, Emoluments and Education of Teachers*: (a) Teachers' character, personal qualities, educational qualifications and professional competence are the foundation of the success of any educational endeavour. Therefore it was proposed that they be accorded the highest place of honour in society and be given adequate emoluments and service conditions. (b) Must enjoy academic freedom to pursue and publish independent studies and research besides speaking and writing on important national and international issues. (c) In-service education for teachers is to get due emphasis.

3. *Development of Languages*: (a) Regional languages: already in use at primary and secondary stages should find suitable place in University education as well as for creative and indigenous thinking. (b) Three languages scheme: i.e., one regional, a second national and a third for international communication. (c) National language: Article 351 of the Constitution required providing the national language as the medium of expression to counterbalance the large number of regional languages in use in different parts of the country. (d) Teaching of classical languages like Sanskrit for cultural unity of the country and for strengthening other regional languages which have a derivative status from Sanskrit. (e) International language: Special emphasis needs to be given to the study of English and other international languages to facilitate sharing of knowledge at the world level in science and technology. The country should make its contributions of significance for the world community to share.
4. *Equal Educational Opportunities*: (a) Regional imbalances in educational facilities should be rectified by providing the same in rural and other backward areas. (b) To promote social cohesion and national integration common schools for all should be adopted so as to prevent segregation of social classes. This will not affect rights of minorities under article 30 of the Constitution. (c) Education of girls is to receive special emphasis, not only on the grounds of social justice, but also because it accelerates social transformation. (d) Intensive efforts are to be provided to develop education among the backward classes and especially among tribal people. (e) Educational facilities for physically and mentally handicapped children should be expanded and attempts should be made to develop integrated programmes enabling handicapped children to study in regular schools.
5. *Identification of Talent*: For the cultivation of excellence, it is necessary that talent in diverse fields is identified at as early an age as possible, and every opportunity provided for its full development.
6. *Work Experience and National Service*: Community Service and national reconstruction is an integral part of education. Emphasis on self help, character formation and a sense of social commitment should be an integral part of all programmes.
7. *Science Education and Research*: Keeping in mind growth of the national economy, science education is to receive the high priority.
8. *Education for Agriculture and Industry*: (a) At least one Agricultural University in every state is to be established with strong departments for the study of one or more aspects of Agriculture. (b) Technical education

and research is to be closely related to industry with flow of personnel both ways for continuous cooperation in provision, design and periodical review of training programme and facilities. (c) There should be continuous review of the agricultural, industrial and other technical manpower needs of the country so as to maintain a proper balance between the output of educational institutions and employment opportunities.

9. *Standard Text Book Production*: There should be a liberal policy of incentives and remuneration for the best talent in writing books of high quality for children and university students, also in regional languages.

10. *Examinations*: The reliability and validity of examinations should be improved. Evaluation is to be a continuous process to improve each student's level of achievement.

11. *Secondary Education*: (a) Educational avenues – a major instrument of social change and transformation should be provided to areas and classes where these have been denied earlier. (b) Provision for Secondary and Vocational Education should conform broadly to the requirements of the developing economy and employment opportunities. Also such facilities for technical and vocational education should be suitably diversified to cover a large number of fields such as agriculture, industry, trade and commerce, medicine and public health, home management, arts, crafts, secretarial training, etc.

12. *University Education*: Adequate funds and proper standards should be maintained keeping in mind the needs for laboratory, library and other facilities as well as for providing strong post-graduate departments in the humanities, social sciences, natural sciences and other technical and professional subjects.

13. *Part-Time Education and Correspondence Courses*: This will benefit teachers, agricultural and industrial workers and such others who have the desire to get educated but cannot do so on a full-time basis.

14. *Spread of Literacy and Adult Education*: Participation in democratic institutions and national development can be accelerated if illiteracy is liquidated. Industrial undertakings and public sectors should take a lead in organizing literacy campaigns as a part of social and national service programmes.

15. *Games and Sports*: Nationwide programmes are needed for excellence in physical fitness and sportsmanship.

16. *Education of Minorities*: Rights of minorities and their educational interests need to be protected in terms of resolutions adopted and constitutional provisions.

17. *Education structure*: A uniform educational structure of 10 + 2 + 3 years from school to college level was adopted by national education policy to be followed throughout the country.

III. EDUCATION AND NATIONAL OBJECTIVES

Education has the honorific task of getting linked with national objectives like self sufficiency in all material needs through economic growth and full employment so that national income per capital can increase.

Education has to play a definite role in achieving social and national integration especially in cases where society is hierarchical, stratified and deficient in vertical mobility. Existence of caste, religious disparity and social distance between classes threaten national unity, social progress and cause social alienation if education is not rooted in tradition.

Therefore, the educational objectives at the national level have to include political development as the primary goal. This is required to strengthen democracy and a socialistic pattern of society wherein 'equality' and 'freedom' have to be kept in the forefront. The objective of political development is to defend the freedom of the country and to create an awareness among the masses of their fundamental rights to equality, freedom, higher standards of living and all civic amenities.

Commitment to democratic socialism requires creation of a new social order. If this change is to be achieved without violent revolution, then the only instrument to do so is *education* as it alone can reach all people of the nation state. It requires strength of will, dedication to work and sacrifice, as the examples of other countries have shown.

In a democracy, the individual is an end in himself and the primary purpose of education is to provide him with the widest opportunities to develop his potentialities to the fullest. However, the path to this goal lies through social organization which can be facilitated through education.

In fact, one of the important principles to be emphasized in the socialistic pattern of society is that individual fulfillment will come through the dedication of all to the national development in all its expressions and develop and deepen the national consciousness through a greater understanding and re-evaluation of our cultural heritage and through a strong faith in the potential achievements of futuristic aspirations. The former can be realized by making languages and literatures, philosophy, religion, history, art, architecture, music, dance, drama, etc., a part of the educational curriculum and the latter by inculcating democratic values and respect for the culture of other national groups as a way of life.

The modernization of education is an essential condition for this democratic and socialistic pattern of society which has accepted the dignity of individual, equality and social justice as the values to be adopted. The western nations have harnessed the liberalizing influences received from the French Revolution, the Welfare States and from the Philosophy of Marx as the main driving force for the rise of socialism. These values, in fact, must be inculcated through Education for a secular, democratic and socialistic society. The political ambience of secularism enhances and enriches the dispositional climate of a country which has in one way or the other lacked in 'equality' and 'social justice' in the past.

IV. THE MATRIX OF SOCIALIST MORALITY AND NATIONAL DEVELOPMENT

Socialism as an ideology has emerged to plead the ideal of the ontological equality of man as a lesson learned from the French Revolution. There have been abstract idealistic formulations of socialism but the most influential has been the Marxist model of socialism which found its place in the National policies of education of many countries for their national development.

These considerations need to be examined as to why socialistic morality found a place in educational policies. If in a democratic set up with a socialist pattern, individual man is the goal for being provided with conditions for his enrichment through education for a free and full development, would it be necessary to know what are the potentialities which need fulfillment as pleaded by social and educational thinkers? Can the ideal nature of man be rendered into a universal value?

Marx sought to bring the "existence" of man in harmony with his "essence." However, must we know what human essence is? Why is there a gulf that divides the two, thereby creating incongruity and the immorality of keeping them apart?

If we glimpse through some classic writings of Marx, we find that the point of departure for Marx is man himself:

> The first premise of all human existence and therefore of all history, the premise, namely, that men must be in a position to live in order to be able to make history.[7]

And again,

> We set out from real, active men, and on the basis of their real life processes we demonstrate the development of the ideological reflexes and echoes of this life process.[8]

[7] Marx-Engels (1964), *The German Ideology*. Moscow: Progress: 39.

V. UNIVERSAL HUMAN NATURE

Marx observed that common man was treated not so much of a human being as a source of work which "unfortunately had to be fueled." Consequently a slave was not included in the definition of a human being, as in Roman law. Therefore, Marx challenged the class-bound concept of man in the following words:

> Is there not a *universal human* nature just as there is a universal nature of plants and heavenly bodies? Philosophy asks what is true, not what is acknowledged as such, what is true for all men, not what is true for individuals."[9] (Italics in original)

In his search for the universal nature of man, Marx explored, first of all, the *Unmensch,* i.e., what he is not. Has he any transcendental, abstract super mundane reality to which he must pay homage? The answer to this Marx found in Aeschylus's *Prometheus Bound* and later in Lucian's *Dialogues*. Prometheus, considered by Marx as 'the noblest of saints and martyrs in the calendar of philosophy,' makes a confession, "In *sooth* all gods I hate." Marx's image of man is cast very much after the rebellious nature of Prometheus who proclaimed:

> I shall never exchange my fetters for slavish servility. 'Tis better to be chained to the rock than bound to the service of Zeus.[10]

Marx's Promethean man also protests against the authority of gods. The criticism of religion ended in a kind of apotheosis of man and was hailed as a penetrating insight into the esoteric truth about man. It led Marx to pronounce the supremacy of man in these words:

> The criticism of religion ends with the doctrine that *man is the Supreme Being for man.* It ends therefore, with the *categorical imperative* to overthrow all those conditions in which man is an abased, enslaved, abandoned, contemptible being [...][11] (Italics mine)

Marx explains the ontic status and onto-genesis of man by the term *Gattungswesen*, i.e. man as a species being.

---

[8] *Ibid.*: 37.

[9] Marx, *The Leading Article of* N° *179 of Kölnische Zeitung*, in Marx-Engels (1955) *On Religion*. Moscow: Foreign Languages: 26.

[10] Marx "Foreword to Thesis: The Difference Between the Natural Philosophy of Democritus and the Natural Philosophy of Epicurus," in Marx "Critique of Hegel's Philosophy of Right", in Marx-Engels *On Religion*: 56.

[11] Caute, David (ed.) (1967) *Essential Writings of Karl Marx*. London: Panther: 56. See also, Marx-Engels, *op. cit.*: 50.

> Man is a species being, [...] he treats himself as a *universal* and therefore a *free being.*[12] (Italics in original)

Marx observed that free, conscious activity is man's species character[13] and man is also an aesthetic being, therefore, he forms things in accordance with the laws of beauty.[14] Being social is part of man's species character and constitutes the molecular basis of the whole society. Therefore Marx spells the moral ideal itself as "the complete return of man to himself as a social (i.e. human) being."

In his sixth thesis on Feuerbach, Marx says:

> The human essence is no abstraction inherent in each single individual. In its reality it is the ensembles of social relations.[15]

VI. DEIFICATION OF MAN AND SOCIALISM

Marx developed a gospel of the supremacy of man, amounting to his deification.[16] Consequently he postulated the emancipation of man as the highest goal of socialism.[17]

In pursuit of this goal, he sought transcendence of alienation,[18] which according to him would resolve the conflict:

> between man and nature, between man and man – the true resolution of the strife between existence and essence, between objectification and self-confirmation, between freedom and necessity, between individual and the species.[19]

This reverence for human dignity and transcendence of human self-estrangement, he politically baptized as the true communism – a society in which the full and free development of every individual forms the ruling principle.[20]

In societies which are in the process of emerging from colonial or dictatorial rules of exploitation, this reverence for human dignity and the

---

[12] Marx (1961) *The Economic and Philosophic Manuscripts of 1844*. Moscow: Foreign Languages: 74.

[13] *Ibid.*: 75.

[14] *Ibid.*: 76.

[15] Marx "VI Thesis on Feuerbach," in Marx-Engels *The German Ideology*: 646.

[16] Parsons, Howard L. (1964) "The Prophetic Mission of Karl Marx," in *The Journal of Religion*, XLIV, I, January, 1964: 70.

[17] Marx *Ec. Phil. MSS*: 82.

[18] Fromm, Erich (1967) *Marx's Concept of Man*. New York: Fredrich Ungar: 58.

[19] Marx *Ec. Phil. MSS*: 102. See also, Schaff, Adam (1964) "Marxism and the Individual," A paper read by the author at an International Symposium on "Morale et Societa" at the Gramsci Institute in Rome, reproduced in *Mainstream*, Dec. 1964: 11.

[20] Marx (1965) *Capital*, I. Moscow: Progress: 592. See also, D. P. Chattopadhyaya (1991) "Roads to World Unity," in *Sri Aurobindo and Karl Marx*. Delhi: Motilal Banarsidass: 160.

return of 'man' to himself – is the ultimate parameter to decide what kind of politics and what kind of education a society must have. In other words a humanistic and a socialistic perspective has constrained the political thinking to converge on an ideology that accepts the supremacy of man as the ultimate value. The humanistic philosophy of education in the 21st century must accept this realistic aspiration of mankind as a point of departure for a further philosophic reflection.

Moral Traditions, Critical Reflection, and Education in a Liberal-Democratic Society

Sergio Cremaschi

1. Politics, that is, Ethics

> If, then, there is some end of the things we do, which we desire for its own sake [...] clearly this must be the good and the chief good. Will not the knowledge of it, then, have a great influence on life? [...] If so, we must try, in outline at least, to determine what it is, and of which of the sciences or capacities it is the object. It would seem to belong to the most authoritative art and that which is most truly the master art. And politics appears to be of this nature.[1]

As the quote illustrates, the very name "ethics" was still unknown to Aristotle, and what has been later named ethics is named by him politics. This is not a detail, neither is to be explained away by such pseudo-Hegelian considerations as that Aristotle has *not yet* reached the genuine concept of the person or the individual and is *still* bound to reasoning in terms of an undivided community.

On the contrary, Aristotle had a clear idea of a *practical* part of philosophy, as opposed to a *purely theoretical* part, the former being the one that not merely satisfies our thirst for knowledge but also helps us in becoming better human beings. He had a clear idea of its subdivision into three levels, which in the Aristotelian tradition have been dubbed *monastica*, *oeconomica*, and *politica*. Note that the threefold division was still alive at Christian Wolff's times, in the eighteenth century. Thus, it was no strange idea that the whole of practical philosophy might be named after the most comprehensive of its three levels, namely politics. But politics as such was, for Aristotle and his followers up to the nineteenth-century discovery of *Realpolitik*, a kind of discourse about the proper goals for human action and the good, and indeed the wider context within which any discourse about goals and the good should be located.

It is no novelty that politics, from the beginning of the eighteenth century on, has been increasingly understood in terms of a technique, more or less as the continuation of war by other means. It is also well-known how, in the aftermath of World War II, a revival of Aristotelian politics as "practical philosophy" has taken place in Germany thanks to

[1] Aristotle, *Nichomachean Ethics*, 1094a 18-1094b 2.

such writers as Joachim Ritter, Hans-Georg Gadamer and others, and in the United States thanks to Leo Strauss and his school. Much of the specific claims advanced by these writers are highly questionable, yet one point is a new/old idea that can be hardly questioned, namely that normative discourse, value judgments, prudential discernment need be exercised firstly about mankind's lot, since no Course of History is out there taking care of it. In a word, the new/old rather obvious idea is that politics is ethics, and any ethic that would be careful in not trespassing into politics would be no ethics at all.

In the real world, and more in detail in the world of educational institutions, such new awareness has produced a couple of distinct phenomena. The first is a number of attempts, perhaps more marked in European countries that have overcome at some point a totalitarian regime, of introducing some kind of political education as a distinct subject in school curricula. Examples of this tendency are the institution in Italy after the fall of Fascism of "civic education," a subject with a somewhat uncertain status, somewhere in between a study of the Constitution and the institutions of the democratic Republic and a kind of education *into* democratic values. In post-Franco Spain an analogous subject was introduced, formerly named "knowledge of the Constitution" and more recently "education to citizenship."

2. The Teaching of "Natural Morality" in Early Modern Europe

There was a time in European history, from the middle of the fifteenth century to the end of the eighteenth, when the study of "natural morality" was believed to be the focus of a humanistic/secular education. This tradition began in Florence at the times of *Rinascimento* and gradually spread toward Northern Europe.

In the Middle Ages, within the framework of Scholasticism, there was hardly any teaching of ethics as a separate subject. Ethics was basically encapsulated within a theological sub-discipline, namely the doctrine of the virtues, both natural and "theological." Yet, something happened that paved the way to the Renaissance revolution, that is, between the thirteenth and the fourteenth centuries a revival of practical philosophy took place gradually in the "minor" faculty, the faculty of arts, carried out by the mostly laymen *magistri* of this faculty. The revival was a consequence of the rediscovery of a few Greek ethical works, first among them Aristotle's *Nichomachean ethics*.

Aquinas, while working within the framework of theological ethics, made a decisive – and still not fully appreciated – improvement on Aristotelian ethics, and Scotus and William of Ockham amended and developed several points in Aquinas's doctrine. The problem with Aquinas was that, while he was clear enough about the claim of existence of a "natural" morality (as contrasted with "revealed" morality) accessible to every human being thanks to the light of reason, no separate treatment of such morality was deemed necessary, and it was presented as a kind of introduction to the treatment of the natural virtues, to be crowned by the discussion of the theological ones.

In the fifteenth century, within the framework of a reaction against Scholasticism by lay *literati*, ethics had a fresh start, at once building on medieval practical philosophy and reading the classical works in a new key. The Florentine *literati* started thinking of moral philosophy as a branch of *Studia humanitatis*, that is, a set of sub-disciplines ranging from rhetoric to grammar, philology and law and supposedly aimed at shaping the character of a wise man and a good citizen. This implied that stress was laid not so much on ethics as a philosophical discipline in a technical sense but instead on "moral discourse" as a part of humanities, which in turn were meant to be the path to a "philosophical" (that is, comparatively secular, albeit compatible with the Christian faith, and besides enlightened and virtuous) way of living. Writings by such authors as Xenophon, Isocrates, Lucianus, Plutarcus, Theofrastus, Sallustius, Titus Livius and Tacitus were assumed to belong to moral discourse, and among professional philosophers Cicero and Seneca, that is, those who were closer to the rhetorical tradition, enjoyed the widest popularity. A tension emerged between the early Renaissance *rhetorical* approach to moral discourse and the later Renaissance programs for a reformed *scientific* ethics (as exemplified by Descartes, Mersenne, Spinoza, and Hobbes), but such tension should not be overstressed, since there was a shared understanding of the goals and comparatively secular character of moral discourse.

It is against this background that the immense popularity of Cicero's *De officiis* during three centuries, as well as the drastic demise of such popularity at about 1800, may be fully appreciated. This work in fact became *the* basic reading for future members of the educated elite. It was praised by virtually everybody up to Voltaire, until it started being underrated at the beginning of the nineteenth century as being, at best, not philosophical enough and, at worst, simply shallow. It may be worth reminding that it had been conceived by Cicero as a synthesis of moral doctrines that he believed to be shared ground for almost all philosophical schools, Epicureanism excluded, even if Panetius the Stoic was his main source. In Cicero's strategy a system of normative ethics might be presented without expatiating on theoretical foundations for two reasons: the first was his own middle-Academic theory of knowledge, i.e. probabilism, which provided a reason why doctrines should be accepted while still waiting for a final argument, since we may hope to provide at best probable proofs, and the second was consensus between major schools about a number of doctrines.

These were a distinction between absolute duty and relative duty, or between the right *(kathòrtoma)*, and social duty *(kathékon)*.[2] The distinction yielded some kind of escape-way for normal people who choose to live a normal life in human society while avoiding the early Stoics' choice to retreat from the world. "Social duty" amounts to pursuing the *honestum*, or what is convenient and appropriate, including four basic goods, namely wisdom, or love of knowledge; social feeling, or preservation of human society implying distributive justice and mutual loyalty; magnanimity, or strength of mind; self-control.[3] Virtue, consisting in "nature itself when led to perfection,"[4] or in reason as the distinctive human faculty,[5] belongs to the domain of *honestum*. Virtue is plural, and in fact it includes the four basic virtues listed by Plato that were to become known as the "cardinal" virtues: wisdom, understood in probabilistic terms, which implies that prudence is a virtue also in theoretical matters, and accordingly assent to unfounded beliefs should be denied and useless speculations should be avoided; justice understood as including benevolence and based on the assumptions of natural sociability and equality; strength of mind; and self-control.[6]

An important change within the Humanistic tradition was the seventeenth-century revival of natural law theory. It implied a less drastic break than several among its proponents wanted us to believe in so far as, firstly, the very idea of natural law was an item from the Ciceronian legacy, secondly, the doctrine held by Grotius and Pufendorf owed something to Spanish baroque Scholasticism. Besides, even if it were true that the proponents of the new natural law theory were influenced by the abovementioned "Cartesian" programs of reforming moral philosophy on the

---

[2] Cicero, *De officiis,* 1.1.8.
[3] *Ibid.,* 1.5.15.
[4] *Ibid.,* 2.5.17.
[5] *Ibid.,* 1.15.49.
[6] *Ibid.,* 1.6.18-19; 1.17.53-58; 1.17.29; 1.19.62; 1.27.93.

blueprint of natural philosophy, and notably Pufendorf was Hobbes's critical follower, all this did not imply any drastic break with Ciceronianism. The reason is that Cicero was not just a rhetorician, but was first of all a Middle-Academic philosopher, a proponent of probabilism, a theory of knowledge that was rather compatible, albeit not with Cartesianism, at least with Baconianism, that is, with one among the philosophical programs inspiring the seventeenth-century "new science."

Samuel von Pufendorf was the author of *De jure naturae et gentium* (1672),[7] where a modified version of Grotius's natural-law theory was presented, less objectivist and more constructivist in its foundations, being grounded in a kind of (non-strictly theological) voluntarism like Hobbes and Locke. Pufendorf's theory up to the time of the French Revolution was assumed to be the paramount account of modern natural law theory and the doctrinal background for modern political revolutions. Precisely for this reason, after the French Revolution, Pufendorf fell suddenly from his high position into oblivion as an effect of Hegel's, Bentham's, and even Kant's criticism of natural law.

A remarkable circumstance is that Pufendorf, after *De jure*, published a shorter work, *De officio hominis et civis* (1673), which amounted to a simplified version of the former, where precisely the theoretical foundations of the doctrine were given for granted, and normative ethics only was illustrated in a rather detailed way.[8] Pufendorf advances three main theoretical claims. The first, taken from Grotius, is the universal validity of natural law, and this implies that the latter is based on Reason instead of Authority. An implication is that natural law is different from positive laws as well as from moral theology, both requiring acknowledgement of some previous authority. Another is that no distinction on principle exists between ethics and natural law. His second claim is that a science of natural law is made possible by the fact that human capacity to know the natural law, the Original Sin notwithstanding, is still alive, or that "our knowledge of this law, yet, may be named natural in so far as its necessary truth may be proved by mental processes or by natural reason."[9] His third claim is that we can reconstruct the natural law only by an *a priori* way, not by an *a posteriori* or empirical way like Grotius, and even less by tracing the good or bad consequences of human actions like

[7] Pufendorf, S. von (1998) *De jure naturae et gentium*, 2 vols., ed. by F. Böhling. Berlin: Akademie Verlag.

[8] Pufendorf, S. von (1997) *De officio hominis et civis*, ed. by G. Hartung. Berlin: Akademie Verlag.

[9] *Ibid.*, Book II, chap. III, § 20.

proto-consequentialist Richard Cumberland. We should start with observation of traits shared by human beings in order to single out a core of unchanging normative principles and then from these we should infer more detailed prescriptions.[10]

On the above theoretical basis, Pufendorf bases his claim that a set of prescriptions may be justified. The first is the prescription of sociability. He declares that human beings never lived outside social life, since the state of nature was, unlike Hobbes, an original peaceful condition. There are indeed kinds of human society, like that of American Indians, that are closer to the state of nature, but human beings need a more complex social life because of their weakness.[11] Human beings are marked by both a need for help and an ability to produce rules. Out of this twofold character of human nature the first precept of natural law follows, namely "every human being should have, as far as he can, a friendly attitude towards other human beings."[12] Such a basic prescription provides the logical premise for more detailed ones. There is a rule for deriving prescriptions from the overarching law of sociability, namely, that if we are bound to pursuing some end we are also bound to pursuing means to such end, and thus "everything that necessarily follows from such sociable attitude should be assumed to be prescribed by the law of nature."[13] By this rule an obligation follows to learn a habit of refraining from damaging others, a duty to benefit them, a duty to improve our talents, a duty to give others free access to those things we can give them at no cost. The mentioned prescriptions are dictates of reason established by observation and rational inquiry on human nature. A theological postulate adds normative force to such dictates and makes the phrase "natural laws" appropriate, namely that human beings were created by God with such dispositions in order to make co-operation and social life possible. On the one hand, the postulate makes the shift from *is* to *ought* possible and, on the other, it does not play the function of a starting-point for *deduction* of moral prescriptions from any divine command. This implies that Pufendorf's doctrine may not be fairly deemed to fall under Kant's censure of "heteronomy."

The *De officio* became an immensely popular work, the text-book for virtually any educated European teenager for 150 years. In fact, from

---

[10] Pufendorf, S. von (1996) "An Hohan Christian von Boineburg 13.1.1677," in *Briefwechsel*, ed. by D. Döring. Berlin: Akademie Verlag: 24-27.

[11] Pufendorf, *De officio hominis et civis*, Book II, chap. II, § 14.

[12] *Ibid.*, Book II, chap. III, § 15.

[13] *Ibid.*

its original language, Latin, it was translated into French, Italian, Danish, Spanish, and Russian. Yet, after 1800 it was soon forgotten, firstly because it had acquired the image of a dangerous work, a Jacobin manual, secondly because Kant forced it into the pigeonhole containing "heteronymous" natural law theories, thirdly because Hegel labelled natural law theory as anti-historical nonsense, and last of all because natural law theory was defined by Bentham as "nonsense upon stilts."

The third and final step in the story of the teaching of natural morality is an unwritten work by Kant, namely his "moral catechism." This Kantian project is, on the one hand, an example of what a popular version of natural morality would have been. On the other hand, the circumstance that the project was abandoned as soon as it was formulated by Kant, that nobody ever tried to write primary-school handbooks of morality, and that no government or – as far as I know – no independent educational institution ever tried to bring Kant's project into practice, illustrates well how far the path undertaken between the fifteenth and the eighteenth centuries was dramatically interrupted at the beginning of the nineteenth century.

The mentioned moral catechism was not one of Kant's unpublished works. It was instead one of his "unwritten doctrines." The moral catechism was in fact a work Kant himself never set out to write but just a subject he wanted to be introduced into basic education. Kant's "pure" moral philosophy, that is Kantian ethics as presented in the *Groundwork* and the *Critique of Practical Reason*, was meant to cover just one half of practical philosophy, the other half being "empirical moral philosophy" or "moral anthropology." This discipline was meant to carry out an empirical study of man not from a theoretical but from a "practical" point of view. Its subject matter is "the subjective conditions in human nature that may help or hinder compliance with the moral law."[14] Kant urges that morality cannot really exist "without anthropology,"[15] for you have to "know first the moral agent in order to realize whether he is able to do what he is expected to do,"[16] and any morality that would try to ignore anthropology would be "just an idea, or a purely speculative subject."[17]

---

[14] Kant, I. (1902) *Metaphysik der Sitten* (1797,) in *Kant's gesammelte Schriften*, ed. by the Berlin-Brandenburgischen Akademie der Wissenschaften. Berlin : Meiner & de Gruyter, (abbr. Ak), vol. VI: 217.

[15] *Ibid.*

[16] Kant, I. *Moralphilosophie Collins*, in Ak, vol. XXVII\1: 244.

[17] *Ibid.*

A presentation of Kant's anthropology is offered in the *Anthropology in a Pragmatic Outlook*. The title reveals that Kant intends to present it not directly as an auxiliary discipline of ethics, but instead as a part of that "knowledge of the world" which is required as a means to happiness. But, since the quest for happiness carries the growth of civilization as an unintended outcome, and since *civilization* is a pre-condition to *moralization*, the discipline's true goal is the formation of character, understood as a "transformation of one's own way of thinking." The later is the decisive aspect of the "doctrine of method" of practical reason, that is the doctrine of the "way" (Greek: *odos*) to virtue.[18] Kant assumes that virtue can be taught, but also that such a teaching does not consist in information about duties and even less in exhortation to their practice. He adds that teaching virtue implies exercise through a never-ending fight against the "inner enemy," but also that such exercise would be meaningless without a former decision for virtue and against vice.[19] Such a teaching may not be given through lectures but should be carried out through dialogue between the teacher and the pupil, aimed at helping the pupil's own discovery of moral truths.[20] And yet the dialogical method cannot be displayed in a void, without any previous notion; a preliminary step is provided by some basic learning, not acquired in an *"acromatic"* way, that is, by lecturing, but instead in an *"erotematic"* one, that is, through questioning, but still addressing the pupil's memory, not yet his reason as the dialogical method will do.

> The first and necessary doctrinal tool by which a still uneducated pupil can be taught the doctrine of virtue is a moral catechism. This should come before religious catechism and should not be included, as a purely accidental item, among other items of religious instruction, but should be taught instead separately and as a self-standing whole; for only by means of purely moral principles the shift from the doctrine of virtue to religion can be made[21].

Contents can be derived "from reason, as it is shared by every human being,"[22] and the catechism should cover all virtues and vices and should be compiled in such a way as to suggest constantly the idea that the motivating force of duty is never grounded in advantages or disadvantages for

---

[18] Kant, I. *Anthropologie in Pragmatischer Sicht* (1798,), in Ak, vol. VII: 291-295; see also the "Methodenlehre der reinen praktischen Vernunft," in *Kritik der praktischen Vernunft* (1788,) in Ak, vol. V: 149-163 ; and the "Ethische Methodenlehre," in *Metaphysik der Sitten*: 477-485.

[19] Kant, *Metaphysik der Sitten*: 477.

[20] *Ibid.*: 478.

[21] *Ibid.*

[22] *Ibid.*: 479.

the agent, and even for other people, but solely in the pure moral principle.

Virtue may be learned and practiced not so much through intellectual learning as by imitation. The latter depends on sensibility, not on the intellect, and its force lies in the force of example as standard *(Exempel)* as distinguished from example as anecdote *(Beispiel)*. Such a motivating force, yet, goes beyond basic imitation mechanisms, since a living *Exempel* gives us a proof "of the possibility of acting according to duty."[23] Accordingly, it does not consist in comparison with any other human being (as he actually is), but just in comparison with the idea of humankind, or with the idea of how a human being should be. The final goal is neither that of teaching a theory, not to say a "technical doctrine" for problem-solving, nor that of improving habits, but instead producing a radical transformation in the individual's "way of thinking."[24] This is the reason why moral education, instead of just fighting vices, should start with a "conversion in the way of thinking, the building of a character."[25] This is why moral theory is no more than a kind of "geometry" of morality while real-world or morality is a matter of judgment, moral motivation depends on the force of Example, and the good moral agent is not an agent trained to *applying* rules but instead an agent who has learned to *interpret* situations, that is to "see" the one salient moral characteristic in a state of affairs, or to answer the question: "what is really going on?"

3. AFTER THE ENLIGHTENMENT: RELIGION *INSTEAD OF* ETHICS

In nineteenth-century Europe a few processes started, both at the level of the history of ideas and at the level of social history, and they influenced each other and mutually reinforced each other's effects.

Firstly, a climate of suspicion against eighteenth-century ideas and ideals established itself. It went with Romanticism, Idealism, and Historicism, not to mention cruder kinds of Traditionalism, all of which tended to deny any validity to universal claims and to attack allegedly a-historical doctrines. The rights of man, natural law, rational or natural morality became targets for opprobrium. Strangely enough, also Utilitarianism and Kantian Ethics, that were in different ways the heirs of the Enlightenment tradition, contributed to this campaign against such au-

---

[23] *Ibid.*: 480; on the role of *Exempel* in Kantian ethics, or better, in Kant's "unwritten ethical doctrines," see Ferrara, A. (2008) *The Force of the Example. Explorations in the Paradigm of Judgment*. New York: Columbia University Press, ch. I.

[24] *Ibid.*: 411; see also *Anthropologie*: 294-5.

[25] Kant, I. *Die Religion innerhalb der Grenzen der bloßen Vernunft* (1793,) in Ak, vol. VI: 55.

thors as Pufendorf, albeit for reasons opposite to those endorsed by the counter-Enlightenment camp. The combined effect was nonetheless oblivions of the natural morality tradition.

Secondly, apart from the Austrian Empire and Scotland, where a universal education system, either state-based or run by local municipal governments or "parishes," had been established in the second half of the eighteenth century, in most European countries a general primary education system was established during the nineteenth century. One of the basic questions for which a solution was sought from the very beginning was that of the place for religious instruction in such a system.

In Britain, a country where an awareness of religious pluralism could less easily be denied than elsewhere, the most enlightened minds tended to converge on a compromise, namely inter-confessional Christian education. This was the proposal endorsed by so different proponents as Richard Whately, an Anglican Bishop, and Sarah Porter née Ricardo, a sister of the economist David Ricardo, a novelist and essayist who was a member of the Liberal elite. Such a solution was commendable for being an attempt to overcome the identification between the Church of England and the State, but it strikingly left out of sight non-Christian minorities including the Jewish community whence Sarah Ricardo herself came.

In most European countries, except France, the obvious solution was believed to be religious instruction in the prevailing Christian Confession. Among them the most liberal version of such a solution was gradually introduced in the Austrian Empire, as far as, at least at the eve of World War I in Austro-Hungarian Gymnasiums two hours a week instruction in the "Mosaic Faith" were scheduled for Jewish students. In France in 1905 an absolute separation of State and Church was established and the teaching of religion as such was banned from public education.

In the course of the above process, no mention of any teaching of morality as distinguished from religious education in Kant's sense was ever made. A need for religious instruction was assumed as a matter of fact, with the modest amendments of the British early solution of inter-Confessional instruction, the Austrian late solution of confessional pluralism, and the striking French "republican" exception. The vague idea was still cherished here and there by some radical Democrat that education should include some teaching of the "duties of man," but it was never taken too seriously. The ruling elites, increasingly secularized and indeed in overt conflict with the Christian Churches, tended everywhere – with the remarkable exception of France – to think that, facing the social issue, tendencies to Durkheimian "anomie" as a result of urbanization, and diffusion of socialist ideas, the local prevailing religion was the easiest means of "educating" the masses to decent behaviour.

A different parallel discussion would deserve a remarkable amount of space about the way of conceiving subjects as history, literature and, in higher education, philosophy. The fact that in virtually all countries in Continental Europe the school was conceived in terms of State school implies, in the historical context, that history was conceived as culminating with National History. On the other hand, literature was National Literature, aimed at cultivating the myth of a National spiritual heritage, and understood as a means of imbibing pupils with supposedly peculiar (Italian, German…) feelings, moral traits, and virtues.

In short, my suggestion is that the result of the compromise between the ruling elites and the Churches was religion as a vehicle of values and models of behaviour for the uneducated masses, and the bulk of education as a means of manipulating the masses into a supposedly shared legacy of national values.

One word may be added on the teaching of philosophy in Gymnasiums and equivalent kinds of high schools. With the remarkable exception of France, where the systematic teaching of philosophy by subdisciplines survived, the German model of Philosophy as the History of Philosophy prevailed, and the subtle message this teaching suggested to future elites was that the course of history, both intellectual and political, was tantamount to the *Coming of Reason* and the only Morality and Religion of the educated (male) man was adhesion to this course, or faith in an identity of freedom and necessity.

As a result of a story of fight and compromise between the ruling elites and the leadership of Christian Churches, three parallel processes took place.

1. Normative ethics, or natural morality, that had been a distinct subject in the education of European elites from the Renaissance times to the end of the eighteenth century, disappeared as such, being partly allotted to the Churches via the teaching of religion in State School, and partly absorbed by the study of history and literature, assumed to be channels for imbibing younger generations with the shared values of the State, the Nation, or the People. Normative ethics as an academic subject became either a battlefield for ideological wars (like the utilitarian campaign for the New Morality, the religious conservative campaign against the modern demise of moral values) or somewhat of a taboo (like the historicist neo-Idealist

view of Philosophy, that is the History of Philosophy, as the educated man's Religion and Morality).

2. Religion, or better the prevailing religion or, in most countries, the "State Religion," became a compulsory subject in the State school. Both the *State* school and *Religion* as a discipline were indeed novelties. The framework, its apparent similarity notwithstanding, was rather the opposite of the Medieval one within which schools were almost invariably Church-based institutions and Religion was not a subject or a discipline but a practice (what was a discipline was instead theology, taught to those who reached the top level in education).

One invisible implication was a division of labour between the lay ruling elite and the Churches, namely a tacit agreement according to which Homer belonged to the secular ruling class and the Bible was the clergy's private property, which would never be made the subject of a critical-historical study as the former instead was expected to be.

3. A result of the mentioned tacit pact between two ruling groups was that the canon of European culture was transformed into something less consistent and less comprehensive than its previous post-Renaissance version had been. In more detail, the tradition to be transmitted to younger generations was construed around a fable, or better a lie, namely that the modern European is the ancient Greek's grandson, and the ancient Hebrew had nothing to bequest to the Modern European. Besides, the canon was reduced to a bark without a kernel, in so far as *literature* and *history* took the place that used to belong to "philosophy" or to *Studia Humanitatis*.

4. Moral Traditions, Religions, Political Institutions, and Critical Reflection

The morale of my story is the following:

A study of the history of moral (and religious and political) ideas combined with critical reflection on social practices should provide the core or the leading subject in education. The large-scale Spanish experiment, and the small-scale Belgian one, in teaching ethics as a subject alternative to the teaching of the Catholic or Protestant religion are not bad examples for possible future developments. The Swedish experiment that made room for comparative religious studies as a subject substituting religious instruction is another interesting example. Yet, both are just interesting starting points, not viable general answers to the question I have asked. The problem with both experiments is being the result of piecemeal social engineering. In the Spanish case ethics is an alternative to religion as if those who want to learn about one religion did not need to learn about ethics and could go on ignoring the existence of more than one religion, and those who want to learn about ethics would better ignore the existence of religions. In the Swedish case the study of religions in a comparative outlook is one half of the right answer but it leaves the other half, *i.e.* morality, aside.

The open questions are: (i) why should *ethics* be an alternative to *religion*? Do those who are educated *into* one religion – which I assume should be done *outside* a public educational system – need not to learn anything about ethics?; (ii) why should children of Protestants, Jews, and Atheists learn about religions and not about morality?; (iii) why should the study of religions be a separate subject, unless it is so just because of historical reasons, that is, the fact of having taken the place of confessional religious instruction? Wouldn't the study of history gain from becoming less a study of political history and more a study of social history as well as of the history of religious/moral/political movements from Buddhism and Judaism to Cynicism, Epicureanism and so on?

My practical recommendations are:

1. Abolishing the teaching of religion in schools where it still exists; this may happen hopefully without ideological wars, as the result of a dialogue between the civil society and the Churches, where the latter may understand that they may forfeit various kinds of control over public education while winning the more valuable promise of a society where citizens will learn in a critical way about the Bible, the Qurān, the Buddhist canon, and Confucius.
2. Abolishing any kind of political education as a separate subject, that is, subjects like the Italian *educazione civica* or the Spanish *educación para la ciudadanía* should go under the heading "ethics."
3. Establishing one subject named "ethics," compulsory for *all*, that is, for children of Islamic no less than of Atheist parents, with a syllabus including: a) critical reflection on values, norms, and institutions regulating private/social lives in our society as well as in other societies starting with examples from everyday life, the media, literature, and history and reaching the study of sources from Confucius and Homer to Cicero, Aquinas, Luther, Calvin, Voltaire... up to Peter Singer; b) critical reflection on the structure and normative justification of national and international political institutions and legal codes.
4. Revising the syllabus of the subject "history" in such a way as to cut down the room assigned to political history and give the spare room to social history and history of religions *and* moralities. This should start with critical reflection on religious beliefs and practices followed by var-

ious communities in our societies (plus rituals, customs, symbolic practices with an apparently non-religious character) compared with those of different societies, reaching a study of sources such as the Bible, the Talmud, the Qurān, Aquinas, Luther, Calvin, Voltaire, Marx, Nietzsche, etc.

5. Revising the syllabus of the subject "literature" in order to transform it into comparative literature, that is: (i) abolishing the dominating notion of "Classics" (that is Hellenic and Roman religious or mythological texts plus some profane poetry which have been falsely believed to be *the* source of secular modern civilization); (ii) establishing the study, besides national and modern European literature, of basic texts from the various world civilizations, Chinese, Indian, Egyptian, and Hebrew, Hellenic, Roman, Christian, Islamic; this would carry a study of the Egyptian *Book of the Dead*, the Indian *Bhagavad Gītā*, the Babylonian *Epic of Gilgamesh* and *Qoheleht* as texts with an equal status to *Ilyad*, *Odyssey*, and *Aeneids*, as well as a study of the latter as *serious* texts, not just as either literature for fun or tools for philological torture.

The rationale of my practical recommendations is that education in a liberal-democratic society may not be socialization *into* the given set of values of a national community but should be just training *to* critical thinking.

DURKHEIM: THE GOAL OF EDUCATION IN A DEMOCRATIC STATE IS AUTONOMY

Asger SØRENSEN

The world is in crisis: Ecologically, financially, and politically. For Émile Durkheim (1858-1917), however, the diagnosis of a societal situation as pathological should not make us just wait for the solution simply to happen by the grace of God, the general equilibrium or the logic of history behind our backs, be it ideal or material. Durkheim is a modern democratic republican, who believes social reality to be the outcome of human activity, and a diagnosis of the pathologies of capitalism must therefore include ideas for a cure. Human beings can cure social diseases, since society is a political reality, which can be different, as already Aristotle made clear.[1]

According to Durkheim the current social disease is partly moral, both in relation to society and to the individual, and part of the cure is therefore education, or to be more specific, *Moral Education*,[2] *L'éducation morale*,[3] which in 1925 became the posthumous title of a collection of Durkheim's lectures. In these lectures his aim was precisely to discuss the educational principles and practices, which were necessary to cope with the challenges of a modernity, which gets its main ideological momentum from enlightenment, i.e. science and rationality, and these are as relevant today as when they were written more than one hundred years ago.[4]

---

[1] Aristotle, *Nicomachean Ethics* in Aristotle (1995) *The Complete Works of* ... New Jersey: Princeton University Press, vol. 2, *Eth. Nic.*, 1139a ff.

[2] Durkheim, Émile (1961) *Moral Education*. New York: Free Press.

[3] Durkheim, Émile (2005) *L'éducation morale* (abbr. *L'éducation*). Paris: Éditions Fabert.

[4] Durkheim's merits in philosophy of education has gone largely unnoticed outside France. There is no mention of him in otherwise very inclusive works such as Wolfgang Fischer & Dieter-Jürgen Löwisch (eds.), *Philosophen als Pädagogen*. Darmstadt: Wissenschaftliche Buchgesesellschaft, 1998; Nigel Blake *et. al.* (eds.), *The Blackwell Guide to the Philosophy of Education*. Oxford: Blackwell, 2003; and Randall Curren (ed.), *Philosophy of Education. An Anthology*. Oxford: Blackwell, 2007. Even in the most comprehensive modern reference work, *A Companion to the Philosophy of Education*, ed. by R. Curren (Oxford: Blackwell, 2006), he is only mentioned once in passing and as a social theorist. Directly on the "unpopularity on Durkheim's work on education," see G. Walford & W. S. F. Pickering, "Introduction," in Walford & Pickering (eds.), *Durkheim and Modern Education*. London: Routledge, 1998: 1-10.

For Durkheim morality is thus not primarily an individual phenomenon, actually quite the contrary. Morality must first be understood at the societal level, and that brings discussions of morality and education in close contact with politics and the challenges from the dynamics of capitalist economy. These political challenges and the proposed answers are dealt with in another collection of lectures, posthumously edited and published in 1950 as *Leçons de sociologie*,[5] which in English has become *Professional Ethics and Civic Morals*.[6] Here we find his arguments for a republican democracy and the ideals of a modern state, and this article will sketch the logic that connects Durkheim's proposals for moral education with his political philosophy.

1. To Moralize Economy and Cure Society We Need a State

To Durkheim the most advanced societies in the beginning of the 20th century are modern societies, and they are in crisis, a crisis that is to be conceived of in terms of both economy and morality. His point is that since early enlightenment in the 18th century economy has developed from a secondary social function to the primary function in society.[7] This becomes a problem to modern society, since contrary to a lot of other social roles and professions, occupation within economy, i.e. trade, industry, entrepreneurship, etc., does not encourage the development of strong moral virtues, values and ideals. To Durkheim the amorality of economic life therefore becomes a public danger to society.[8] Liberating economy means that a still larger part of human life is lived without or beyond morality, and the result will eventually be a demoralization of society. To Durkheim the answer is to moralize the economy, and that means to regulate it. This is the only way to make sure that economic activities are organized collectively and rationally, conducted according to rules determining rights as well as duties, detailed and concisely, and not just improvised according to individual whims.[9]

To moralize economy thus means to accept a regulation of economy by something, we would normally call a state. As a good Aristotelian, Durkheim thinks that human beings always live in groups. These groups can be more or less organized, but they are all particular and real in the strongest sense, since they are constituted by people, who have things in

---

[5] Durkheim, Émile (1997) *Leçons de sociologie* (abbr. *Leçons*). Paris: P.U.F.

[6] Durkheim, Émile (1992) *Professional Ethics and Civic Morals*. London: Routledge.

[7] *Leçons*: 50.

[8] *Ibid.*: 51.

[9] *Ibid.*: 52

common, things which are part of their common consciousness, that is, common representations or common ideas.[10] In a global perspective humanity as such is therefore neither a group nor a society. For Durkheim the highest possible human organisation must be thought of as within a particular society, and in a descriptive perspective the most highly organized human group is the modern state.[11] The state is characterized by being a political society, which means a society composed of various secondary groups such as those mentioned and families, professions, local communities, castes, etc.[12] Such a political society can also be composed of other political societies, and one can therefore have a continuity or better, a hierarchy of political societies, which means that what is considered a state can actually be subordinate to higher political society,[13] as for instance is the case today in the USA and the EU.

In one sense the state is thus itself a political society. Durkheim, however, also thinks of the state as a special function within a society, namely the organ for societal thinking, deliberation and decision. Durkheim's idea is that the state in this sense should be separated from society in order to think and decide for society. The state should develop the representations common to society and change the diffuse common consciousness into a clear self-consciousness of the society in question, making thereby society aware of its causes and goals. To accomplish this Hegelian task the state constitutes organs for deliberation, namely councils, commissions, parliaments, where it can develop the representations most valuable for society. The state then is an organ for social deliberation, which is precisely not just speculative, but practical in its ambitions, namely to govern the collective behaviour of society.

It is important here to underline that the state thus conceived is neither the monopoly of power, nor the apparatus which serve to hold the population in order. The state is thus not the executive power,[14] and neither is it the judicial power. According to Durkheim both the legal system and the army are to be considered secondary groups in relation to the state thus conceived.[15] Since Durkheim is a scholar of Montesquieu,[16] he

[10] Durkheim, Émile (1996) "Représentations individuelles et représentations collectives," in Durkheim, *Sociologie et philosophie*. Paris: Presses Universitaires de France: 1-48. [In English, *Sociology and Philosophy*. New York: Free Press, 1974.]

[11] *L'éducation*: 113-15.

[12] *Leçons*: 79-81.

[13] *Ibid.*: 84.

[14] *Ibid.*: 87.

[15] *Ibid.*: 85.

must be supposed to be familiar with the separation of powers recommended by the latter. Claiming that the state is neither a judicial nor an executive power thus amounts to saying that the state ought to be the legislative power. The state thinks, decides and communicates its decisions by issuing orders to the executive powers, which then take action.[17] The state is a society in itself and as such it is an organ for authority, or better: an agent for sovereign authority.[18] As an authority, however, the state is not necessarily authoritarian. On the contrary it can be both valuable and desirable for its citizens.

2. The Bigger The State The Greater The Freedom

This is the basic structure of the state that is supposed to moralize the economy and cure the modern society of its current illness. The societal necessity of a state thus conceived can of course vary. Durkheim notes the difference between states at peace and states at war, where the extent of control and authority is much bigger in the latter than in the former. In this case the functions of the state multiply, they become more important, and Durkheim notes that just as the human brain can be developed so can the social. What is interesting is that this growth is not just temporary and limited to times of war; actually such a development has been constant up through human history.[19] For a classical liberalist big government – i.e. the state – is the biggest threat to human freedom, and Durkheim notes that if this was descriptively correct, then human freedom should have diminished up through history. Instead he wants to argue that actually the opposite is the case; namely, the bigger the state the greater the freedom.

Historically Durkheim recognizes the obvious fact that the division of labour has been developed both quantitatively and qualitatively, meaning that more and more people in modern societies are highly specialized in their particular skills. Since civilisation means that our needs have been developed in numbers and refined each by themselves, this means that more and more individual specialists are indispensable to the smooth functioning of a modern civilisation such as ours. To Durkheim it is therefore understandable that the individual is more highly valued in a modern society than in less developed societies. Already at the time of Durkheim one could recognize a modern "cult of the individual," an es-

---

[16] Durkheim, Émile (1953) *Montesquieu et Rousseau, précurseurs de la sociologie*. Petite Bibliothèque Sociologique International. [In English: *Montesquieu and Rousseau: Forerunners of Sociology*. Ann Arbor, Mich.: University of Michigan Press, 1960.]

[17] *Leçons*: 86-87.

[18] *Ibid.*: 84.

[19] *Ibid.*: 88-90.

teem of the individual as the highest "moral reality," protected by awe and "respect."[20] Modern morality thus holds individual human beings highly in regard. Durkheim, however, wants to stress this does not mean a threat to the cohesion of society, quite the contrary. Since modern individuals in general share the respect for the individual as a common value, it can be considered the basis of a specific kind of solidarity, which Durkheim calls 'organic' and considers normal for the modern society.[21]

For Durkheim this is the reason to value modernity and the actual historical development of society. He wants to argue for the possibility of individual freedom without unacceptable liberalistic and legalistic assumptions. Individuality must be a collective moral project, which is part of the moralization and regulation of capitalist economy. Durkheim thinks practically, aiming to entrench the moral respect for the individual, and this can be thought of in two ways, individually and collectively. Individually the entrenchment is brought about by formation, education, and upbringing in general; collectively by the creation of such values as common and institutionalising them, that is, entrenching them with legitimacy in the customs and behaviour accepted by society, maintaining the thing-like character of the moral respect without its religious overtones. Durkheim wants both as part of the same socialization process.

Durkheim declares himself to be a rationalist in the sense that no part of reality is inaccessible to human reason.[22] This should be understood in the Aristotelian way, as comprising both the theoretical and the practical relation to reality. Durkheim is not quite clear on this point however. He thus argues that reality can be understood rationally without being changed substantially.[23] The ambition of Durkheim is, first, to study the respect for the individual rationally, and then, second, on this basis to secularize it as reasonable, and this must be done without losing its moral imperative force. So Durkheim actually does want to change something, namely rationalizing morality and thereby moral thought and action. This may sound rather optimistic, but Durkheim would argue that part of the

---

[20] *Ibid.*: 92.

[21] 'Normal' is here to be understood as 'ideal.' Durkheim was well aware that social solidarity in reality was threatened by class conflict, and he regarded social justice as an "indispensable" "condition" for the realization of organic solidarity (Durkheim, Émile (1893) *De la division du travail social*. Paris: Félix Alcan: 420-34). [In English: *The Division of Labour in Society*. New York: Macmillan, 1933.] For a standard account of organic solidarity, see Lukes, Steven (1985) *Emile Durkheim. His Life and Work*. Stanford Univ. Press: 146-66.

[22] *L'éducation*: 34.

[23] *Ibid.*: 161-62.

job is actually done by the historical development of modern societies, politics and science, which favours the individual as the bearer of reason.

This leads to the other part of the answer, namely the faith in the potentialities of both human beings and societies, cherishing them both as something valuable, which can nevertheless be otherwise. The individual can raise itself to something beyond itself, precisely because the individual is never just an individual, but, as it is often put in dialectics, always already social and historical. As Durkheim puts it, the best in us comes from society,[24] but this is not a static thing; just as human beings can improve so can societies, and they both do so by improving on the other.

What is interesting is that Durkheim is convinced that the growth of the state adds to this improvement, saying that the stronger the state, the better the conditions for the individual and its personal freedom. Durkheim would therefore recommend continuing the development of the state even more, precisely to add to the freedom of the individual, and that is interesting considering the political discussions and the societal development in the wake of post-modernity, which all have pointed in the opposite direction.

Durkheim admits that apparently this is a paradox,[25] but the solution is ready at hand: namely, recognizing that the individual is not given as a human individual by nature. We have rights, values, prices, because they are given to us by society, not because of the natural constitution of things.[26] Durkheim explicitly criticises Kant for thinking human rights as natural, given once and for all, making the human being something not to be violated.[27] Humans are only humans because of society, and when the individual is not given by nature, the sovereign cannot be restricted to being a simple arbiter. If the individual is a product of society, and the state is the brain of society, the state is also responsible for the creation of the individual. It is therefore quite right that society is experienced as valuable and that the individual experience becoming social as being elevated by society.[28]

Durkheim, however, is very conscious of the fact that human groups tend to absorb their members. To Durkheim it is first of all a matter of social density. The more extensive the group is, the lesser are the possibilities of such an absorption by elevation. Put in another way, the

---

[24] *Ibid.*: 106.
[25] *Leçons*: 93.
[26] *Ibid.*: 102.
[27] *Ibid.*: 101.
[28] *Ibid.*: 96.

possibilities of social control and thus the tyranny of the collective diminish simply because of the lesser social density.[29] Modern societies, however, are very dense societies, so this does not offer a general solution, and the general point is that one cannot rely on human groups to regulate this balance by themselves. We need a state to regulate society in order to secure freedom within society. The modern individual is a creation of the modern state, and it is only this creature that can realize freedom.

It is important to notice that this was not Durkheim's position in the first version of *De la division du travail social*, *The Social Division of Labour* from 1893. Here society does not need a political state in order to moralize economy, and this early position can be seen as an even more advanced liberal vision than Adam Smith's, since Durkheim did not even have to rely on God's invisible hand. A few years later, though, he recognized that he had been too optimistic, and in the second edition of the book from 1902 he added a new introduction, where he argues for the development of intermediary groups to secure the unity of society.[30] This, however, does not mean that Durkheim turns from a liberal into a communitarian. In his political lectures these secondary groups are recognized as potentially and often really suppressive, and to secure the freedom of the individual it is therefore necessary to institute a counterbalance. This counterbalance is the state.

For Durkheim it is thus the balance of power between the state and the secondary groups that is to secure the freedom of the individual. It is, however, important to emphasize that it is not just the balance of power that secures individual freedom; the state is valuable in itself to the freedom of the individual. Since secondary groups like families, clans and religious communities are formed by society before the state, Durkheim can regard the state as liberating the individual by bestowing the individual with rights and value simply as an individual, namely as a person. It is in this sense that the state constitutes and creates the individual. Durkheim can therefore declare that the essential function of the state is to liberate the individual. Still, the state is also a particular social group itself, and to avoid that it becomes despotic and absorbing as such, it is necessary that secondary groups ounterbalance the state, and it is out of these complex webs of conflicting balances within the state that the freedom of the individual is born.[31] From Montesquieu, Durkheim thus inher-

---

[29] *Ibid.*: 97.

[30] See Lukes, *Emile Durkheim*: 539. See also *Leçons*: 134-35.

[31] *Leçons*: 97-98.

its the idea of using power against power to secure the freedom of the citizens.

An individual with natural, political, legal or civil rights is an individual recognized and thus protected as such by a state. Such an individual is the product of a state, and actually the state is liberating for the individual since the state recognizes the rights of individuals, whereas secondary groups are less permissive. As mentioned, one of the reasons for this is the lesser size of secondary groups. Another reason, however, is more interesting. The basic idea is that the state is the thinking centre of society, an organ for clarity and reason. As such it can legitimately intervene in secondary groups, since clarity is valuable and the collective consciousness of secondary groups by definition is more diffuse. The reason is simply that secondary groups are not preoccupied with ruling a heterogeneous political society, but can rely on the traditional morality of a homogeneous group to simply rule itself.

3. A Strong Democratic State is The Best Defence Against Capitalist Economy

The state is thus both the conscious creator and the reasonable protector of the individual. What can be said of government and democracy on those conditions? Durkheim criticizes Aristotle and Montesquieu for occupying themselves too much with the number of persons involved in government. Both the representatives in the parliament and the government are always in the minority, and the main point is not their numbers, but to mark the difference between those in government and those governed.[32] As we have seen, the state is a social group, which must take it upon itself to think for society. Social and political thought is common in society at large, consisting of hopes, beliefs and feelings, which mostly are diffuse, but which can be made clear by the state, that is, in the hands of a government.

Society and state are closely related and should be so. They represent two different kinds of collective psychic life, the first diffuse, unconscious, spontaneous, and automatic, whereas the latter is highly organized, centralized, reflective and takes place in deliberations and discussions, both by individuals themselves and in collective session. The aim of this Hegelian scheme is to develop the collective consciousness to become conscious of itself and thus ready to make decisions motivated by reason. The state helps society to be more disciplined, and the analogy is in this case for Durkheim the individual. The distinction between two

[32] *Ibid.*: 110-11.

kinds of psychic life is the same as for individuals; just as our behaviour can be more or less conscious, more or less governed, so can the behaviour of society.[33]

As mentioned, the state can be more or less involved in the life of society, meaning that government can extend its deliberations to greater or lesser areas. It can, however, also be expansive in another dimension, namely by the number of those involved in the deliberations, just as noticed by Aristotle and Montesquieu. Durkheim's point, however, is different. When the government extends its deliberations to the social groups affected by its decisions, it gets more information and can thus make better informed judgements. Governmental questions can be posed to society in various ways, and one way is simply to consult the population by making referendums from time to time. The communication, however, can also be made both more intense and continual, and that makes both the state and the government lose their sacred character. This, however, must not be taken as an ideal of dissolving the state into society. The state should still be clearly distinguished from society, since it is important that there is an organ dedicated to ruling society, which can reach an exceptional clarity in these matters. The ideal of democracy must not be made equivalent with society ruling itself, since society has many functions and cannot be trusted to develop a clear consciousness about itself.[34]

Durkheim's point about democracy is not just that more people are involved in the government of society, whereby it is closer to the ideals of collective popular sovereignty of the people. It is just as important that democracy means that governmental deliberations become more extensive in society, and that in itself makes government better. As mentioned, modern government expands the state into still more areas, and taken together these developments expand the domain of clear and conscious decisions in society. Such political enlightenment eventually makes development and progress possible in all areas of social life, since one can only improve what is conceived in a clear way. The more civilized a society thus becomes, the more democratic it becomes, and the better it can be governed in all corners of the social life.[35]

Democracy does not mean that the state is weak. Quite the contrary. It is true that democracy means the extension of consultations and communication to more people, more often and with more affairs left to ra-

---

[33] *Ibid.*: 113-14.
[34] *Ibid.*: 115.
[35] *Ibid.*: 117.

tional agreement; but at the same time democracy also means the extension of state authority into areas of social life, which were left to private decisions before.[36] This is what provokes modern libertarians. Apart from those areas already mentioned, Durkheim in this connection adds health and education,[37] and precisely these areas are often put in dispute by libertarians. The typical arguments are that the education of the individual is the responsibility of the family, not the state, and that health is the responsibility of the individual, not the state. To Durkheim this is simply nonsense, since there is no individual before the state. The state must therefore be developed even more, and democracy must also be understood as what history is actually progressing towards. Societies become more complex the more modern they become and thus more difficult to govern. In such societies the government would be in need of more and more information to make the right decisions, and Durkheim therefore considers democracy the only right way to govern future societies. Only the clarity about societal matters, which can be achieved in democracies, will enable a society to be flexible and adjust rapidly to changing circumstances.[38]

4. To Such a State One Needs Citizens Educated to Be Autonomous

For Durkheim the regulation by the state of society should thus be a regulation by society itself. This, however, does not mean letting everybody do as they please and then hoping for the best. In order to fulfill its role the state must be the most rational part of society, and this does not come by itself. A democratic society governed by a rational state is something that has to be formed intentionally and rationally, and according to Durkheim this is best done by developing the moral education of the inhabitants. To a democratic society education should be taken care of by the state in order to liberate the individual human being from secondary groups such as the family and the religious communities. The teacher must therefore meet the pupil already at an early age and treat the pupil accordingly. To Durkheim the right education must be a gradual actualization of the moral character, which at every step takes into account the emotional and cognitive potentialities of the child.

---

36 *Ibid.*: 122.
37 *Ibid.*: 120.
38 *Ibid.*: 124.

For Durkheim it is important to stress that the ideal is a rational education.[39] To be rational, however, does not mean that there is always a final answer on moral matters. We have to prepare children that morality changes in a society such as ours, and that they also have to contribute to that development.[40] To be rational means that we should not let religious prejudice or emotional haste determine our final verdicts. As potentially rational beings we should strive to make ourselves master of ourselves through moral education, which can be reconstructed into three elements, discipline, attachment to groups and autonomy. The school must form the child for the social life by stimulating these elements to become general dispositions.[41] They are all necessary for maturing human beings to become reasonable, but they should be encouraged at the right stages of development and in the right proportions.

Discipline is the basic condition, which should lead education in the early years, and since discipline today has some unpleasant connotations, it is important to understand it in the right sense from the start. First of all, Durkheim argues very strongly for an "absolute prohibition of corporal punishment," since it violates the modern idea of the human being as worthy of "religious respect."[42] According to Durkheim primitive people do not use violence in education, and modern educationalists like Tolstoy argue against the necessity of violence in education. According to Durkheim the problem, however, is the social structure of the school: "Because this society naturally has a monarchic form, it easily degenerates into despotism."[43] It is the closure of schools and classes that makes violent abuses possible. To avoid violence schools should therefore be made more open to the public, and classes should not be left alone too much with only one teacher. Durkheim recognizes the need for punishment, but it should be applied with great care. It is important to signal that there is a law, and that it ought to be obeyed, but already back then it was well known from criminology that punishment cannot be used to prevent transgressions of the law,[44] and Durkheim adds that punishment works best as a threat.[45]

---

[39] *L'éducation*: 35.
[40] *Ibid.*: 45.
[41] *Ibid.*: 53.
[42] *Ibid.*: 233-34.
[43] *Ibid.*: 249.
[44] *Ibid.*: 210-11.
[45] *Ibid.*: 251.

When Durkheim talks about discipline and authority the idea is to prepare the child for living in a democratic society, which offers a lot of freedom, but also demands a lot of inhibition. The aim of the education in school is that the children should learn to respect a non-personal law. In the family there is emotion and lenience, mildness and a lot of exceptions. In contrast to this the school represents “the first initiation to the austerity of duty. This is where the serious life begins.”[46] Discipline is valuable as a disposition since morality is the area of duties,[47] and duties require an ability to repeat actions under the same conditions,[48] almost like a habit. The duty refers to a rule, which refers to something beyond the single individual, and this something we acknowledge as an authority. Authority is to Durkheim a “moral power”[49] or “a quality of a human being raised beyond the merely human.”[50] We act in a certain way, because we accept the prescription of the authority, which appears as a moral rule or law.

Durkheim is well aware that this is controversial, and that one might very well consider discipline just a necessary evil. As he puts it, if life is good, how can it be desirable to constrain it?[51] There is no doubt that discipline is necessary to moderate desire and limit the appetites, and that moral education gives us the power to resist ourselves, to master ourselves.[52] Durkheim’s point is, however, that this is not against our nature, but a condition for the development of our nature.[53] Discipline is the condition for the development of our nature as reasonable beings, individually and collectively, as free citizens in a democratic society.[54] Human nature needs discipline. Freedom is not simply to do what one pleases at every moment, letting oneself be guided by impressions and whims. Freedom is to raise oneself above, what is merely corporal, emotional and animalistic. Without discipline autonomy, individual as well as collective, would be impossible.

The second element, attachment to groups, also calls for some remarks. Durkheim’s idea is that we must encourage children to love something beyond themselves. They already love their parents, but we want to

---

46 *Ibid.*: 197.
47 *Ibid.*: 56.
48 *Ibid.*: 60.
49 *Ibid.*: 62.
50 *Ibid.*: 130.
51 *Ibid.*: 60.
52 *Ibid.*: 79-80.
53 *Ibid.*: 87.
54 *Ibid.*: 85.

get beyond that. As Durkheim puts it, the domain of morality starts where the social starts.[55] Children should learn to love the specific groups to which they are actually attached, i.e. apart from the family also the school class, the school itself, the town or city and eventually the modern nation state. Durkheim's point is that society transgresses the individual both materially and morally.[56] Human beings are therefore only completed by being attached to more groups than one, and morality only when there is solidarity with all those groups.[57]

As mentioned above the state is something particular and real; but as the rational centre of society the state is also the highest possible human organization. Durkheim does not want to exclude the possibility that a global state one day would be able to comprise the whole of humanity, and one could say that the ideal state would be the global state, which automatically would make all citizens world citizens. Durkheim, however, emphasizes that the condition of both human morality and of a political order is a real society defined by its common representations about language, religion, custom, etc., and humanity is still not a society in this sense. And actually he is not sure whether this is actually an ideal to be realized.[58] In other words: maybe the ideal global state will then be a totality excluding the differences between groups and thus totalitarian, which means that it would not be desirable after all.

In relation to the ideal attachments there is thus a conflict – both conceptual and real – between patriotism and cosmopolitanism, which Durkheim, however, deals with in a very elegant dialectical way. The idea is to say that any actual state ought to realize the ideals of humanity; if this is made the case, then the conflict between particularistic patriotism and universalistic cosmopolitanism disappears. This, however, presupposes a distinction between two forms of patriotism. One form is turned against the outside, expansive and thus potentially always in conflict with its neighbours. The other is turned towards the inside, improving qualitatively what is already the patrimony and peacefully focused on the progress of national science, art and industry, thereby improving the lot of the population living there.[59] And it is of course the latter kind of patriotism that can be reconciled with cosmopolitanism.

---

[55] *Ibid.*: 96.
[56] *Ibid.*: 128.
[57] *Ibid.*: 112.
[58] *Ibid.*: 120.
[59] *Ibid.*: 114-15.

A state must by nature aim to maintain itself, and as such it must be patriotic. But patriotism can be turned inward to develop the patrimony within existing borders. That means that more areas of societal life will be the made the subject of public deliberation, and that clarity and reason will be demanded of the collective representations of the secondary groups in question. Traditional legitimacy is not enough anymore. The domain of the state will thus be extended into areas normally considered part of civil society, that is, religion, family, health, education, the labour market, and private economy in general.

Since the individual is becoming still more valuable in modern societies, the modern state must have the goal to govern the collective machine, as Durkheim formulates it, so that it will be felt less burdensome for the individual, securing peaceful exchange and the harmony of the individual good wills. But since modern society is also becoming still more complex in the same process, the state must spend more and more energy governing its own interiors. As a result the state becomes less and less occupied with the exterior and therefore also more peaceful in relation to its neighbours. It does not mean that wars simply disappear, only that they will tend to mean less for the modern states, relatively speaking.[60]

This makes it also more likely that one can actually experience the conflation of the two opposing ideal attachments, namely the particularistic patriotism and the universal cosmopolitanism. The modern state actually recognizes the individual in a way that approaches recognizing the individual as a human being, *simplicter*. The modern state has as its goal that its citizens become educated as human beings, i.e. that their civilian duties become particular forms of universal human duties. There is still patriotism and it is still love for a particular nation, but it is now connected with the pride that the state is the best organized, most just, and most moral society among the nations known. Durkheim does not only think that such a patriotism can easily be accepted as legitimate, but also that it should be encouraged for the sake of the individual, its rights and its liberties.[61]

For Durkheim the two first elements of moral education both refer to society, although in different ways. The discipline is required by the order of society, whereas the ideal of being attached to groups calls attention to society as something valuable beyond the individual. Society is at

---

[60] *Leçons*: 105.

[61] *Ibid.*: 108-09.

the same time something which we must have duties towards and something which is desirable.[62] Durkheim emphasizes that we never act morally only out of either duty or love for the good. A duty is a desirable constraint, and we could never raise ourselves above ourselves without the discipline forced upon us by society.[63] In terms of moral education these elements, however, should be thought of as sequential, meaning that discipline comes first and encouraging attachment to still wider groups comes second. This brings us to the last element, autonomy.

Autonomy is the goal of moral education in the democratic state.[64] The rationality of education is not only a goal, but actually demonstrated in the process, namely by explaining to the children along the way, how morality actually functions. For Durkheim formulating the moral reality in rational terms does not endanger morality,[65] quite the opposite. Moral education makes morality in modern societies intelligent.[66] It is reason and science, which is the basis of autonomy. When we understand the nature of morality, we are masters of the moral law, and then moral authority ceases to be heteronomous.[67] We can understand morality as good and natural, even though it constrains. We are part of society and therefore we accept morality as both desirable and necessary in an enlightened manner, and that is the end of humiliation and slavery.[68] Durkheim stresses that thought is liberating for will, and the conclusion is that it is the consciousness of the nature of human morality that make us autonomous.[69]

5. END

In this small sketch I have attempted to argue that a dialectical democratic republicanism like Durkheim's is still a suitable political answer to the challenges of modernity and global capitalism. With Durkheim we can argue morally and politically for a strong state without giving up on the ideals of rationality, individual freedom and democracy. Only a strong

---

[62] *L'éducation*: 132.

[63] *Ibid.*: 141.

[64] Unfortunately Durkheim never completed his construction of the logic of this third element, and the sketches he left are now lost. Still we have some indications, on which we can base a reconstruction, and a very good account can be found in W. Watts Miller, "Teaching autonomy," in Walford & Pickering, *Durkheim and Modern Education*: 72-91.

[65] *L'éducation*: 147-48.

[66] *Ibid.*: 164.

[67] *Ibid.*: 161.

[68] *Ibid.*: 162.

[69] *Ibid.*: 164.

state can develop humanity through education, science and social interventions, just as it alone has the power to counter the human desires united behind free market capitalist economy. With Durkheim we can thus fight capitalism without giving up on the ideals and achievements of modernity.

IMAGINATIVE FORCES IN LAW AND EDUCATION

Peter KEMP

Today, educational institutions from primary schools to universities are subjected more and more to political pressures to transform themselves into management institutions that can "sell knowledge" and promote competitiveness not only between educational institutions but also between nations. This political transformation of education means that the goal of teaching and research is less and less about the cultivation and moral formation of the human being to create and encourage the good life in society and more and more about training in technical and scientific performativity in order to increase the production of material goods and prevail in national and international competition. As a result, education is becoming dehumanized by reducing the cultivation of what is human to what is useful for competition on the world market; cultivation is no longer about how to contribute to establishing and maintaining a global human community and peace in the world.

The question is how to oppose this dehumanization of education. What must the politics be for an education that does not reduce cultivation to nothing other than learning about how to adapt to national and global competition but, rather, makes an appeal to responsibility for a global community? My answer is that this politics should not only prescribe an ethics of care for the good life with others in personal relationships but also a sense of global justice, implying a world order of national and transnational laws.

But one must ask whether such a world order with a minimum of common values is not impossible – given the plurality of values connected with different cultures and traditions in our world?

The French professor of international law at the Collège de France in Paris, Mireille Delmas-Marty, has written a major work on *The Imaginative Forces of Law (Les forces imaginantes du droit)* in four volumes that try to answer this question. They are entitled *The Relative and the Universal* (volume I), *Ordering Pluralism* (volume II), *The Restoration of Powers* (volume III) and *Towards a Community of Values?* (volume IV).[1]

[1] Delmas-Marty, Mireille *Les forces imaginantes du droit*. Paris: Ed. du Seuil, Vol. I, *Le relatif et l'universel*, 2004, Vol. II, *Le pluralisme ordonné*, 2006, Vol. III, *La refondation des pouvoirs*, 2007, et Vol. IV, *Vers une communauté de valeurs?*, 2011. Volume II has been

In this work, Delmas-Marty scrutinizes the obstacles and barriers to the establishment of a common legal world order and points out what we can do to surmount them and where we can find a basis for a belief in the possibility of a world community in which diversity is preserved without giving up on a common legal order. Nothing could be more important for education today than to aim at creating responsible citizens of the world.

1. THE SPIRIT OF COMMERCE AND THE LAW OF THE MARKET

Since our question has to do with education for the possibility of constructing or establishing a cosmopolitan community that will lead to a peaceful world or a world without wars, let us start by considering a remark by Immanuel Kant in his writing *Perpetual Peace*, which he called *A Philosophical Sketch*, published in 1795 and in an expanded edition in 1796.

What is important in our context is the idea in Kant that "just as nature wisely separates nations which the will of every state, sanctioned by the principles of international law, would gladly unite by artifice or force, nations which could not have secured themselves against violence and war by means of the law of world citizenship unite because of mutual interest."[2] And Kant defines this idea by referring to "the spirit of commerce." He believes that this spirit "is incompatible with war," so that, sooner or later, it "gains the upper hand in every state."[3] And he explains this by saying: "As the power of money is perhaps the most dependable of all the powers (means) included under the state power, states see themselves forced, without any moral urge, to promote honorable peace and by mediation to prevent war wherever it threatens to break out […] In this manner nature guarantees perpetual peace by the mechanism of human passions. Certainly she does not do so with sufficient certainty for us to predict the future in any theoretical sense, but adequately from a practical point of view, making it our duty to work toward this end, which is not just a chimerical one."[4]

Today, the question is the following: Can we still believe in the idea that the spirit of commerce is incompatible with war? According to her work on *The Imaginative Forces of Law*, the answer of Mireille Del-

---

translated separately by Naomi Norberg, *Ordering Pluralism: A Conceptual Framework for Understanding the Transnational Legal World*. Portland, USA: Hart Publishing, 2009.

[2] Kant, Immanuel *Perpetual Peace*, in *On History*, ed. by Lewis White Beck. Englewood Cliffs, NJ: Macmillan/Library of Liberal Arts: 114 (*Zum ewigen Frieden*, Akad. Ausgabe, VIII: 368).

[3] *Ibid.*

[4] *Ibid.*

mas-Marty is apparently negative. Right from the first volume, she asserts the ambiguity of the relationship of commerce to peace. If, she writes, commerce together with war is at the origin of the appearance of the law of peoples *(jus gentium)*, it seems that economic globalization also has the "pretension" of making a call to "the law of the market."[5] And this "law of the market" aims to establish a universal law that is equivalent "to the law of the strongest."[6]

In claiming that this law prevails today in our societies, Delmas-Marty recognizes that this is not conducive to a legal world community that respects an ordered plurality and, consequently, is not conducive to a global order of peace that presupposes that peoples are guided by a totality of values recognized globally by the most powerful political actors.

But what, according to Delmas-Marty, is precisely the danger of the law of the market? It is not only the fact that this law says that the strong shall triumph over the weak but also that, in so doing, nothing prevents it from uniting with a nationalist spirit. It follows that this will exacerbate the battle between business people who enter into world commerce and the fight between nations that relate to each other as actors in competition on the world market. Following Delmas-Marty, the law of the market implies that "the States that organize the competition are [...] themselves subjected to a competitive order that determines, at least, a part of their activities."[7] Thus, she says, they become involved in a dual process of expanding the logic of the market and generalizing market value to include things outside the commerce.

2. THE COMPETITIVE STATE

With this description of the socio-economic state of the world today, Delmas-Marty approaches the analysis made by the Danish professor of political science Ove Kaj Pedersen in his book *The Competitive State (Konkurrencestaten)*. The author compares the welfare state with what he calls the competitive state in order to show what has happened since the appearance of the idea that competition between companies and nations would be the social and economic force to unify all peoples of the world. Initially, the idea of competition penetrates the market as an idea of a dynamic relationship between companies that increases production. It is conceived not only as a force within a nation but also and particularly as fertile on the world market. Moreover, it drives these companies to merge

---

[5] *Les forces imaginantes du droit*, vol. I, *Le relatif et l'universel*: 54.

[6] *Ibid.*: 106.

[7] *Les forces imaginantes du droit*, vol. III, *La refondation des pouvoir*: 148.

into bigger and bigger commercial organizations called multinational corporations in which every enterprise becomes a branch. But after the Cold War and the dissolution of the Soviet Union, the reunification of Germany, and the opening of the Chinese economy, competition has penetrated the relationships between nations, and States – beginning with the United States of Bill Clinton – have thrown themselves into competition with each other as if nations were companies.[8]

In 1994, the economist Paul Krugman, who later won the Nobel Prize, called this idea of competition between nations "a dangerous obsession," arguing that a nation is not a company.[9] Nevertheless, it is this idea that leads politicians today to talk about putting their country on the top of some ranking. And, in so doing, they claim not only that the State must stimulate the competition between companies on a national and global level but also that they must transform themselves into a competitive state. That means that competition is more than technological in the sense of promoting technological innovations; it is also structural and institutional, aiming to foster the best conditions for the companies of that State by creating economic, political, cultural, and educational institutions to strengthen the competitive capacities of the State.

Ove K. Pedersen is not convinced that States or nations are really in competition, but he does not deny that there are expert systems and political programs "that make it possible for politicians and others to act *as if* they were."[10] This is the reason the idea of competition penetrates more and more into public discussions and modes of thinking in international commercial and economic institutions. Institutional reforms are imposed in order to promote competition in society and between nations.

Thus, public institutions for education, health, information, etc., are transformed more and more into commercial institutions that must enter into competition with each other. The university, for instance, becomes an enterprise that only searches for the knowledge it can "sell" and is less interested in reliable, credible knowledge. In addition, students in primary schools and high schools are educated for competition, while cultural and moral education are considered "useless." Their performance is constantly tested and the results published in ranking lists. The goal of all education then becomes to make the person capable of asserting him- or herself as the strongest in competition on the market, not only the national but

---

[8] Pedersen, Ove K. (2011) *Konkurrencestaten*. Copenhagen: Hans Reitzels forlag: 14.

[9] Krugman, Paul (1994) "Competiveness: A Dangerous Obsession," *Foreign Affairs* 73 (2): 28-44.

[10] *Konkurrencestaten*: 50.

also the global market. Everything is done in order to serve the struggle between nations.

In this way, the competitive state eliminates the welfare state more and more. The welfare state took care of the welfare of every citizen and assured everyone equal justice under the law and the possibility of the co-determination of all citizens in the affairs that concern them, whereas the competitive state aims at rewarding those who are the best and the most powerful.

According to Ove K. Pedersen, the welfare state has not yet been defeated by the competitive state, and the outcome of the battle between the two ideologies is not assured. It is true that, since the 1970s, the welfare state has suffered from some serious system errors in that it was too expensive and too anarchistic and, therefore, impossible to govern; but the competitive state also suffers from system errors – in particular, a deficit of democracy and unqualified and random forms of leadership. In other words, this form of State suffers from a lack of legitimacy and good leadership. It does not express a general will.

From the analysis in Ove K. Pedersen's book, one can conclude that, if we do not succeed through political and educational measures in confining the power of the competitive state and maintaining a certain public system of care for citizens and if the spirit of competition is not controlled by care of citizen welfare, the whole life of society will end up on an insane course in which all solidarity has disappeared in a war of all against all without anybody knowing why they are participating in this war.

This analysis implicitly confirms the claim of Delmas-Marty that, if the law of the market becomes the only law that governs society, it would obstruct a true legal community between human beings – not only because it implies that they would be reduced to commodities, as she claims, but also because it would involve all human activity in an endless loop to beat anyone who is not a brother-in-arms.

3. THE FEAR OF TERRORISM

However, it is not only competition that threatens the real global community; another obstacle – in particular, after the 9/11 in 2001, i.e. in the last decade of our world history – is the fear of terrorism that has developed into a whole "culture of fear." Indeed, this fear has produced the idea that the citizen of a State, whether it is a welfare state or a competitive state, is implicated in a war against Evil, a war against a horrific crime that threatens to dissolve or explode society. This citizen now tries to ensure his or her own security, which is considered more urgent than to show respect for human rights in a case in which a human being may be dangerous and represent the Empire of Evil. In this way, Delmas-Marty claims, people "re-nationalize the inhumane and justify it in their inner selves on the basis of the gravity of the crime."[11] It was, unfortunately, the Security Council of the UN that opened the way for such justifications by its resolution of September 12, 2001. This resolution, which considered terrorists as a "threat to international peace and security," recognized "the inherent right of individual or collective self-defense." As a result, as Delmas-Marty mentions, it was up to every State to determine whether it was in a situation of legitimate self-defense and to judge for itself, "in the absence of a global court for human rights, the means and the extent of the riposte."[12]

According to Delmas-Marty, it is this extension of the concept of legitimate self-defense to cover the fight against terrorism without framing it in reference to common values that has brought States to "legitimize torture in a discreet way."[13] It is true that, later, the UN General Assembly tried, as Delmas-Marty says, to "reconstruct the relationship between terrorism and torture around common values by linking, instead of opposing, the fight against terrorism and the prohibition of the inhumane."[14]

However, the paradigm of a "war on crime" is radically different from two other paradigms for the relationship to war, i.e. the prohibition of war crimes and the prohibition of crimes against humanity. The courts at Nuremberg and Tokyo criminalized the violation of these two prohibitions in 1945 just after the Second World War. These prohibitions have been developing since the Middle Ages from the idea of the *jus gentium* (the Law of Peoples) about what one does not have the right to do *ad bellum* (before the war) and what one does not have the right to do *in bello* (during the war). But what one does not have the right to do *post bellum* (after the war) has never really been clarified, although it implicitly remains a "question whether any aggression may justify war crimes committed by those having suffered aggression, after they have become the victors."[15]

---

[11] *Les forces imaginantes du droit*, vol. IV, *Vers une communauté de valeurs?*: 72.
[12] *Ibid.*
[13] *Ibid.*
[14] *Ibid.*: 72-73.
[15] *Ibid.*: 46.

However, through the notions of war crimes and crimes against humanity and supported by the Geneva Conventions from 1949 and the additional protocols from 1977 on the treatment of prisoners of war and civilians during war, the prohibition of the inhumane has progressively developed towards being considered valid in periods of peace. Nevertheless, since 9/11, the justification of legitimate defense has been applied to terrorist aggressions in such a way that Delmas-Marty can claim, along with Giorgio Agamben[16] and others, that the exception has become the rule. It follows that "what was launched as a political slogan, 'war on crime,' is no longer a simple metaphor but has become the substratum of a banal penal logic and even a legitimization of the inhumane that constitutes a break with the paradigms of Nuremberg."[17]

However, the situation changed in 2004 when the unacceptable treatment of prisoners in the American camp Abu Ghraib in Iraq was revealed. Delmas-Marty can quote what Chateaubriand declared in his *Memories from beyond the Grave* when he describes the massacre of the prisoners in Jaffa by Napoleon Bonaparte's troops : "The moral truth of an action is only uncovered in the details."[18] It was indeed "an image shock,"[19] transmitted to the public at large by the media, that provoked the conscience in such a way that the UN resolution of 19 September 2005 recognized that there are limits to the fight against terrorism and that the measures applied should conform to international law. It is then up to the imaginative forces of the humanitarian international law to expound the prohibition of the inhumane.

4. THE FEAR OF THE OTHER

Today, the fear of terrorism makes people prioritize to their own security rather than cherish the dignity of the Other. In politics and education, we must, therefore, not only think about the possibility of convincing people – particularly, the younger generation – to escape the logic of the market but also about how to resist the logic of the fear of the Other. Therefore, it is worthwhile to follow Delmas-Marty's reflection on the role of fear in society.

She recognizes that the will to live together may find support in the fear of risks and catastrophes. However, even if this fear, which she calls

---

[16] Agamben, Giorgio (2003) *Stato di Eccezione. Homo sacer*, 2,1. English transl.: *State of Exception*. University of Chicago Press, 2005.

[17] *Vers une communauté de valeurs?*: 46-47.

[18] Quoted by M. Delmas-Marty *Vers une communauté de valeurs?*: 37.

[19] *Ibid.*: 80.

"solidarity fear," may give rise to a common legality and even if it is different from the fear of an enemy or of an Other supposed to be an enemy, it "does not provide the key to a real common destiny."[20] She is well aware of the fact that the task remains "to convince those politically responsible and sensible to public opinion who worry about the situation that fear is always insufficient to give meaning to human action; it must be completed by an ethics of solidarity that is expressed in concentric circles from the closest to the most distant desire for a common destiny."[21] It follows that she thinks that we must "oppose solidarity to market values."[22]

The question is whether, with this idea of a common destiny, Delmas-Marty inscribes her reflection in the logic of a global social contract. She recognizes the fictive character of the idea of a social contract, and she agrees with me in calling it a "faction," i.e. a fiction ordering facts.[23] Moreover, she appreciates the splendid way in which Kant speaks about the social contract when he claims that we must act "as if it exists."[24] However, she doubts the utility of the idea of a contract to conceive "all the specificities of a global social contract that, in reality, are added onto national, international, regional, and transnational structures that, for the most part, did not exist at the time of the Enlightenment."[25] It would be necessary to conceive the global contract "as a multidimensional contract that connects actors and institutions in different ways from one level to another or from one sector to another,"[26] but she doubts that it would then still be a contract. She believes that, in a social contract, the desire to live together in a spirit of solidarity and peace is associated with "the fear that incites people to stick together to defend themselves in a spirit of war."[27] However, the global contract in our time is facing terrorism not from outside the community but from within; and, in that situation, the contract has no external enemy. Is it then still a contract including a desire to unite and a fear that excludes?

An objection to this doubt about using the idea of a global contract today might be that Delmas-Marty refers to an idea of contract that does

---

[20] *Ibid.*: 11.
[21] *Ibid.*: 390.
[22] *Ibid.*: 392.
[23] *Les forces imaginantes du droit,* vol. III, *La refondation des pouvoir*: 257.
[24] *Idem.*
[25] *Ibid.*: 257.
[26] *Idem.*
[27] *Ibid.*: 258.

not correspond to the way Hobbes, Rousseau and Kant, for instance, understood the contract. In fact, a social contract is not primarily an exclusion of the Other in Hobbes, Rousseau, or Kant. On the contrary, it was understood to be an inclusion of every citizen (conceived in Hobbes and Rousseau in a national framework) and not, essentially, directed against an external enemy. To Hobbes, the idea of a contract was supposed to replace the civil war in England with peace. The political world outside the country did not really interest him (although he wrote his great books in Paris). It is true that fear in Hobbes, which is a fear of the violent death in a war of all against all, may be used to justify totalitarianism and the exclusion of others who do not obey the power of the State. It is also true that Hobbes thought that fear of the Other could bring these wars to an end. However, Delmas-Marty's claim is that, if the idea of the social contract is transferred to the global level, it might result in a "global civil war" (as Hannah Arendt, Carl Schmitt, and Giorgio Agamben have imagined it), which is contrary to Hobbes' idea of the contract, whose intention was precisely to end civil wars.

In opposition to Hobbes, Rousseau wrote a book especially about *The Social Contract* in which the fear of the individual Other plays no role. According to Rousseau, it is no longer this individual but the State that is dangerous, and this danger makes a contract necessary in order to protect the individual. Moreover, in Kant, the absence of the citizen as co-legislator in a republic is dangerous, and this is exactly the point of his argument against Hobbes.[28]

In addition, neither Hobbes nor Rousseau can imagine an extension of the idea of the contract to a global level, which explains why only Kant – who, in fact, conceived the idea of a global social contract – could accept the idea of the citizen of the world. And this contract was not based on the fear of the Other but, rather, on what Adam Smith called sympathy for the Other. In fact, the idea of the contract in Kant expresses the desire to live together and justifies a global common law. However, Kant could not imagine that this law would mean more than a right to free movement around in the world, the "right to visit." Today, we are in a totally different situation; we are obliged to take into account several major global problems unknown to Kant concerning finance, culture, and

[28] Kant, Immanuel "Über die Gemeinspruch: das mag in der Theorie richtig sein, taugt aber nicht für die Praxis" (II, "Gegen Hobbes"), in *Werke in sechs Bänden*. Insel Verlag, Band VI: 150.

environment that only can be dealt with by a complicated elaboration of global legal norms.[29]

5. From Law to Ethics

It is as if Delmas-Marty considers problematic the move from ethics to law and does not give it much weight in the fight to surmount the barriers and "overcome the fear."[30] The vision of the good life seems too weak to influence the world of law. She rather believes in the construction of law by the imaginative force of judges who express their imagination in legal judgments and, in so doing, influence ethics through law.[31]

It is true that, in the fourth volume of her work on *The Imaginative Forces of Law*, she recognizes that the influence between ethics and law can go both ways. She notices: "Sometimes, the path – that is, apparently, the most logical – goes from values to law […] sometimes, which is the most surprising, the path goes in reverse from law to ethics."[32] However, she does not explain more about this mutuality. Her interest is, first of all, the path from what she calls "founding prohibitions" to law and ethics; these are the prohibition of *war crimes* that develops from the law of peoples and international law to the prohibition of *crimes against humanity*, which implies that humanity is, at the same time, a victim and a value to defend.[33] Moreover, she is interested in what comes out of the development of the "fundamental rights" formulated in the declarations of human rights since the revolutions in North America and France at the end of the 18th century. These human rights "also create prohibitions in their ways, but with a focus on the States."[34] In fact, they protect the individual against the State. They "offer an instrument in order to 'rationalize *la raison d'État*' and to found a true world community that is a community both between States and between individuals."[35]

However, according to Delmas-Marty, the challenge from terrorism has given rise to the false idea that a state of equilibrium between security and freedom must be found.[36] This idea erases all the prohibitions that were proclaimed absolute and without exception, and it permits no invio-

[29] Kemp, Peter (2011) *Citizen of the World: The Cosmopolitan Ideal for the Twenty-First Century*. New York: Humanity Books.
[30] *Les forces imaginantes du droit,* vol. IV, *Vers une communauté de valeurs?*: 290.
[31] *Ibid.*: 84.
[32] *Ibid.*: 20-21.
[33] *Ibid.*: 331.
[34] *Ibid.*: 23.
[35] *Ibid.*
[36] *Ibid.*: 71.

lable rights.[37] Delmas-Marty has devoted an entire book to this question, showing how responsible politicians today are tempted to question the liberties included in the rule of law because they think terrorism justifies their search for an equilibrium between security and freedom.[38] It is true that, by referring to the legal idea of *jus cogens* (a peremptory norm), several supreme courts, including the Supreme Court of the United States, have defended some inviolable rights against State power and, in several cases, have been able to oppose the tendency toward the inhumane.

Delmas-Marty is well aware of the fact that we cannot consider the foundations of fundamental rights as stable and cannot take them for granted. Nevertheless, she believes that they are justified by values implicit in some prohibitions that are in the process of being claimed universally, such as the prohibition of human cloning and the more and more universal abolition of the death penalty. Moreover, she finds values implying a global community in the idea of global common goods such as good health and a good climate without global warming ending in an "eco-cide."[39] Here, values about our relationships to the world appear in "collective preferences."[40]

On several occasions, Delmas-Marty resumes her position by focusing on the interaction between biological evolution aiming at the survival of the species, which she calls "hominization" (French: *hominisation*), on the one hand, and, on the other hand, cultural learning (implying the recognition of the human dignity), which she calls *humanization*.[41] In fact, without humanization, all that is possible becomes permitted (for instance, in the medical field: human cloning, genetic manipulation, the creation of chimeras, etc.).[42] In addition and more generally, if hominization and humanization are not intertwined in the technological evolution of globalization, social life will become a tyrannical system in which human beings cannot breathe anymore.[43]

The aim of the imaginative forces of law in which Delmas-Marty has faith is to imagine "a new humanism that is both plural and open." She thinks that this renewal is surely "one of the conditions for making

---

[37] *Ibid.*: 171 & 335.

[38] Delmas-Marty, M. (2010) *Libertés et sûreté dans un monde dangereux*. Paris: Éd. du Seuil.

[39] *Ibid.*: 98.

[40] *Ibid.*: 335.

[41] *Ibid.*: 97 and *Les forces imaginantes du droit,* vol. III, *La refondation des pouvoir*: 31.

[42] *Ibid.*: 17.

[43] *Ibid.*: 203.

the human community beginning to appear capable of overcoming fear and its paradoxes in order to express its solidarity and assume its common destiny."[44] It follows that she ends up with an eco-ethics, i.e. an ethics for the human community in our time.

CONCLUSION

We began by contrasting Delmas-Marty with Kant. And there are certainly obstacles to the cosmopolitan community and to the new humanism that Kant did not realize, not only because the spirit of commerce is not so innocent as he believed but also because he lived in a pre-globalized and pre-technologized world. In this world, there were no big questions about global finance, about the global co-existence of cultures, or about the ecological interdependencies of all beings – all questions that necessarily demand a renovation of law. It follows that Delmas-Marty is right in claiming that the logic of the market cannot save us, and she is even more right than she believes because this logic not only transforms living beings into commodities, it also becomes a spirit of competition that pulls people into a whirlwind of nonsense.

However, to the extent that global commerce means that "we are all in the same boat," it may open our eyes to the truth that, without a will to live together, we are all lost and destroyed by the forces of things. It may teach us that we cannot survive without recognizing a certain global legal order to ensure the peace of the world. In so doing, commercial and economic life in our time may help open our eyes to the practical necessity of this order. In that way, Kant is right. But Delmas-Marty is also right in claiming that we need imaginative forces so that the law can express not only hominization (Kant's "mechanism of human passions") but also a humanization that, in politics and education, may triumph over the logic of the market. In other words, in order to avoid the subversion of our schools and universities into fatuous factories, politics and education need a "faction," i.e. a fiction that orders the facts of human plurality into a new global community and transforms our world into a human dwelling *(oikos)*.

And as Delmas-Marty observes: "International criminal law gives an example of a fiction that becomes reality."[45]

---

[44] *Ibid.*: 378.
[45] *Ibid.*: 12.

About the Authors

Blaise Bachofen (b. 1967): Tenured Associate Professor of Philosophy at Cergy-Pontoise University (France). His research interests include the philosophy of Rousseau and modern political philosophy. He has published six books, among them *La condition de la liberté. Rousseau, critique des raisons politiques* [The Condition of Freedom. Rousseau, Critique of Political Reasons] (Paris: Payot, 2002); *Le libéralisme au miroir du droit* [Liberalism in the Mirror of Law] (Lyon: ENS, 2008); (in collaboration) *Cornélius Castoriadis, réinventer l'autonomie* [Cornélius Castoriadis. Reinventing Autonomy] (Sandre, 2008); *Rousseau, Politique et esthétique* [Rousseau, Politics and Aesthetics] (Lyon: ENS, 2011); and many articles, most recently "Why Rousseau Mistrusts Revolutions," in *Rousseau and Revolution* (ed. by H. R. Lauritsen & M. Thorup, London/New York, Continuum, 2011).

Bhuvan Chandel (b. 1941): Professor of philosophy, Dean, Faculty of Arts, Chief Editor, *Journal of Social Sciences*, Panjab University, Director, Indian Institute of Advanced Study, Shimla, Awardee, University Grants Commission Nationl Lecturship, Annual President, Indian Philosophical Congress, Vice-President, International Council for Philosophy and Human Sciences, (CPHS), UNESCO, Member, Steering Committee, FISP, Member, IIP and Russian Academy of Research in Humanities. Her published works include: *Marxian Ethics: Some Preliminary Considerations* (Delhi: Munshiram Manoharlal, 1979); *Nature of Violence* (Chandigarh: P.U. Publication Bureau, 1980); *Philosophy of Daya Krishna* (Delhi: Indian Council of Philosophical Research, 1994); *In Quest of Peace* (Pune: Maharashtra Institute of Technology, 1996); *Samanvaya* (Pune: Maharashtra Institute of Technology, 1997); *Cultural Traditions and the Idea of Secularization* (Ankara & Delhi: FISP & Centre for Studies in Civilizations 1998) and *History, Time and Truth: Essays in Honour of D. P. Chattopadhyaya* (Delhi: Kalki Prakash, 1998).

D. P. Chattopadhyaya (b. 1933): Professor, Jadavpur University, Calcutta. Founder-Chairman, Indian Council of Philosophical Research, Chairman of the Teachers' Commission of India, and Centre for Studies in Civilizations. Published 96 multidisciplinary volumes. Union Cabinet Minister, State Governor, Member of the Russian Academy of Research in Humanities, Member of the International Institute of Philosophy. Last publications: *Philosophical Consciousness and Scientific Knowledge: Conceptual Linkages and Civilizational Background* (2004); *Self, Society* *and Science: Theoretical and Historical Perspectives* (2004); *Religion, Philosophy and Science* (Shimla: Indian Institute of Administrative Studies, 2006), and *Aesthetic Theories and Forms in Indian Tradition* (Delhi, 2008).

Sergio CREMASCHI (b. 1949): Associate Professor of Moral Philosophy at the "Amedeo Avogadro" University (Alessandria, Novara, Vercelli) Italy. His research focuses are the history of ethics and economic ethics. His latest books are: *L'etica del Novecento* [Twentieth-Century Ethics] (Rome, 2005); *L'etica moderna* [Modern Ethics] (Rome, 2007); *Normativity Within the Bounds of Plural Reasons. The Applied Ethics Revolution* (Uppsala, 2007). Articles in English in *History of Political Economy, Journal of Pragmatics, Croatian Journal of Philosophy, The European Journal of the History of Economic Thought* and *The Journal of Philosophical Economics*.
www.lett.unipmn.it/docenti/cremaschi/default en.htm

Enrique DUSSEL AMBROSINI (b. 1934 in Argentina): Professor at the Dpt of Philosophy, Metropolitan Autonomous University (UAM), Campus Iztapalapa in Mexico City. Among his books in English are *Towards an unknown Marx: A Commentary on the Manuscripts of 1861-63* (Routledge, 2001); *Twenty Theses on Politics* (Duke UP, 2008). Major works are: *Ética de la liberación en la Edad de la Globalización y de la Exclusión* [Ethics of Liberation in the Age of Globalization and Exclusion] (Madrid, 1998); *Política de la Liberación I-II* [Politics of Liberation I-II] (Madrid, 2007-2009) and (with others) *Historia del Pensamiento Filosófico Latinoamericano, del Caribe y "Latino" (1300-2000)* [History of Latinamerican, Caribean and "Latino" Thinking] (Mexico D.F., 2009). Articles in English in *Philosophy and Social Criticism, Radical Philosophy Review, Philosophy Today* and *Constellations*.
www.enriquedussel.com.

Gordon FINLAYSON (b. 1964): Director of the Centre for Social & Political Thought, and Senior Lecturer in the Dept. of Philosophy at the University of Sussex, UK. He works on social and political philosophy and critical theory. He is author of *Habermas: A Very Short Introduction* (OUP 2005), and co-author/editor of *Habermas and Rawls: Disputing the Political* (Routledge 2010). His most recent articles appeared in *Telos* (2009) *Review of Politics* (2010), and *Harvard Theological Review* (2012). He has articles forthcoming on Habermas in *Constellations*, and Adorno in *European Journal of Philosophy*.

Tuktuk GHOSH (b. 1955): M.A., Ph. D., Taught at Delhi University, later got selected for highly competitive Indian Administrative Service, Senior Educational Administrator in Ministries of Culture and Education, Headed all Universities of Buddhist studies, Research Institutions, Museums, Art Galleries, national Archives and Libraries in the Country. Representative of India in forums of world organizations. She was Principal Secretary for Women and Children (Welfare and Education); and is currently Additional Chief Secretary in the Government of West Bengal. Has published books including *Early History of Rice in India* (Delhi: Gian Publishing House, 1985) which has been accepted as the matrix for a National Project on *Paddy Cultivation and ancient Indian Culture* by the Ministry of Culture, Government of India. Also published several articles on selective educational themes.

Athanasia GLYCOFRYDI-LEONTSINI (b. 1946): Professor of Modern European and Neohellenic Philosophy at the National and Kapodistrian University of Athens, Greece. Head of Philosophy and Deputy Head of the Department of Philosophy, Psychology and Pedagogy at the same University (2011-2013). She is Vice President of the Institut International de Philosophie. Her research interests are in Neohellenic philosophy, Byzantine and post-Byzantine philosophy, philosophy of the Scottish Enlightenment, modern and contemporary aesthetics, moral and political philosophy. Among her books in Greek are *The Epistemological Foundations of Thomas Reid's Aesthetics* (Athens, 1988); *Neohellenic Aesthetics and the European Enlightenment* (Athens, 1989); *Neohellenic Philosophy: Moral and Political Questions* (Athens, 2001); *Aesthetics and Art: Critical Reconsiderations* (Athens, 2006), *An Introduction to Aesthetics* (Athens 2008) She is jointed general editor of the *Corpus Philosophorum Graecorum Recentiorum*.

María José GUERRA PALMERO (b. 1962): Associate Professor of moral philosophy at the University of La Laguna, Tenerife, Spain. Among her publications are *Mujer, identidad y reconocimiento. Habermas y la crítica feminista* [Woman, Identity and Recognition. Habermas and the Feminist Critique] (Instituto Canario de la Mujer, 1998) and *Breve introducción a la ética ecológica* [A Brief Introduction to Ecological Ethics] (Madrid, 2001). She has co-edited *Globalización y neoliberalismo: ¿un futuro inevitable?* [Globalization and neoliberalism: an inevitable future?] (Oviedo, 2002), *Los laberintos de la responsabilidad* [The labyrinths of responsibility] (Madrid, 2006) and *20 pensadoras del siglo XX* [20 Female Thinkers of the Twentieth Century] (Oviedo, 2006). Articles in Spanish and international philosophical journals such as *Isegoría, Bioethics, Daimon* and *Theoria.*

Jørgen HUGGLER (b. 1956): Associate Professor of philosophy, Aarhus University. He is the author of *Hegels skeptiske vej til den absolutte viden* [Hegel's Sceptical Path to Absolute Knowing] (Copenhagen, 1999); "Das absolute Wissen in der *Phänomenologie des Geistes*" [The Absolute Knowledge in the *Phenomenology of Spirit*]; *Hegel-Jahrbuch*, 2001; "Hegel's Phenomenology of Rationality," in *Dialectics, Self-consciousness, and Recognition* (ed. Sørensen *et al.*, Malmö, 2009); "Der Anfang und das Sollen. Über Kierkegaards Fichte-Deutung in *Über den Begriff der Ironie*", *Kierkegaard Studies, Monograph Series* 22 (De Gruyter, 2010); "Culture and Paradox in Kant's Philosophy of Education," in *Kant and Education. Interpretations and Commentary* (ed. Roth & Surprenant, Routledge, 2012).

Per JEPSEN (b. 1976): post-doctoral fellow at the Department of Eduation, Aarhus University, Denmark. PhD in philosophy from Copenhagen University 2010. His research interests range from the history of modern philosophy to the concept of autonomy in moral and educational philosophy. A particular research interest is modern critical theory. Among his publications are "'Frihedens skyggespil' – Spinoza og oplysningens dialektik" [The Shadow Play of Freedom – Spinoza and the Dialectics of Enlightenment], *Slagmark* (Aarhus, Denmark), n° 39, 2004 and *Adornos kritische Theorie der Selbstbestimmung* [Adornos' Critical Theory of Selfdetermination] (Würzburg, Königshausen & Neumann, 2012).

Peter KEMP (b. 1937): Emeritus Professor of Philosophy at Faculty of Arts, University of Aarhus, Campus Copenhagen, Denmark. Executive Director for the Centre for Ethics and Law, Copenhagen. President of the XXIInd World Congress of Philosophy, Seoul, 2008. Major works: *Théorie de l'engagement,* I-II [Theory of Engagement] (Paris, 1973); *Das Unersetzliche. Eine Technologie-Ethik* [The Irremplacable. An Ethics of Technology] (Berlin, 1992); *La mundialización de la ética* [The Globalisation of Ethics] (Mexico D.F., 2007); *Sagesse pratique de Paul Ricœur* [Pratical Wisdom of Paul Ricœur] (Paris, 2010) and *Citizen of the World* (New York, USA, Prometheus Books, 2011).

Evanghelos MOUTSOPOULOS (b. 1930): Professor, University of Athens since 1969, Rector thereof, 1977. Visiting professor at several foreign universities and research centres. Author of more than 50 philosophical volumes and translated into many languages. He has presented papers in more than 800 international philosophical conferences, very frequently, as an invited speaker. Research interests: Kairology, philosophy of art, philosophy of Greek culture, history of modern Greek philosophy, philosophy of cosmic space, and philosophy of music. As president of the Foundation for Research and Editions of Modern Greek Philosophy he has created the *Corpus Philosophorum Graecorum Recentiorum* (1966). Founder and editor of the international philosophical review *Diotima* since 1973. Since 1984 he has also been the editor of the international philosophical review *Philosophia*, an official publication of the Academy of Athens.

TONG Shijun (b. 1958): Professor of Philosophy and University Council Chairman of East China Normal University, Shanghai. Main interests are political philosophy and philosophy of science. Among his books are *Chinese Philosophy: Practical Reason and Dialectical Logic* (Bergen, Norway, 1989); *Epistemology and Methodology in the Post-Hegelian European Philosophy of 19th Century* (Bergen, 1993); *Dialectics of Modernization* (Sidney, 2000); *Critique and Practice* (Beijing, 2007) and *Theoretical Dialogues in Practice* (Malmö, 2009). Among his translations into Chinese are Hilary Putnam's *Reason, Truth and History* (co-transl., Shanghai, 1997) and Jürgen Habermas' *Faktizität und Geltung* [Between Facts and Norms] (Beijing, 2003).

Asger SØRENSEN (b. 1960): Associate Professor of philosophy of education, University of Aarhus, Denmark. Main interests are political and social philosophy, ethics, and philosophy of science. Major works are: *Forskning, etik, konsekvens* [Research, Ethics, Consequence] (Copenhagen, 2003) and *Om videnskabelig viden* [On Scientific Knowledge] (Frederiksberg, 2010). He has edited Enrique Dussel: *Frigørelsesfilosofi* [Philosophy of Liberation] (Copenhagen, 2008), coedited *Excesser – om Bataille* [Excesses – on Bataille] (Aarhus, 1994); *Dialectics, Self-Consciousness, and Recognition* (Malmö 2009) and *Rawls politiske filosofi* [The Political Philosophy of Rawls] (Malmö 2009). Articles in English in *Philosophy and Social Criticism*, *Public Reason* and *Danish Yearbook of Philosophy*.

INDEX